CONTENTS

Part 1:   *Comment from 1662 to 1920*

Part 2:   *Articles and Essays from 1925 to the Present*

Part 3:   *Reviews of Productions, 1930 to the Present*

ACKNOWLEDGEMENTS

The editor and publishers wish to thank the following, who have kindly given permission for the use of copyright material : G. Gregory Smith extract from *Ben Jonson* (Macmillan, 1919); Faber & Faber Ltd and Harcourt Brace Jovanovich Inc. for 'Ben Jonson' from *Selected Essays* (1951) by T. S. Eliot; the Clarendon Press for Introduction to *Volpone* from *Ben Jonson*, vol. II (1925) ed. C. H. Herford and Percy Simpson, and 'Jonson's Tortoise' by Ian Donaldson from *Review of English Studies*, XIX (1968); Chatto & Windus Ltd for extract from *Drama and Society in the Age of Jonson* (1937) by L. C. Knights; *Philological Quarterly* for 'Jonson's Metempsychosis' by Harry Levin from *P.Q.* XXII (1943); University of Chicago Press for 'The Double Plot in *Volpone*' by Jonas A. Barish from *Modern Philology*, LI (1953); University of Auckland for 'Tragical Mirth : *King Lear* and *Volpone*' by S. Musgrove from *Shakespeare and Jonson*, the Macmillan Brown Lectures, *Auckland University College Bulletin*, no. 51, English Series, no. 9 (1957); John J. Enck, 'The Artificer', from chap. vi of *Jonson and the Comic Truth*, by permission of the University of Wisconsin Press, copyright © 1957 by the Regents of the University of Wisconsin; Chatto & Windus Ltd and Columbia University Press for extract from *The Broken Compass* (1958) by Edward B. Partridge; *Modern Language Quarterly* for 'Folly into Crime : The Catastrophe of *Volpone*' by S. L. Goldberg from *M.L.Q.* XX (1959); Yale University Press for Introduction to *Volpone* by Alvin B. Kernan, copyright © 1962 by Yale University; Ernest Benn Ltd and Hill & Wang Inc. for Introduction to *Volpone*, ed. Philip Brockbank (New Mermaid Series, 1968); *The Times* for '*Volpone* at the Festival Theatre, Cambridge', 28 April 1930, '*Volpone* at the Malvern Festival', 31 July 1935,

8   ACKNOWLEDGEMENTS

'*Volpone* in Sir Tyrone's Best Style', 11 November 1964, and 'Black Comedy Still Has Too Much' by Henry Popkin, 17 January 1968; *New Statesman* for '*Volpone* Revived' by Desmond MacCarthy, 29 January 1938, and 'The Fox' by T. C. Worsley, 26 July 1952; George G. Harrap & Co. Ltd for review of the Wolfit revival of *Volpone* from *The Amazing Theatre* (1939) by James Agate; The Observer Ltd for 'Viewhalloo *Volpone*' by Ronald Bryden, 21 January 1968.

GENERAL EDITOR'S PREFACE

Each of this series of Casebooks concerns either one well-known and influential work of literature or two or three closely linked works. The main section consists of critical readings, mostly modern, brought together from journals and books. A selection of reviews and comments by the author's contemporaries is also included, and sometimes comments from the author himself. The Editor's Introduction charts the reputation of the work from its first appearance until the present time.

The critical forum is a place of vigorous conflict and disagreement, but there is nothing in this to cause dismay. What is attested is the complexity of human experience and the richness of literature, not any chaos or relativity of taste. A critic is better seen, no doubt, as an explorer than as an 'authority', but explorers ought to be, and usually are, well equipped. The effect of good criticism is to convince us of what C. S. Lewis called 'the enormous extension of our being which we owe to authors'. A Casebook will be justified only if it helps to promote the same end.

A single volume can represent no more than a small selection of critical opinions. Some critics have been excluded for reasons of space, and it is hoped that readers will follow up the further suggestions in the Select Bibliography. Other contributions have been severed from their original context, to which some readers may wish to return. Indeed, if they take a hint from the critics represented here, they certainly will.

A. E. DYSON

INTRODUCTION

Jonson's darkest comedy, *Volpone*, has had, along with *The Alchemist*, the brightest critical fortunes of any of his plays. Jonson wrote it with unaccustomed speed, in five weeks, for performance at the Globe in 1606, and it appears to have pleased its first audiences greatly. A few months later, played at Oxford and Cambridge, it was received with such 'love and acceptance' that Jonson gratefully dedicated the published quarto of 1607 'to the two most noble and most equal sisters, the two famous Universities', providing it with a critical preface of exceptional weight and seriousness, in which he expounded some of his most deeply pondered views on the nature of poetry.

The high regard shown the play by its first audiences continued through most of the seventeenth century. Jonson's garrulous 'son', James Howell, assured his master in a letter that he had been 'mad' when he wrote it – mad with the inspiration of *furor poeticus*[1] – and a widely circulated jingle linked it with two other Jonson comedies in a trinity of masterpieces: 'The Fox, The Alchemist, and Silent Woman,/ Done by Ben Jonson and outdone by no man.'[2] References amassed in two volumes of Jonson allusions testify to the speed with which some of the play's characters became creatures of folklore. Pepys, the most indefatigable playgoer of the century, pronounced the century's verdict: 'a most excellent play; the best I think I ever saw'.[3] Despite a rising tide of sentimentalism and bardolatry, which would ultimately engulf it, *Volpone* held the stage till nearly the end of the century following.

The play's first true critic was Jonson himself, who in his dedicatory epistle singled out the harsh judgements imposed on the knaves as a crux requiring special explanation. But criticism as a whole did not return seriously to this point until the present century. For the most part seventeenth-century comment tends to be desultory. We hear the anecdotal voice of John Aubrey, seconded – or possibly parroted – by Winstanley, informing us that the character of Volpone was modelled on that of Sir Thomas Sutton, a Jacobean merchant tycoon, a bit of gossip which shed so little light on the play that – true or false – it never aroused the faintest critical interest. We hear the moralising voice of John Dennis, seconded by Congreve, complaining of the ridicule of a 'Personal defect' in the figure of Corbaccio, on the ground that personal defects cannot be amended, and hence cannot further the corrective aim of comedy. But there is a literal-mindedness in this view which rather misses the point. What makes Corbaccio ridiculous is not his deafness as such but the fact that this never interferes with his avarice. No bodily infirmity deters this ferocious oldster from pursuing the objects of his greed as furiously as a younger man might pursue sensual pleasure – not his deafness, not his gout, not his weak eyes or his missing teeth. Avarice, in effect, has *supplanted* his other faculties. It has become his method of apprehension and his vital principle, the air he breathes and the thing for which he lives, an all-sufficient replacement for a decaying sensory apparatus. This is what prompts our laughter. The deafness itself takes on the quality of a moral failing; it is no more a simple physical defect than Falstaff's fatness.

Apart from their somewhat quirky interest in character, the early critics concern themselves with questions of structure. Dryden, in a generally admiring notice on Jonson's dramaturgy, makes unfavourable mention of the fact that the last act does not, in his view, spring naturally enough from the first four: events having reached a momentary equilibrium at the end of the first trial scene, a fresh jolt is required to set them in motion again and bring on a catastrophe. But in the act of lodging this indictment, Dryden supplies the basis for a refutation. Volpone's last fatal prank, he points out, 'though it suited not with his character as a crafty or covetous person, agreed

well enough with that of a voluptuary'. Volpone, that is, is not
to be confined by the will of the critic solely to the character
of the crafty or covetous man; he is actuated by other, sometimes murkier and more interesting, impulses. For John
Dennis, who follows Dryden's lead, '*Volpone* in the fifth Act
behaves himself like a Giddy Coxcombe, in the Conduct of that
very Affair which he manag'd so Craftily in the first four'.
But Dennis has been viewing Volpone even more narrowly
than Dryden as an emblem of miserly cunning. If we look at the
play we find plenty of reason to question the formula. Has
Volpone truly proceeded up to this point with the exemplary
discretion pretended by Dennis? Is there nothing of the 'giddy
coxcomb' in his disguise as a mountebank? Does his treatment
of his victims – his Bubbles, as Dennis calls them – in the early
scenes in no way forecast his later behaviour towards them? Is
it sufficient to say of him at *any* point in the action, as Dennis
so heavily says, that his 'design' is simply 'to Cheat'?

Criticism in general often finds itself more at ease discussing
shortcomings than successes. Failure lends itself more readily
to the analytic process. It invites the critical putting asunder of
elements which the artist may have imperfectly joined, whereas success confronts us with elements too closely fused to be
easily disjoined. Jonson's early champions often had difficulty
specifying the grounds of his greatness even when they were
firmly convinced of it. The fact that Jonson himself placed a
premium on 'reason' and 'judgement', moreover, seemed to
license a critical discussion conducted in such terms, so that for
much of the eighteenth century positive evaluation tends to
reduce itself to the ritual repetition of a few eulogistic epithets.
Dennis praises *Volpone* for its 'strength of . . . Judgment';
Davies, eighty years later, considers the fable 'chosen with
judgement'. Other writers declare their approbation of the
'correctness' of the plot, or of its adherence to decorum – the
strictness with which the characters are made to talk and act
like themselves : so Steele, so Whalley. For still others it is the
'erudition' of the play, its synthesising of bits and pieces trans-

lated from ancient writers, which commands respect. 'Judgement', 'correctness', 'erudition' : however irrelevant and inadequate these terms may seem to us to suggest the inner life of Jonsonian comedy, in the eighteenth century at least they constituted high praise. In the nineteenth they lived on to become the kiss of death.

In contrast to their somewhat unfocused and uncertain expressions of approval, eighteenth-century critics followed Dryden and Dennis in drawing up a highly specific bill of complaint against particular faults. They censured the subplot so relentlessly as an 'excrescency' that they drove it from the stage : the Covent Garden revival of 1771 reduces it to a ghost. They disparaged the character of Corbaccio as 'caricature', without considering whether Corbaccio himself, for all his grotesqueness, was in fact conceived differently from the other characters, whom they professed to admire. They condemned the last act as an 'absurd and improbable' violation of realism, without pausing to assess the realism of the play as a whole. We may grant, certainly, the claim that the play has a realistic basis. Greedy fortune-hunters do, it appears, prey on rich childless old men in order to inherit their wealth, and doubtless they always will. But that any rich old man should devise such a counter-hoax as Volpone's, that he should order his whole existence around it, engineer events so that one hopeful legatee disinherits his son, another prostitutes his wife, and a third commits perjury on a monumental scale – all this, plainly, must be accounted improbability alongside which the improvisations of Act v are as a mere pinch of sand flung on to a vast beach.

Occasionally, in their praise, the commentators do descend to particulars, to refute adverse criticism from other quarters; close scrutiny of the play's virtues thus arises as part of the critical dialogue. Cumberland, for example, defends Mosca's hasty invitation to Bonario as not only no lapse from his usual adroitness, but as an enhancement of it, affording 'a very brilliant occasion for setting off his ready invention and

presence of mind in a new and superior light'. On the other
hand, Cumberland also shows us criticism beginning to lose its
way down a false trail. He seconds Dennis's disapproval of
Volpone's 'unseasonable' insults in Act v 'to the very persons,
who had witnessed falsely in his defence, and even to the very
Advocate, who had so successfully defended him'. But does any
spectator in his right mind suppose that Volpone will be *grateful* to his victims? Do we think he *ought* to be grateful to them,
when he knows, and we know, that their intervention was
totally – even pathologically – selfish? Cumberland clearly expects characters in plays to act from motives that ordinary,
decent folk will recognise as reasonable ones – the kind that
presumably govern their own behaviour – even after those
characters have been fully established as moral monsters. The
implication comes out even more strongly in his comments on
the final punishments, which he finds to be 'just and solemn',
so much so that he charges Jonson with a 'wanton' breach of
decorum 'when he violates the dignity of his court of judges
by making one of them so abject in his flattery to the Parasite
upon the idea of matching him with his daughter'. But is the
'dignity' of the court a reality? Do the judges, at any moment
prior to the final sentencing, show much aptitude for their
job? Has Jonson portrayed them as genuinely worthy of
reverence, or is it simply that Cumberland wishes them to
be so?

Even Gifford, Jonson's first scholarly editor, who sweeps
away a good many critical cobwebs with a vigorous hand,
bungles his attempted vindication of the judges. Trying to
justify the matrimonial scheming of the fourth judge, he does
so in the worst possible way. He tries to defend his good character, instead of defending him *as a character*. And he proceeds
ineptly at that. For the fact that Volpone is presumed dead at
this juncture in no way mitigates or extenuates the magistrate's
behaviour; it simply makes it plausible : it provides a concrete
objective for his toadying and fawning. More perverse still is
Gifford's evident acceptance of Cumberland's premiss that the

magistrates ought to be upright and incorruptible. No doubt they ought, as all men ought to be. The question is whether Jonson has so portrayed them. Comedy exists because there are rascals who do *not* behave as men ought, including some lodged in posts of high trust and authority. Whoever finds this proposition intolerable has seen too little of both life and literature.

Gifford falters in a different way in his attempted defence of the subplot. Here he can muster only the pious wish that Sir Politic Would-be, 'through his wife', is 'in some measure, connected with the plot; and both are occasionally subservient to the poet's main design'. The hollow generality here, 'subservient to the poet's main design', together with the timid qualifiers, 'in some measure', 'occasionally', coming from the fiery quill of Gifford, betray a total lack of conviction and illustrate the fact that so long as unity of design was thought of solely in terms of plot mechanics, little could be done to acquit the characters of the subplot from the charge of being interlopers.

Gifford's reasonings, in any case, keyed largely to eighteenth-century objections, could do little to rescue *Volpone* from icy death at the hands of the romantics. Charles Dibdin had struck the new note in 1800 – grudging, chill, and uncomprehending. Against most of the evidence available to us, and citing none of his own, Dibdin affirms that the play 'has never greatly succeeded', for the reason that 'Quaint, dry, studied correctness, unsupported by quickness, spirit, and fire, can never satisfy'. Here the correctness which had once been a mark of excellence is in process of turning into a fault, and being rechristened 'dry, studied correctness', while 'quickness, spirit, and fire' are on the road to becoming its antithesis. If *Volpone* possessed the former – so runs the underlying logic – it could scarcely have had much of the latter. Obstacles in the path of intelligent appreciation mount as critics evolve a new and apocryphal criterion for judging dramatic characters. Formerly the demand had been that they be lively, consistent and natural. The new requirement is that they be likeable as well, that they display 'goodness of heart', that they prompt one to wish to associate convivially with them. Coleridge hints at a rewritten *Volpone* in which Celia and Bonario would assume the roles of the young lovers: so Jonson's scathing vision of folly would be sugared over with a sentimental frosting of innocence and charm.

Except for rare moments, such as the performances of *Every Man in His Humour* in which Charles Dickens played Bobadil, interest in Jonson stagnated during the nineteenth century. It revived towards the end under the unlikely stewardship of Swinburne, who, with his flair for iconoclastic judgement, came to the aid of the neglected author in an essay remarkable for its unapologetic enthusiasm. If Swinburne sometimes seems to get Jonson slightly wrong – as when he finds in *Volpone* 'a savour of something like romance' – he at least abandons the old puzzles over the mechanics of the action, and discards the outworn rules of thumb for interpreting character. He sees that what is central in the principals is not their simple cleverness in deceit, but something more arresting, 'the serious fervour and passionate intensity of their lurid and resourceful wickedness', which lends a 'distorted dignity to the display of their doings and sufferings'. If this exaggerates the sombreness of the play, at least it constitutes a live response to its poetry, and not an owlish pronouncement on the clockworks of its plotting. Swinburne rightly refuses to countenance the hoary canard according to which Jonson spoiled the play when he made Volpone assume a new disguise in Act v. Instead of a sign of feebleness, he finds that 'the haughty audacity of caprice which produces [Volpone's] ruin out of his own hardihood and insolence' forms a 'master-stroke' of the plot.

With Swinburne newly alert to the poetic texture, and with Germanic and neo-Germanic scholarship beginning to recover the play's sources and historical points of reference, the moment was ripening towards the twentieth-century re-

discovery of this slighted masterpiece, which we may date with
T. S. Eliot's essay of 1919, and C. H. Herford's Introduction
of 1925. Eliot's revolutionary remarks begin by throwing over-
board the whole notion of 'exaggeration' as a way of account-
ing for Jonson's dramatic power, even when that notion is
sanctified by transposition into the scholarly concept of
'humours'. He goes on to explain how differently Jonsonian
characters function from Shakespearian, and how differently
criticism must therefore approach them. For the first time
since Jonson's own day Eliot links Jonson's mastery as a
dramatist to his brilliance as a poet, focusing on two representative passages from *Volpone* to illustrate the qualities of
Jonsonian verse. So eager is he indeed to discredit the hack-
neyed emphasis on plot which had dogged Jonson criticism
that he nearly denies the importance of plot altogether, concluding, in a famous formula, that what holds the plays
together is 'a unity of inspiration that radiates into plot and
personages alike'.

Eliot thus supplies a set of fresh terms, a renewed interest in
the expressive powers of the verse, and an altered awareness
of how character operates in comedy. Herford provides a con-
spectus of critical opinion on the play, and a sense of its place
in the Jonson corpus. Reopening the question of the catastrophe, he concurs with Swinburne in finding it 'wonderfully
contrived'. He analyses the characters with a vivid sense of
their individual identities, even if he also clings to the romantic
habit of speaking of them as though they enjoyed an indepen-
dent existence of their own. And he works out the first reasoned
defence of the subplot, as a case of the artistic relevance of
irrelevancy.

Together Eliot and Herford catapult *Volpone* criticism into
the twentieth century. Subsequent commentators have followed them both, with more intensive scrutiny of the verse –
its texture, tone, and imagery – and with closer analysis of
components such as the first-act jig, the subplot, and the finale.
They have also located new areas for investigation, notably

the relations between the play and various aspects of its historical context. A series of one-volume editions has been accompanied by a corresponding series of critical introductions of a
high order, in which the findings of scholarship have been re-
synthesised into fresh interpretations. If it is true, as William
Empson complains, that recent criticism has dealt too pietisti-
cally with the play, producing 'crippled or perverted moral
judgements, wholly out of contact with the basic tone of feeling',[4] it is also true that the determination to account for
everything that is there, to grasp the serious purposes behind
comic techniques, to give Jonson the benefit of the doubt by
crediting him with artistic responsibility rather than assuming
him guilty until proved innocent, has produced an unpre-
cedented attentiveness in critical discourse.

Perhaps the surplus of moralising in recent critical commentary (not, it is hoped, unduly represented in the selections
below) has also been partly offset by the return of the play to
the stage, and the consequent growing body of informed
reporting on productions. Reviews serve not only to record
performances that may be valid interpretations in their own
right; they also remind us of the strange amphibious nature of
our dramatic classics, which simultaneously inhabit two distinct and partly incompatible worlds. In reviews of productions of *Volpone* one is struck by how often the critics express
surprise that a play which seemed so dark, forbidding, and
verging on the tragic in reading proved so hilarious in the
theatre. Doubtless one would be right in concluding that no
production has succeeded as yet in fusing the play's darker
with its lighter tones. Yet one may also doubt whether a perfect fusion is possible. Can a lone reader in his armchair ever
feel the full impact of the play as farce, which depends so
directly on the physical presence and comic inventiveness of
the actors, and on the gregariousness of the playhouse? Inside
the theatre one always becomes something more, and less, than
one's ordinary self, a molecule in a larger human community.
Conversely, can the theatre audience, caught up in jokes and

collective laughter, its eyes glued on the visual pleasures of the stage, ever feel all the nuances of the verse, however firmly it may believe in them? Empson himself once ruefully admitted that he believed 'what the notes say about the mad talk of Ophelia, that it had most elaborate connections with the story', though he had 'never heard a modern actress make it seem anything but raving'.[5] But probably no modern actress could bridge the inherent gulf between the play as dramatic poem and the play as theatrical experience. It might be juster to conclude that certain details, certain aspects, will be bound to register differently under differing conditions, and that neither mode of realisation need be viewed as definitive. Each, rather, may be said to realise certain values of the play more fully than the other.

Many old ghosts have vanished from the current critical debate over *Volpone*. Sir Thomas Sutton disappeared in the seventeenth century, and so, in the eighteenth, did the pseudo-problem of Corbaccio as 'caricature'. The inquest opened by Dryden into the structural peculiarities of Act v would seem to be closed; few today would dispute Swinburne's and Herford's verdict, that Volpone's compulsive resumption of his hoaxing, far from being a desperate shift to galvanise a flagging plot, forms one of the master-strokes of the action. Romantic sentimentalism dies harder, but presumably few would wish to endorse the protests of Coleridge and Hazlitt against the wickedness of the characters, especially in the face of such telling rejoinders as that of James Agate. Less categorically, it may be ventured that the Act i interlude, the mountebank scene, and the Sir Politic Would-be scenes have been rescued from the charge of irrelevance, as well as from the scorn of those for whom farce is too low-minded a form of comedy to consort with the more intellectual level of the rest. The once belittled digressions have been restored in the theatre with increasing sureness of touch, and (it would seem) to the increasing approval of judicious spectators.

Certain other critical issues remain unresolved, notably the

one broached by Jonson himself concerning the fitness of the
final punishments. Dryden conceded the utility of Volpone's
disguise in Act v because it helped fulfil Jonson's aim of 'the
punishment of Vice, and the reward of Virtue'. A century
later Cumberland varied the theme : the fable is 'of moral
tendency, female chastity and honour are beautifully displayed
and punishment is inflicted on the delinquents of the drama
with strict and exemplary justice'. But neither Dryden nor
Cumberland speaks to the point Jonson himself raises :
whether punishment *ought* to be inflicted on comic characters
in such 'strict and exemplary' fashion. Neither, that is, asks
whether the ending, however wholesome its morality, con-
forms to the spirit of the rest of the play, and to the spirit of
comedy. It is odd to find Dryden extenuating an aesthetic
lapse so primly, given his usual casualness towards moral con-
siderations. But Jonson himself has supplied the precedent.
For to allege, as he does, that the harsh verdicts are meant 'to
put the snaffle' in the mouths of unfriendly critics – evidently
the Puritans – who 'cry out, we never punish vice in our interludes', is to urge an extrinsic, moralistic basis for an aesthetic
decision, and thus to beg the question. The question the
friends of the comic theatre would wish to ask would be
whether, indeed, we should 'punish vice in our interludes' at
all? And if so, whether there are not punishments and punishments, whether penalties suited to an actual court of law may
not be inappropriate in the freer and more autonomous
tribunals of comedy? Or wherein lies the greater freedom and
autonomy of the creator-artist?

Debate persists, also, with respect to the roles of Celia and
Bonario, who must sustain the cause of virtue unaided among
the Venetian predators. For Cumberland, as we have seen,
'female chastity and honour are beautifully displayed'. For
Swinburne, 'the tone of villainy and the tone of virtue' both
soar to an exceptional pitch. But does Jonson, in truth, intend
us to take these characters straight? Does he never invite our
laughter or tolerate a reaction of callous amusement towards

them? Recent criticism and stage performance have tended to see these victim figures in an equivocal light, their claim on our indignant sympathies by no means so self-evident as older commentary tended to assume. John J. Enck has suggested that Jonson's peculiar triumph as a playwright consisted in his practice of 'negative comedy', from which positive standards have been erased, even though they may confront us at every turn by implication. Is it possible that the two exemplars of virtue in Venice are not meant as exemplary at all?

A final question, interlinked with these others, concerns the name and nature of the force governing the action. Do the good characters win out, as they believe, through heaven's intervention? By miracle, as the *avvocatori* think? Or does evil obey an inner logic that causes it to overreach and destroy itself? In that case, do we therefore assume some guiding intelligence in the cosmos, or merely the operation of the laws of chance? Confronted with the mazes of the final scene, critics have been tempted either piously to endorse the pious conclusions of Celia and Bonario, or to throw up their hands with the second *avvocatore* – 'This same's a *labyrinth*!' – and declare the question unanswerable. Whatever the answer, and whatever the answerability of the question, it has asked itself with mounting insistence in our own generation, and critics have increasingly sought the key to it in the inner dynamics of the plot. The problem of the play's final moments has become, as Jonson was the first to understand, but in ways beyond those he foresaw, the crucial problem for the play as a whole.

Despite the moralism of which Empson complains, which has vitiated some recent criticism, and introduced, no doubt, an element of high strenuousness into a great deal of it, it is hard not to feel that recent investigations have also greatly clarified our sense of the play's nature, formerly obscured in a smog of irrelevancy. To discriminate the properties of the verse, to ponder the moral and aesthetic implications of the finale, is to draw near the heart of the mystery much more directly than by trading random impressions on the likeability of this character or that, or indulging in chit-chat about the propriety of this detail or that. If criticism in our day has not arrived at final answers, it has at least begun to ask the right questions. It is in the conviction that *Volpone* is a masterpiece, inspiriting to read and exhilarating to experience in the theatre, and with the desire to keep debate on it alive and flourishing, that the present samplings from its critical fortunes are collected and offered.

JONAS A. BARISH

NOTES

1. J. F. Bradley and J. Q. Adams (eds), *The Jonson Allusion-Book* (Yale, 1922) p. 153.

2. G. E. Bentley, *Shakespeare and Jonson* (Chicago, 1945) II 273. I am heavily indebted to this volume, as to the Bradley–Adams *Allusion-Book*, for material from the early period. Indispensable, likewise, for tracing the critical progress of *Volpone* in the eighteenth century is R. G. Noyes, *Ben Jonson on the English Stage 1660–1776* (Harvard, 1935) pp. 39–102.

3. See below. Most citations in this Introduction will be to excerpts and essays reprinted below, for which no specific page references will be supplied.

4. 'Volpone', *Hudson Review*, xxi (1968–9) 653.

5. *Some Versions of Pastoral* (Chatto & Windus, 1935) p. 39.

PART ONE

Comment from 1662 to 1920

Likewise my Playes may be Condemned, because they follow not the Antient Custome, as the learned sayes, which is, that all Comedies should be so ordered and composed, as nothing should be presented therein, but what may be naturally, or usually practiced or Acted in the World in the compass of one day; truly in my opinion those Comedies would be very flat and dull, and neither profitable nor pleasant, that should only present the actions of one day; for though *Ben. Johnson* as I have heard was of that opinion, that a Comedy cannot be good, nor is a natural or true Comedy, if it should present more than one dayes action, yet his Comedies that he hath published, could never be the actions of one day; for could any rational person think that the whole Play of the *Fox* could be the action of one day? or can any rational person think that the *Alchymist* could be the action of one day? as that so many several Cozenings could be Acted in one day, by Captain *Face* and *Doll Common*; and could the *Alchymist* make any believe they could make gold in one day? could they burn so many Coals, and draw the purses of so many, or so often from one person, in one day? and the like is in all his Playes, not any of them presents the actions of one day, although it were a day at the Poles, but of many dayes, nay I may say some years.

(from *Playes*, the third preface, 'To the Readers', 1662)

SAMUEL PEPYS

January 14th. . . . Home to dinner, thence with my wife to the King's house, there to see *Vulpone*, a most excellent play; the best I think I ever saw, and well acted.

(from *Diary*, 1665, ed. H. B. Wheatley)

JOHN DRYDEN

'Tis evident that the more the persons are, the greater will be the variety of the Plot. If then the parts are manag'd so regularly that the beauty of the whole be kept intire, and that the variety become not a perplex'd and confus'd mass of accidents, you will find it infinitely pleasing to be led in a labyrinth of design, where you see some of your way before you, yet discern not the end till you arrive at it. And that all this is practicable, I can produce for examples many of our English Plays : as the *Maids Tragedy*, the *Alchymist*, the *Silent Woman*; I was going to have named the *Fox*, but that the unity of design seems not exactly observ'd in it; for there appear two actions in the Play; the first naturally ending with the fourth Act; the second forc'd from it in the fifth : which yet is the less to be condemn'd in him, because the disguise of *Volpone*, though it suited not with his character as a crafty or covetous person, agreed well enough with that of a voluptuary : and by it the Poet gain'd the end at which he aym'd, the punishment of Vice, and the reward of Virtue, both which that disguise produc'd. So that to judge equally of it, it was an excellent fifth Act, but not so naturally proceeding from the former.

(from *An Essay on Dramatic Poesy*, 1668)

NICOLAS BOILEAU

Observe the town, and study well the court;
For thither various characters resort.
Thus 'twas great Jonson purchased his renown,
And in his art had borne away the crown,
If less desirous of the people's praise,
He had not with low farce debased his plays;
Mixing dull buffoonery with wit refined,
And Harlequin with noble Terence joined.
When in the *Fox* I see the tortoise hist,
I lose the author of the *Alchemist*.

(from *The Art of Poesy*, trans. Sir William Soames
and John Dryden, 1683)

JOHN AUBREY

Thomas Sutton (1532–1611)

. . . 'Twas from him that B. Johnson tooke his hint of the fox, and by Seigneur Volpone is meant Sutton. (II 246)

(from *Brief Lives*, 1670–99)

WILLIAM WINSTANLEY

I have conversed with some of the Wits, who credibly informed me, that *Ben Johnsons* Play of the *Fox* under the name of *Vulpone*, had some allusion to Mr [Thomas] *Suttons* manner of treating of his kindred.

(from *England's Worthies*, 1684)

JOHN DENNIS

Dear Sir,

I Have now read over the *Fox*, in which thô I admire the strength of *Ben Johnson*'s Judgment, yet I did not find it so accurate as I expected. For first the very thing upon which the whole Plot turns, and that is the Discovery which *Mosca* makes to *Bonario*; seems to me, to be very unreasonable. For *I* can see no Reason, why he should make that Discovery which introduces *Bonario* into his Masters House. For the Reason which the Poet makes *Mosca* give in the Ninth Scene of the third Act, appears to be a very Absurd one. Secondly, *Corbaccio* the Father of *Bonario* is expos'd for his Deafness, a Personal defect; which is contrary to the end of Comedy Instruction. For Personal Defects cannot be amended; and the exposing such, can never Divert any but half-witted Men. It cannot fail to bring a thinking Man to reflect upon the Misery of Human Nature; and into what he may fall himself without any fault of his own. Thirdly, the play has two Characters, which have nothing to do with the design of it, which are to be look'd upon as Excrescencies. Lastly, the

Character of *Volpone* is Inconsistent with it self. *Volpone* is like *Catiline, alieni appetens, sui profusus*; but that is only a double in his Nature, and not an Inconsistence. The Inconsistence of the Character appears in this, that *Volpone* in the fifth Act behaves himself like a Giddy Coxcombe, in the Conduct of that very Affair which he manag'd so Craftily in the first four. In which the Poet offends first against that Fam'd rule which *Horace* gives for the Characters.

Servetur ad imum,
Qualis ab incepto processerit, et sibi constet.

And Secondly, against Nature, upon which, all the rules are grounded. For so strange an Alteration, in so little a time, is not in Nature, unless it happens by the Accident of some violent passion; which is not the case here. *Volpone* on the sudden behaves himself without common Discretion, in the Conduct of that very Affair which he had manag'd with so much Dexterity, for the space of three Years together. For why does he disguise himself? or why does he repose the last Confidence in *Mosca*? Why does he cause it to be given out that he's Dead? Why, only to Plague his Bubbles. To Plague them, for what? Why only for having been his Bubbles. So that here is the greatest alteration in the World, in the space of twenty-four hours, without any apparent cause. The design of *Volpone* is to Cheat, he has carried on a Cheat for three years together, with Cunning and with Success. And yet he on a sudden in cold blood does a thing, which he cannot but know must Endanger the ruining all.

I am,/Dear Sir,/Your most Humble/Servant.

(from *Letters on Several Occasions*, 1696)

WILLIAM CONGREVE

Sometimes *Personal Defects are misrepresented for Humours.*
I mean, sometimes Characters are barbarously exposed on

the Stage, ridiculing Natural Deformities, Casual Defects in the Senses, and Infirmities of Age. . . . But much need not be said upon this Head to any body, especially to you, who, in one of your Letters to me concerning Mr *Johnson's Fox*, have justly excepted against this Immoral part of *Ridicule* in *Corbaccio's* Character; and there I must agree with you to blame him whom otherwise I cannot enough admire for his great Mastery of true Humour in Comedy. . . .

(from *Letter to Dennis on Humour in Comedy*, 1695)

JEREMY COLLIER

Ben Johnson's Fox is clearly against Mr *Dryden*. And here I have his own Confession for proof. He declares the *Poets end in this Play was the Punishment of Vice, and the Reward of Virtue. Ben* was forced to strain for this piece of Justice, and break through the *Vnity of Design*. This Mr *Dryden* remarks upon him : How ever he is pleased to commend the Performance, and calls it an excellent *Fifth Act*.

Ben Johnson shall speak for himself afterwards in the Character of a Critick. . . .

1*st*. Monsieur *Rapin* affirms 'That Delight is the End that Poetry aims at, but not the Principal one. For Poetry being an Art, ought to be profitable by the quality of it's own nature, and by the Essential Subordination that all Arts should have to Polity, whose End in General is the publick Good. This is the Judgment of *Aristotle* and of *Horace* his chief Interpreter.' *Ben Johnson* in his Dedicatory Epistle of his *Fox* has somewhat considerable upon this Argument; And declaims with a great deal of zeal, spirit, and good Sense, against the Licentiousness of the *Stage*. He lays it down for a Principle, 'That 'tis impossible to be a good *Poet* without being a good *Man*. That he (a good Poet) is said to be able to inform Young Men to all good Discipline, and enflame grown Men to all great Virtues &c. – That the general complaint was that the *Writers* of

those days had nothing remaining in them of the Dignity of a
Poet, but the abused Name. That now, especially in Stage
Poetry, nothing but Ribaldry, Profanation, *Blasphemy*, all
Licence of Offence to God and Man, is practised. He confesses a great part of this Charge is over-true, and is sorry he
dares not deny it. But then he hopes all are not embark'd in
this bold Adventure for Hell. For my part (says he) I can, and
from a most clear Conscience affirm; That I have ever
trembled to think towards the least Profaneness, and loath'd the
Use of such foul, and unwash'd Bawdry, as is now made the
Food of the *Scene*. The encrease of which Lust in Liberty,
what Learned or Liberal Soul does not abhor? In whole
Enterludes nothing but the Filth of the Time is utter'd – with
Brothelry able to violate the Ear of a *Pagan*, and Blasphemy,
to turn the Blood of a Christian to Water. He continues, that
the Insolence of these Men had brought the *Muses* into Disgrace, and made *Poetry* the lowest scorn of the Age. He
appeals to his Patrons the *Vniversities*, that his Labour has
been heretofore, and mostly in this his latest Work, to reduce
not only the antient Forms, but Manners of the *Scene*, the
Innocence and the Doctrine, which is the *Principal End* of
Poesy, to inform Men in the best Reason of Living. Lastly he
adds, that 'he has imitated the Conduct of the Antients in this
Play, The goings out (or Conclusions) of whose *Comedies*,
were not always joyful but oft-times the Bawds, the Slaves,
the Rivals, yea and the Masters are multed, and fitly, it being
the Office of a *Comick Poet* (mark that!) to imitate Justice,
and Instruct to Life &c.' Say you so! Why then if *Ben Johnson*
knew any thing of the Matter, Divertisement and Laughing is
not as Mr *Dryden* affirms, the *Chief End* of *Comedy*. This
Testimony is so very full and clear, that it needs no explaining,
nor any enforcement from Reasoning, and Consequence.

(from *A Short View of the Immorality and
Prophaneness of the English Stage*, 1698)

RICHARD STEELE

Will's Coffee-house, May 27.

This night was acted the comedy, called, the *Fox*; but I wonder the modern writers do not use their interest in the house to suppress such representations. A man that has been at this will hardly like any other play during the season : therefore I humbly move, that the writings, as well as dresses, of the last age, should give way to to the present fashion. We are come into a good method enough, (if we were not interrupted in our mirth by such an apparition as a play of Johnson's) to be entertained at more ease, both to the spectator and the writer, than in the days of old. It is no difficulty to get hats and swords, and wigs and shoes, and every thing else, from the shops in town, and make a man shew himself by his habit, without more ado, to be a counsellor, a fop, a courtier, or a citizen, and not be obliged to make those characters talk in different dialects to be distinguished from each other. This is certainly the surest and best way of writing : but such a play as this makes a man for a month after overrun with criticism, and enquire, 'What every man on the stage said? What had such an one to do to meddle with such a thing? How came t'other, who was bred after this or that manner, to speak so like a man conversant among a different people?' These questions rob us of all our pleasure; for, at this rate, no sentence in a play should be spoken by any one character, which could possibly enter into the head of any other man represented in it; but every sentiment should be peculiar to him only who utters it. Laborious Ben's works will bear this sort of inquisition; but if the present writers were thus examined, and the offences against this rule cut out, few plays would be long enough for the whole evening's entertainment.

But I do not know how they did in those old times : this same Ben Jonson has made every ones passion in this play be towards money; and yet not one of them expresses that desire, or endeavours to obtain it any way but what is peculiar to him only: one sacrifices his wife, another his profession, another his posterity, from the same motive; but their characters are kept so skilfully apart, that it seems prodigious their discourses should rise from the invention of the same author.

(from *The Tatler*, 1709)

RICHARD HURD

The *Volpone*, is a subject so manifestly fitted for the entertainment of all times, that it stands in need of no vindication. Yet neither, I am afraid, is this Comedy, in all respects, a complete model. There are even some Incidents of a farcical invention; particularly the *Mountebank Scene* and *Sir Politique's Tortoise* are in the taste of the *old comedy*; and without its rational purpose. Besides, the *humour* of the dialogue is sometimes on the point of becoming inordinate, as may be seen in the pleasantry of *Corbaccio's mistakes through deafness*, and in other instances. And we shall not wonder that the best of his plays are liable to some objections of this sort, if we attend to the *character* of the writer. For his nature was severe and rigid, and this in giving a strength and manliness, gave, at times too, an intemperance to his satyr. His taste for ridicule was strong but indelicate, which made him not over-curious in the choice of his *topics*. And lastly, his *style* in picturing characters, though masterly, was without that elegance of *hand*, which is required to correct and allay the force of so bold a colouring. Thus, the biass of his nature leading him to Plautus rather than Terence for his model, it is not to be wondered that his wit is too frequently caustic; his raillery coarse; and his humour excessive.

(from *A Dissertation on the Provinces of the Drama*, 1753)

PETER WHALLEY

(*a*) A note on the mountebank scene (II ii)

This whole episode of *Sir Politick Would-be* never did, nor ever can please. He seems to be brought in merely to lengthen out the play. Perhaps too 'tis particular satire.   Mr Upton.

I cannot help thinking this episode to be rather an excrescence than a beauty, as it has no sort of connection with the rest of the play : yet the character is not destitute of humour, and possibly might be intended for some particular person. However, it exposes with great life the taste of that state-intriguing age, in which it was easier to find a politician, than a man.

(*b*) A note on Lady Would-be in the court (iv vi)

There never was a character supported with more propriety, than this of Lady Would-be. She comes into the court in all the violence of passion, and having vented her rage in a hasty epithet or two, she relapses into her usual formality, and begins to compliment the judges. Tired with her breeding and her eloquence, they are obliged not to give her a reply, and proceed to the examination of the other parties. The preceding scene is a great instance of the power of avarice, when the poet brings the father and the husband, to bear testimony against the son and the wife.

(*c*) A note on Mosca and Volpone in the last scene (v xii)

There is true comic humour in these dealings between Mosca and Volpone : and one cannot help observing, that at a time so critical to them both, the covetousness in their tempers defeats their several designs. An instance of great decorum in the poet, whose intention was to display an inherent avarice in every human breast. I do not see why Mr Dryden should say there are two actions in this play; the first naturally ending with the fourth act; the second forced from it in the fifth. The action indeed is something varied, but it still tends to the disappointment and mortification of the pretenders to Volpone's wealth. Yet, as he adds, this disguise of Volpone, tho' not suited to his character, as a crafty or covetous person, agreed

well enough with that of a voluptuary : and, by it, the poet
gained the end at which he aimed, the punishment of vice, and
the reward of virtue, both which that disguise produced.

(from Ben Jonson, *Works*, 1756)

ANONYMOUS

Covent-Garden Theatre, *Nov.* 26.
The Fox

A Comedy, by Ben Jonson.

Ben Jonson, as a Dramatic Writer, seems, by some, to have
been unjustly placed in Competition with the immortal
Shakespear. The number of his Pieces is, indeed, very considerable, and some of them deserve a very high rank in
literary Fame; but his Comedies are infinitely superior to his
Tragedies. . . . Of these *Volpone* has been generally considered
as the principal, in point of Merit; and certain it is, that with
respect to Character and Language, it is very highly finished.
The Plot is perfectly original; in the Conduct of which, the
Author has discovered great Erudition and Correctness. The
circumstance of *Volpone*'s taking advantage of the depravity
of human Nature in others, yet suffering himself to be duped
and overreached by the subtility of *Mosca*, (a Creature of his
own raising) is happily imagined, and executed in a very
masterly manner. But, with all these perfections, it seems
better calculated to afford pleasure in the Closet, than on the
Stage, as there is an evident deficiency of incident, and interest
in the Catastrophe, which renders it incapable of giving that
satisfaction in the Representation, it undoubtedly must afford
on a perusal. It is only for real Genius to taste that redundance
of inexpressible beauties, which appears through the whole,
and which must render it, as *Hamlet* says, '*Caviare to the
Multitude*' – After all, though the Piece before us will not
produce those pleasing sensations on the Stage, arising from
the Flashes of Nature, Passion and Genius which the Plays of

Shakespear never fail to bestow, the present lamentable dearth of good Comic Writers, will sufficiently justify the revival of it. . . .

As this Comedy is now represented, most of the obsolete Passages, and many blameable intrusions upon delicacy of idea, and expression in the original, are sensibly omitted, the latter being unsuitable to the professed chastity of the present age; and some Scenes are transposed, and others omitted as superfluous, by which judicious alteration, the appearance of new Characters, and the quicker succession of incidents, contributes more agreeably to heighten and promote the progress of the main design. . . .

With respect to the Representation of this Play, the principal Characters, viz. *Volpone, Mosca, Voltore, Corvino, Corbachio,* and *Bonario,* are well performed by Messrs *Smith, Bensley, Hull, Clarke, Shuter,* and *Wroughton,* so well, that they appear to fill the Author's Ideas very pleasingly and very justly, except, that Mr *Hull,* who is generally natural and correct in his playing, rather over-acts his Part in the capacity of the *Advocate,* in the Scenes before the *Avocatori,* in the Senate. With respect to Mr *Shuter,* in the Character of *Corbachio,* we are glad to remark, that his Performance throughout, is chaste and attentively correct, without the least taint of that over-strained luxuriancy of humour, he too frequently displays, and which almost perpetually runs into buffoonery. His strokes of Bye play, of endeavouring to hasten the death of *Volpone,* (whom he supposes to be sick, and near his end, on the Couch) by pressing his stomach with his cane, while *Mosca* is engaged with *Voltore,* are well imagined, when we consider, that in this Character, Nature is rather caricatured, which is the general, tho' only fault of this Author, in his Comic Writings. . . .

(from *The Theatrical Review,* 1771)

The Fable of *Volpone* is chosen with judgement, and is founded upon avarice and luxury. The paying obsequious and constant courtship to childless rich people, with a view to obtain from them bountiful legacies in return, has been a practice of all times, and in all nations. There is in Lucian, the father of true ridicule, an admirable dialogue, on this subject, between Pluto and Mercury. An old man of ninety is assiduously courted by several young fellows, who, in hopes of being his heirs, perform the lowest and meanest offices to him. Pluto orders Mercury to carry off these rascals, who are dividing, in their minds, the old fellow's riches, to the infernal shades, but commands him to double, nay, treble, the age of him who is the object of their obsequiousness. Lucian has no less than five or six dialogues on the same subject.

In the comedy of *The Fox*, there is not much to be censured, except the language, which is so pedantic and stuck so full of Latinity, that few, except the learned, can perfectly understand it. 'Jonson, says Dr Young, brought all the antients upon his head : by studying to speak like a Roman, he forgot the language of his country.'

The conduct of the plot in the first four acts, except the mountebank scene, is truly admirable. The last act is, in my opinion, quite farcical. That a man of Volpone's sagacity should venture to appear in public, in the disguise of a mountebank, to be an eye-witness of a lady's beauty, of which he had heard only from report, and after escaping from the apprehended consequences of this exorbitant frolic, which had brought him within the censure of a court of judicature, upon the bare declaration of the judges in his favour, and against those he had caused to be unjustly accused; that he should again assume another shape, that of an apparitor or tipstaff; make a pretended will; leave all his money, jewels, and effects, pretendedly to so wretched a fellow as a pimp and parasite; and all this with no other view than to mortify, insult, and

abuse, those whom he had gulled, while yet the sentence of
the court was depending, is a matter as absurd and improbable
as any thing acted at the Italian comedy.

(from *Dramatic Miscellanies,* 1783)

RICHARD CUMBERLAND

. . . After all it will be confessed that the production of such a
drama as *The Fox* in the space of five weeks is a very wonderful performance; for it must on all hands be considered as the
master-piece of a very capital artist, a work, that bears the
stamp of elaborate design, a strong and frequently a sublime
vein of poetry, much sterling wit, comic humour, happy
character, moral satire and unrivalled erudition; a work –

> Quod non imber edax, non aquilo impotens
> Possit diruere, aut innumerabilis
> Annorum series et fuga temporum.

In this drama the learned reader will find himself for ever
treading upon classic ground; the foot of the poet is so fitted
and familiarized to the Grecian sock, that he wears it not with
the awkwardness of an imitator, but with all the easy confidence and authoritative air of a privileged Athenian:
Exclusive of Aristophanes, in whose volume he is perfect,
it is plain that even the gleanings and broken fragments
of the Greek stage had not escaped him; in the very first
speech of Volpone's, which opens the comedy, and in
which he rapturously addresses himself to his treasure, he is to
be traced most decidedly in the fragments of Menander,
Sophocles and Euripides, in Theognis and in Hesiod, not to
mention Horace. . . .
    The Fox is indubitably the best production of it's author,
and in some points of substantial merit yields to nothing,
which the English stage can oppose to it; there is a bold and
happy spirit in the fable, it is of moral tendency, female chas-

tity and honour are beautifully displayed and punishment is inflicted on the delinquents of the drama with strict and exemplary justice : The characters of the *Hæredipetæ*, depicted under the titles of birds of prey, *Voltore, Corbaccio* and *Corvino*, are warmly coloured, happily contrasted and faithfully supported from the outset to the end : *Volpone*, who gives his name to the piece, with a fox-like craftiness deludes and gulls their hopes by the agency of his inimitable Parasite, or (as the Greek and Roman authors expressed it) by his *Fly*, his *Mosca*; and in this finished portrait Jonson may throw the gauntlet to the greatest masters of antiquity; the character is of classic origin; it is found with the contemporaries of Aristophanes, though not in any comedy of his now existing; the Middle Dramatists seem to have handled it very frequently, and in the New Comedy it rarely failed to find a place; Plautus has it again and again, but the aggregate merit of all his Parasites will not weigh in the scale against this single *Fly* of our poet : The incident of his concealing *Bonario* in the gallery, from whence he breaks in upon the scene to the rescue of Celia and the detection of *Volpone*, is one of the happiest contrivances, which could possibly be devised, because at the same time that it produces the catastrophe, it does not sacrifice *Mosca's* character in the manner most villains are sacrificed in comedy by making them commit blunders, which do not correspond with the address their first representation exhibits and which the audience has a right to expect from them throughout, of which the *Double Dealer* is amongst others a notable instance. But this incident of *Bonario's* interference does not only not impeach the adroitness of the Parasite, but it furnishes a very brilliant occasion for setting off his ready invention and presence of mind in a new and superior light, and serves to introduce the whole machinery of the trial and condemnation of the innocent persons before the court of *Advocates* : In this part of the fable the contrivance is inimitable, and here the poet's art is a study, which every votarist of the dramatic muses ought to pay attention and respect to; had the same

address been exerted throughout, the construction would have
been a matchless piece of art, but here we are to lament the
haste of which he boasts in his prologue, and that rapidity of
composition, which he appeals to as a mark of genius, is to be
lamented as the probable cause of incorrectness, or at least the
best and most candid plea in excuse of it: For who can deny
that nature is violated by the absurdity of *Volpone*'s unseasonable insults to the very persons, who had witnessed falsely in
his defence, and even to the very *Advocate*, who had so
successfully defended him? Is it in character for a man of his
deep cunning and long reach of thought to provoke those, on
whom his all depended, to retaliate upon him, and this for the
poor triumph of a silly jest? Certainly this is a glaring defect,
which every body must lament, and which can escape nobody.
The poet himself knew the weak part of his plot and vainly
strives to bolster it up by making *Volpone* exclaim against his
own folly –

I am caught in my own noose –

And again –

To make a snare for mine own neck, and run
My head into it wilfully with laughter!
When I had newly 'scap'd, was free and clear,
Out of mere wantonness! Oh, the dull devil
Was in this brain of mine, when I devis'd it,
And Mosca gave it second . . .
        . . . These are my fine conceits!
I must be merry, with a mischief to me!
What a vile wretch was I, that cou'd not bear
My fortune soberly! I must have my crotchets,
And my conundrums! . . .

It is with regret I feel myself compelled to protest against so
pleasant an episode, as that which is carried on by *Sir Politic
Wou'd-be* and *Peregrine*, which in fact produces a kind of
double plot and catastrophe; this is an imperfection in the

fable, which criticism cannot overlook, but *Sir Politic* is altogether so delightful a fellow, that it is impossible to give a vote for his exclusion; the most that can be done against him is to lament that he has not more relation to the main business of the fable.

The judgment pronounced upon the criminals in the conclusion of the play is so just and solemn, that I must think the poet has made a wanton breach of character and gained but a sorry jest by the bargain, when he violates the dignity of his court of judges by making one of them so abject in his flattery to the Parasite upon the idea of matching him with his daughter, when he hears that Volpone has made him his heir; but this is an objection, that lies within the compass of two short lines, spoken aside from the bench, and may easily be remedied by their omission in representation; it is one only, and that a very slight one, amongst those venial blemishes –

    ... quas incuria fudit.

It does not occur to me that any other remark is left for me to make upon this celebrated drama, that could convey the slightest censure; but very many might be made in the highest strain of commendation, if there was need of any more than general testimony to such acknowledged merit. *The Fox* is a drama of so peculiar a species, that it cannot be dragged into a comparison with the production of any other modern poet whatsoever; it's construction is so dissimilar from any thing of Shakespear's writing, that it would be going greatly out of our way, and a very gross abuse of criticism to attempt to settle the relative degrees of merit, where the characters of the writers are so widely opposite : In one we may respect the profundity of learning, in the other we must admire the sublimity of genius; to one we pay the tribute of understanding, to the other we surrender up the possession of our hearts; Shakespear with ten thousand spots about him dazzles us with so bright a lustre, that we either cannot or will not see his faults; he

gleams and flashes like a meteor, which shoots out of our sight
before the eye can measure it's proportions, or analyse it's
properties – but Jonson stands still to be surveyed, and presents so bold a front, and levels it so fully to our view, as seems
to challenge the compass and the rule of the critic, and defy
him to find out an error in the scale and composition of his
structure.

Putting aside therefore any further mention of Shakespear,
who was a poet out of all rule, and beyond all compass of
criticism, one whose excellencies are above comparison, and
his errors beyond number, I will venture an opinion that this
drama of *The Fox* is, critically speaking, the nearest to perfection of any one drama, comic or tragic, which the English
stage is at this day in possession of.

(from *The Observer*, no. cx, 1788)

CHARLES DIBDIN

Volpone; or the Fox, was performed in 1605, and has been
generally considered as Jonson's best production. Certainly the
plot is upon a very meritorious principle, and the characters
are forcibly drawn. A knave who feigns illness in order to
impose upon knaves, and cheat them of their money by working up their credulity into a belief that each shall become his
heir, is one of the boldest ideas of a character that can be conceived, and yet moral justice is rendered more complete by
making that knave imposed upon by another of yet superior
cunning; shewing that the machinations of the wicked, be they
ever so subtle, are constantly counteracted by the same devil
that inspired them.

The group of characters that are introduced to work up
those materials, are full of contrast, strength, and nature;
would not one think it, therefore, very extraordinary that this
piece, even supported by admirable acting, has never greatly
succeeded? Nothing, considered superficially, can be so un-
accountable; but, when the subject is fairly investigated,

nothing can be more clearly comprehended. Quaint, dry, studied correctness, unsupported by quickness, spirit, and fire, can never satisfy. The author in this piece conducts us into a uniform and proportionable building, presents us with an entertainment, and introduces us to company, but the apartments are cheerless vaults, the viands are carved marble, and the guests are statues.

(from *A Complete History of the English Stage*, 1800)

WILLIAM GIFFORD

(*a*) From the General Introduction

The *Fox* was received, as it well deserved to be, with general applause. The author's enemies however were not inactive: they could not venture to question his talents; they therefore turned, as usual, their attacks against his character, and asserted that, under the person of Volpone, he had satirized Sutton, the founder of the Charter House, his friend and benefactor.[1] It is not a little amusing to see the calumniators of our poet in that age, driven to the same absurdities as those of the present day. Two characters more opposite in every respect than those of Sutton and Volpone are not to be found in the history of mankind. Sutton inherited a large estate; he was one of the greatest traders of his time, he had agents in every country, and ships on every sea: he had contracts, mines, mills, ploughs, he was a naval commissioner, and master of the ordnance in the north; in a word, one of the most active characters of an active period. Now mark the description of Volpone, as given by himself, in the opening of the play:

> ... I glory
> More in the *cunning purchase* of my wealth
> Than in the glad possession; since I gain
> No *common* way. I *use no trade*, no *venture*,
> I wound no earth with *plough-shares*, fat *no beasts*
> To feed the shambles; have no *mills* for iron,

Oil, corn, or men, to grind them into powder;
I blow no subtle glass, expose no *ships*
To threatnings of the furrow-faced seas;
I turn no monies, &c. &c.

Sutton was a meek and pious man, Volpone is a daring
infidel; Sutton was abstemious, but kind and charitable; Volpone is painted as the most selfish and unfeeling of volup-
tuaries:

> ... prepare
> Me music, dances, banquets, all delights:
> The Turk is not more sensual in his pleasure
> Than will Volpone be.

Again: Volpone is a creature of ungovernable lust, a monster of seduction; Sutton was the husband of one wife, to
whose memory he was so tenderly attached, that upon her
death, which took place about two years before the date of this
piece, he had retired from the world, to a life of strictness and
reserve; he was, at this time, nearly fourscore, and bowed down
to the grave with sorrow for his loss, while Volpone, in the full
vigour of manhood, exclaims –

> what should I do
> But cocker up my genius, and live free
> To all delights? – See, I am now as fresh,
> As hot, as high, and in as jovial plight,
> As when, in that so celebrated scene,
> For entertainment of the great Valois
> I acted young Antinous?

In a word, the contrast is so glaring, that if the commentators on Shakespeare had not afforded us a specimen of what
ignorance grafted on malevolence can do, we should be lost in
wonder at the obliquity of intellect which could detect the
slightest resemblance of Sutton in the features of Volpone.

The *Fox* is dedicated, in a strain of unparallelled elegance
and vigour, to the two Universities, before whom it had been

represented with all the applause which might be anticipated from such distinguished and competent judges of its worth.[2] The English stage had hitherto seen nothing so truly classical, so learned, so correct, and so chaste.

NOTES

1. 'Sutton's biographer (S. Herne) after noticing this report, says – "It is probable the poet never intended what they think : for in that age several other men were pointed at, and who was the true person, was *then* a matter of doubt!" (*Dom. Carthus.,* p. 42). It is no longer so – we are better judges of these matters than the contemporaries of Sutton, and decide without difficulty.' I regret to find Mr D'Israeli among the poet's accusers; for he is an anxious inquirer after truth, and brings, as far as I have been able to discover, an unprejudiced mind to his investigations. His fault is too great a deference for names unworthy of his trust. This is an evil which every day will contribute to abate. Twice in one page (*Quarrels of Authors,* III 134) he charges Jonson with bringing Sutton on the stage.

2. There is an allusion to this circumstance in the verse of Jonson's friend E. S. (Edward Scorey?) :

> . . . now he (the *Fox*) hath run his train and shown
> His subtile body, where he best was known,
> In both Minerva's cities, he doth yield
> His well-form'd limbs upon this open field, &c.

(*b*) From the afterword to *Volpone*, following quotation of a portion of the essay of Richard Cumberland, reprinted above (pp. 39–43)

This excellent analysis of the *Fox*, was written by Mr Cumberland, a man peculiarly fitted by nature for dramatic criticism; but who wasted his ingenuity and his talents in an eager and excessive chase after general notoriety, which frequently led him beyond the sphere of his knowledge. . . . The point on which Mr Cumberland chiefly rests, is the injury done to the unity of the plot by the disguise of Volpone in the last act, which he terms a violation of nature. Now it is evident, I think, that this forms the great moral of the play, and that Jonson had it in view from the beginning. 'Is it in character', Mr Cumberland asks, 'for a man of Volpone's deep cunning, and long reach of thought to provoke those on whom his all depended, to retaliate upon him, and this for the poor triumph of a silly jest?' Mr Cumberland shall answer his own question. In his review of the *Double Dealer* (ibid., p. 244), he finds Maskwell, like Volpone, losing his caution in the exultation of success; upon which he observes: 'I allow that it is in character for him to grow wanton in success; there is *a moral in a villain out-witting himself.*' This appears a singular change of opinion in the course of a few pages: but, whatever may be Mr Cumberland's versatility, Jonson is consistent with himself and with the invariable experience of mankind. 'See', says Falstaff, 'how wit may be made a jackanapes when 'tis upon an ill employ!' The same sentiment is to be found in Beaumont and Fletcher:

> Hell gives us *art* to reach the depths of sin,
> But leaves us *wretched fools* when we are in.
> *(Queen of Corinth)*

This, too, is the moral of the *New Way to Pay Old Debts,* so strikingly pointed out by Massinger:

> Here is a precedent to teach wicked men,
> That when they quit religion and turn atheists,
> Their own abilities leave them.

And, finally, this is inculcated by Butler in the quatrain already given, and which its shrewdness and applicability, will justify me in giving once more:

> But when he'd got himself a name
> For fraud and tricks, he spoil'd his game;
> And forced his neck into a noose,
> To shew his play at Fast-and-Loose.

Mr Cumberland allows Sir Politick to be 'a delightful fellow', and will not, therefore, hear of his exclusion. But could he find nothing to say for his lady, the most finished, and amusing female pedant which the stage ever produced? – Through her, Sir Politick is, in some measure, connected with the plot; and both are occasionally subservient to the poet's main design.

With regard to 'the breach of character, in making one of the judges conceive the idea of matching his daughter with Mosca', Mr Cumberland himself admits that the objection is confined to the 'compass of two lines spoken aside'. But in justice to this learned personage, let it be further remarked that his determination is founded upon the actual demise of Volpone, in which case, as he justly concludes, the parasite is freed from all suspicions of fraud and imposture. It seems to have escaped Mr Cumberland's recollection that Mosca is not the servant, but the humble friend of Volpone; and it is quite certain that he has not penetrated into the author's views in this part of the scene.

Mr Cumberland pronounces the *Fox*, 'indubitably the best production of its author', and this appears to be the prevailing opinion. I venture, however, to declare my dissent, and to place that prodigy of human intellect, the *Alchemist*, at the head of Jonson's labours. The opinion of Mr Cumberland may be candidly accounted for, from his more intimate acquaintance with the illustrious originals which furnished much of the strength and beauty of the *Fox*, than with the obscure and humble sources, from which this mighty genius derived the rude materials of the *Alchemist*. With respect to the popular decision on this subject, it has no better foundation, perhaps, than the accidental collocation of his plays in the homely couplet so often repeated :

The Fox, the *Alchemist*, and *Silent Woman*,
Done by Ben Jonson, and outdone by no man.

But it is time to draw to a conclusion. I shall therefore only subjoin a few lines from Hurd (a man seldom just to Jonson, never friendly), and leave the reader to wonder at the perversity which could maintain that the author of the *Fox* had 'stalked for two centuries on the *stilts of artificial* reputation'.

'Later writers for the stage have, no doubt, avoided these defects (the sporting with Corbaccio's deafness, &c., p. 192) of the exactest of our old dramatists. But do they reach his excellencies? Posterity, I am afraid, will judge otherwise, whatever may be now thought of some fashionable comedies. And if they do not, – neither the state of general manners, nor the turn of public taste appears to be such as countenances the expectation of greater improvements.' – Μαντι κακων! – 'To those who are not over sanguine in their hopes, our forefathers will perhaps be thought to have furnished (what, in nature, seemed linked together) the fairest example of dramatic, as of real manners.' (*Hor.* II 244).

(from Ben Jonson, *Works*, 1816)

WILLIAM HAZLITT

His portraits are caricatures by dint of their very likeness, being extravagant tautologies of themselves; as his plots are improbable by an excess of consistency; for he goes thorough-stitch with whatever he takes in hand, makes one contrivance answer all purposes, and every obstacle give way to a predetermined theory. For instance, nothing can be more incredible than the mercenary conduct of Corvino, in delivering up his wife to the palsied embraces of Volpone; and yet the poet does not seem in the least to boggle at the incongruity of it : but the more it is in keeping with the absurdity of the rest of the fable, and the more it advances it to an incredible catastrophe, the more he seems to dwell upon it with complacency and a sort of wilful exaggeration, as if it were a logical discovery or corollary from well-known premises. . . .

The Fox, or *Volpone*, is his best play. It is prolix and improbable, but intense and powerful. It is written *con amore*. It is made up of cheats and dupes, and the author is at home among them. He shews his hatred of the one and contempt for the other, and makes them set one another off to great advantage. There are several striking dramatic contrasts in this play, where the Fox lies *perdue* to watch his prey, where Mosca is the dextrous go-between, outwitting his gulls, his employer, and himself, and where each of the gaping legacy-hunters, the lawyer, the merchant, and the miser, eagerly occupied with the ridiculousness of the other's pretensions, is blind only to the absurdity of his own : but the whole is worked up too mechanically, and our credulity overstretched at last revolts into scepticism, and our attention overtasked flags into drowsiness. This play seems formed on the model of Plautus, in unity of plot and interest; and old Ben, in emulating his classic model, appears to have done his best. There is the same caustic unsparing severity in it as in his other works. His patience is tried to the utmost. His words drop gall.

> Hood an ass with reverend purple,
> So you can hide his too ambitious ears,
> And he shall pass for a cathedral doctor.

The scene between Volpone, Mosca, Voltore, Corvino, and Corbaccio, at the outset, will shew the dramatic power in the conduct of this play, and will be my justification in what I have said of the literal tenaciousness (to a degree that is repulsive) of the author's imaginary descriptions.

(from *Lectures on the English Comic Writers*, 1819)

⅄ SAMUEL TAYLOR COLERIDGE

This admirable, indeed, but yet more wonderful than admirable, play is from the fertility and vigour of invention, character, language, and sentiment the strongest proof, how impossible it is to keep up any pleasurable interest in a tale, in which

there is no goodness of heart in any of the prominent characters. After the third act, this play becomes not a dead, but a
painful, weight on the feelings. Zeluco is an instance of the
same truth. Bonario and Celia should have been made in some
way or other principals in the plot; which they might have
been, and the objects of interest, without having been made
characters. In novels, the person, in whose fate you are most
interested, is often the least marked character of the whole. If
it were possible to lessen the paramountcy of Volpone himself,
a most delightful comedy might be produced, by making Celia
the ward or niece of Corvino, instead of his wife, and Bonario
her lover.

(from *Literary Remains*, 1836)

ALGERNON CHARLES SWINBURNE

In 1605 the singular and magnificent coalition of powers
which served to build up the composite genius of Jonson displayed in a single masterpiece the consummate and crowning
result of its marvellous energies. No other of even his very
greatest works is at once so admirable and so enjoyable. The
construction or composition of *The Alchemist* is perhaps more
wonderful in the perfection and combination of cumulative
detail, in triumphant simplicity of process and impeccable
felicity of result : but there is in *Volpone* a touch of something
like imagination, a savour of something like romance, which
gives a higher tone to the style and a deeper interest to the
action. The chief agents are indeed what Mr Carlyle would
have called 'unspeakably unexemplary mortals' : but the
serious fervour and passionate intensity of their resolute and
resourceful wickedness give somewhat of a lurid and distorted
dignity to the display of their doings and sufferings, which is
wanting to the less gigantic and heroic villainies of Subtle, Dol,
and Face. The absolutely unqualified and unrelieved rascality
of every agent in the later comedy – unless an exception should
be made in favour of the unfortunate though enterprising

Surly – is another note of inferiority; a mark of comparative
baseness in the dramatic metal. In *Volpone* the tone of villainy
and the tone of virtue are alike higher. Celia is a harmless lady,
if a too submissive consort; Bonario is an honourable gentleman, if too dutiful a son. The Puritan and shopkeeping scoun-
drels who are swindled by Face and plundered by Lovewit are
viler if less villainous figures than the rapacious victims of
Volpone. . . . Nor can I admit, as I cannot discern, the blemish
or imperfection which others have alleged that they descry in
the composition of *Volpone* – the unlikelihood of the device by
which retribution is brought down in the fifth act on the
criminals who were left at the close of the fourth act in im-
pregnable security and triumph. So far from regarding the
comic Nemesis or rather Ate which infatuates and impels
Volpone to his doom as a sacrifice of art to morality, an
immolation of probability and consistency on the altar of
poetic justice, I admire as a master-stroke of character the
haughty audacity of caprice which produces or evolves his ruin
out of his own hardihood and insolence of exulting and daring
enjoyment. For there is something throughout of the lion as
well as of the fox in this original and incomparable figure. I
know not where to find a third instance of catastrophe comparable with that of either *The Fox* or *The Alchemist* in the
whole range of the highest comedy; whether for completeness,
for propriety, for interest, for ingenious felicity of event or for
perfect combination and exposition of all the leading characters at once in supreme simplicity, unity, and fullness of cul-
minating effect.

(from *A Study of Ben Jonson*, 1889)

G. GREGORY SMITH

When, after four years, Jonson returns to the comic stage with
Volpone, he betrays the effects of his sullen retreat to tragedy.
Personal animosities have lost their bitterness, though, in the
Prologue and once in the play (II i), the insults on his slow

art, his collaboration, and his plagiarism still rankle. Yet he
would claim that

> All gall and copperas from his ink he draineth,
>   Only a little salt remaineth. (Prologue)

In the Dedication to the Universities, he declares that those
who cater for 'the multitude' may 'do it without a rival, for
me', and promises, 'if my Muses be true to me', to 'raise the
despised head of Poetry again, and stripping her out of those
rotten and base rags wherewith the times have adulterated her
form, restore her to her primitive habit, feature, and majesty,
and render her worthy to be embraced and kist of all the great
and master-spirits of our world'. There is temper in this mood,
but more dignity, or at least a staying of personal clamour
against poetasters. Jonson's resolve carried with it one serious
risk, that he might overstrain the functions of comedy, as
reserved for the lighter faults of men; and another, more personal to himself, that he might throw the weaknesses of his
'humorous' method into stronger relief. The theme of *Volpone*
is the familiar story of the machinations of a cunning, greedy
man and his clever parasite, the follies of their dupes, and the
final undoing of all parties; but Jonson, notwithstanding his
liberal allowance of good fun, tunes it to a pitch unexpected in
comedy, and in one place at least, where Corvino (not the
wittol of Restoration comedy) would force his wife to shame,
strikes the note of tragedy. All the chief characters, indeed all
except the English knight and his lady and the unhappy Celia,
are so ill-conditioned, that they forbid the 'sporting' sympathy
on which comedy, by Jonson's own rule, must rely. Their
deeds are 'crimes' rather than 'follies'. The Fox and his friends
are never mere mischief-makers; they are villains of the stuff
of which tragedy makes use, but without the dignity conveyed
in her treatment, playing with a natural frankness, with no
suggestion of the discrepancy between real and assumed
character which gives comedy its great opportunity. It matters

not that there is a happy ending to the sorrows of minor characters. The excess in depravity is here never a reasonable cause of entertainment, as it might be, and can be shown to be, in certain plays, when a character admitting poor defence on general grounds may be useful in serving the purpose of innocent pleasure. The satirical intensity rarely, if ever, permits that laughter at vice, which is 'the greatest of all possible incongruity'. The piece is a dramatic satire, or, better, a satirist's comedy. Not a single character in it is real, even in the sense proclaimed by Jonson himself. Everything is drawn to exaggeration : the scene is laid in Venice, the mother-city of splendid vice; there is one continuous suggestion of luxury, in Volpone's surroundings, in his wooing of Celia in terms out-Marlowing Marlowe. The intrigue is slight and the *dénouement* is reached by the weak dramatic device of making triumphant villainy overreach itself or be suddenly pricked in conscience; but the play, thanks to its observance of the unity of time, moves easily, notwithstanding such minor faults as the unnecessary tedium of the Fox's rôle as a mountebank, or the inexplicable entry of Bonario into the Magnifico's house, and it gathers some dramatic strength, if only in a reflex way, from the cumulative extravagance of the satire. Jonson's introduction of Sir Politic Would-be, his wife, and Peregrine in a comic underplot with little or no connexion with the main story is a confession and amends to Comedy for giving in her name this unrelieved sketch of human depravity. The soul of the piece is the parasite Mosca, Volpone's 'witty mischief'. But we suspect his humanity, as we suspect Volpone's, and, it may be, Voltore's, and Corbaccio's, and Corvino's, and only listen to him with the respect we give to a well-contrived hyperbole.

(from *Ben Jonson*, 1919)

T. S. ELIOT

Largely on the evidence of the two Humour plays, it is sometimes assumed that Jonson is occupied with types; typical

exaggerations, or exaggerations of type. The Humour definition, the expressed intention of Jonson, may be satisfactory for
these two plays. *Every Man in His Humour* is the first mature
work of Jonson, and the student of Jonson must study it; but
it is not the play in which Jonson found his genius : it is the last
of his plays to read first. If one reads *Volpone,* and after that
re-reads the *Jew of Malta*; than returns to Jonson and reads
Bartholomew Fair, The Alchemist, Epicœne and *The Devil is
an Ass,* and finally *Catiline,* it is possible to arrive at a fair
opinion of the poet and the dramatist.

The Humour, even at the beginning, is not a type, as in
Marston's satire, but a simplified and somewhat distorted
individual with a typical mania. In the later work, the Humour
definition quite fails to account for the total effect produced.
The characters of Shakespeare are such as might exist in
different circumstances than those in which Shakespeare sets
them. The latter appear to be those which extract from the
characters the most intense and interesting realization; but
that realization has not exhausted their possibilities. Volpone's
life, on the other hand, is bounded by the scene in which it is
played; in fact, the life is the life of the scene and is deriva-
tively the life of Volpone; the life of the character is insepar-
able from the life of the drama. This is not dependence upon a
background, or upon a substratum of fact. The emotional
effect is single and simple. Whereas in Shakespeare the effect is
due to the way in which the characters *act upon* one another,
in Jonson it is given by the way in which the characters *fit in*
with each other. The artistic result of *Volpone* is not due to
any effect that Volpone, Mosca, Corvino, Corbaccio, Voltore
have upon each other, but simply to their combination into a
whole. And these figures are not personifications of passions;
separately, they have not even that reality, they are constituents. It is a similar indication of Jonson's method that you
can hardly pick out a line of Jonson's and say confidently that
it is great poetry; but there are many extended passages to
which you cannot deny that honour.

> I will have all my beds blown up, not stuft;
> Down is too hard; and then, mine oval room
> Fill'd with such pictures as Tiberius took
> From Elephantis, and dull Aretine
> But coldly imitated. Then, my glasses
> Cut in more subtle angles, to disperse
> And multiply the figures, as I walk. . . .

Jonson is the legitimate heir of Marlowe. The man who
wrote, in *Volpone* :

> for thy love,
> In varying figures, I would have contended
> With the blue Proteus, or the hornèd flood. . . .

and

> See, a carbuncle
> May put out both the eyes of our Saint Mark;
> A diamond would have bought Lollia Paulina,
> When she came in like star-light, hid with jewels. . . .

is related to Marlowe as a poet; and if Marlowe is a poet,
Jonson is also. And, if Jonson's comedy is a comedy of
humours, then Marlowe's tragedy, a large part of it, is a
tragedy of humours. But Jonson has too exclusively been considered as the typical representative of a point of view toward
comedy. He has suffered from his great reputation as a critic
and theorist, from the effects of his intelligence. We have been
taught to think of him as the man, the dictator (confusedly in
our minds with his later namesake), as the literary politician
impressing his views upon a generation; we are offended by
the constant reminder of his scholarship. We forget the comedy
in the humours, and the serious artist in the scholar. Jonson
has suffered in public opinion, as anyone must suffer who is
forced to talk about his art.

If you examine the first hundred lines or more of *Volpone*
the verse appears to be in the manner of Marlowe, more deliberate, more mature, but without Marlowe's inspiration. It
looks like mere 'rhetoric', certainly not 'deeds and language

such as men do use'. It appears to us, in fact, forced and flagitious bombast. That it is not 'rhetoric', or at least not vicious rhetoric, we do not know until we are able to review the whole play. For the consistent maintenance of this manner conveys in the end an effect not of verbosity, but of bold, even shocking and terrifying directness. We have difficulty in saying exactly what produces this simple and single effect. It is not in any ordinary way due to management of intrigue. Jonson employs immense dramatic constructive skill : it is not so much skill in plot as skill in doing without a plot. He never manipulates as complicated a plot as that of *The Merchant of Venice*; he has in his best plays nothing like the intrigue of Restoration comedy. In *Bartholomew Fair* it is hardly a plot at all; the marvel of the play is the bewildering rapid chaotic action of the fair; it is the fair itself, not anything that happens in the fair. In *Volpone*, or *The Alchemist*, or *The Silent Woman*, the plot is enough to keep the players in motion; it is rather an 'action' than a plot. The plot does not hold the play together; what holds the play together is a unity of inspiration that radiates into plot and personages alike.

(from 'Ben Jonson', 1919, reprinted in *Selected Essays*, 1951)

PART TWO

Articles and Essays from 1925 to the Present

C. H. Herford

INTRODUCTION TO *VOLPONE* (1925)

I

Volpone, the amazing product of five weeks' labour, was most probably written during the first months of 1606.[1] It was acted shortly after its completion by the King's Men at the Globe; and later on, perhaps in the autumn term of the same year, with great 'love and acceptance' before the two Universities. Early in 1607–8[2] Jonson published it in quarto, with a stately and pregnant dedicatory address, the most important document we possess of his notions in criticism, and of his mind about his own art in this early phase of his career.

With *Volpone* Jonson returned, in his own view at least, to comedy. But it was to comedy widely different from all previous work of his own in that kind, and rather hard to accommodate not merely to the elastic Elizabethan notions of comic art, but (what Jonson cared much more for) to 'the strict rigour of' ancient '*comick* law'. In the sternness of the catastrophe, as Jonson felt, it approached tragedy. And in its whole conception and conduct, in the lurid atmosphere which pervades it from beginning to end, in the appalling and menacing character of the principal movers of the plot, it approaches, not indeed the profound and human-hearted tragedies of Shakespeare, but, very obviously and significantly, his own grandiose and terrible tragedy of two years before. *Sejanus* opened up to him that new technique in drama of which *Volpone* was to be the finest fruit. History, in the great example of Sejanus' career and fall, brought home to him anew the immense value of a continuous and close-knitted plot, with terror and scorn for its ruling motives; it perhaps impressed him also, anew, with the wealth, in dramatic material of this kind, of the records of imperial Rome, still unexplored and unexploited by his dramatic contemporaries. Among Roman institutions thus capable of yielding terror and scorn, yet rich too in the grim and sardonic comedy which suited Jonson's present mood, that of legacy-hunting (*captatio*) stood in the front rank. The Roman *captator* who presented his fortune to the legatee in the expectation of a more than corresponding reward, and the prospective legatee who played maliciously on the greed of rival candidates for his bequests, might seem to be ready-made sources for Jonsonian comedy, so aptly do they fall into his standing categories of the cheated and the cheat. His earlier comedy had 'sported' with the comparatively naïve follies and pretensions of his day. His later applied its more elaborate technique to organized humbug and corruption, – alchemy, the news-staple, Bartholomew Fair. The Roman institution of legacy-hunting provided an example of organized humbug better fitted perhaps to call into play the energies of Jonson's comic satire than any of these, – save in the one respect that it was un-English, and that his powerful realism was thus deprived of one of its sustaining sources. On the other hand, like the career of Sejanus, the institution of legacy-hunting was illuminated by a mass of ancient literature; for the scholar the satire of the first and second centuries had left brilliant and incisive pictures of this vice of the early empire, the *captator* was derided by Horace, Juvenal, and Pliny;[3] he provided the theme of an amusing episode in Petronius' *Satiricon*; and, in particular, his appetences and mortifications, and the strategy on both sides evolved in this conflict of base interests, provided the material for some of the wittiest of Lucian's *Dialogues of the Dead*.

It was on this strategical aspect of legacy-hunting, with its rich development of make-believe, of criminal invention and resource, that Jonson fastened. He found especially in Lucian amusing pictures of the legator who meets game with counter-game, the laugh being regularly with him, not with his persecutors.[4] Thus in *Pluto and Mercury*, an old man, Eucrates,

with no children, but fifty thousand *captatores*, plays upon
their hopes, feigning death when he is actually in the best of
health. Pluto orders that he shall be restored to youth, while
the *captatores* are forced, instead of becoming his heirs, to go
to Hades before him. In another case, a *captator*, Callide-
midas, tries to hasten matters by poisoning Ptoeodorus, the
expected legator, but accidentally takes the poison himself.
Similarly Cnemon leaves his fortune to Hermolaus, expecting
to be made his heir; unluckily he is himself killed by accident
before his time. Terpsion complains loudly in the underworld
of the hardship of having to die at thirty, when old Thucritos,
whom he had besieged with gifts, has lived beyond ninety.
While in the *Simylus* we are introduced to one, Polystratos,
who has lived for thirty years on the gifts of his expectant
heirs.[5]

A more ambitious but scarcely more effective use of the
legacy-hunting motive was made by Petronius, the *arbiter
elegantiarum* of Nero's Court. Petronius, as little as Jonson,
was a mere observer; and he put into his book the same gifts
of ingenious combination and piquant elaboration which,
applied to the entertainment of Nero, had made his fortune
and were to cost him his life. The 'Supper of Trimalchio', the
most famous of all the extant scenes, is a little masterpiece of
Aristophanic invention. The story of the adventures of Eumolpus at Croton is less effective, partly because it is more frag-
mentary; but we easily trace the outline of an even more
audaciously fashioned plot. Eumolpus, a white-haired poet,
with a *rusé* countenance and a past career of successful dissimulation, is the arch-strategist of the company. Wrecked off
the south coast of Italy, he and his comrades escape with difficulty to the shore. A bailiff informs them that they are in the
neighbourhood of Croton. On their inquiring the character
and pursuits of the inhabitants, 'Gentlemen,' puts in the bailiff,
'if you are men of business, change your purpose and seek
other means of support. But if you are men of wit and refinement, able to keep up a fraudulent pretence, you are come to

a regular El Dorado. For in this city learning gets no reward, eloquence has no place, grave and honest manners avail nothing, but the whole population is divided into two classes, *aut captantur aut captant*; – legacy-hunters and their prey. In this city no one rears children, since whoever has heirs of his own is excluded from all feasts and games, refused all the conveniences of life and hides his head among the outcasts of society. Whereas bachelors with no near kin are advanced to the highest honours. . . . You are entering a town which is like a pestilence-stricken plain, filled with nothing else but crows and corpses, the tearing and the torn' (§ 116). Eumolpus accordingly proceeds to pose as a hapless old man who has just lost his son, and has left his native place in order to avoid being daily harrowed by the sight of his son's friends and burial-place. In the shipwreck he has just lost all his equipment, but he owns vast estates and hosts of slaves in Africa. It is further arranged that he is to cough violently, to talk of gold and silver, complain of the miserable yield of his estates, to sit every day at his accounts, and make a new will every month (§ 117). Thus prepared, Eumolpus and his party enter Croton and presently fall in with a throng of *captatores*, who, on hearing their story, immediately vie with one another in heaping their wealth upon Eumolpus and entreating his favour (§ 124). Eumolpus and his companions plunge into wild licence and luxury. Only one incident need be specified. An aged and 'honourable' matron, Philomela, in her youth an adept at legacy-hunting, introduces her children, a clever boy and girl, to Eumolpus for this purpose. The issue of the adventure cannot clearly be made out from the extant fragments.

It will be seen that neither Lucian nor Petronius can be said to have provided the plot of *Volpone*. But to one or both Jonson doubtless owed the fundamental situation of the legator who makes game of the legacy-hunters, and a few details of the execution.

II

In choosing such a subject as this Jonson, then, necessarily abandoned one of his surest holds upon the play-going public, his powerful presentment of the London life at their doors. In Jacobean London similar concoctions of greed, cunning, and credulity were not perhaps much less rife than in imperial Rome; but this particular variety of them was not yet at home there. Yet the very unfamiliarity of this 'folly' touched the vein of a Jacobean audience at another point. If they enjoyed seeing London gallants and prentices, country simpletons and City wives, made sport of, they were at least as accessible to the romantic fascination of strange or exotic crime. This kind of interest, however, would have been much deadened had the plot been laid in a vanished society, known only to the learned and by books. Jonson therefore took a most politic step in transferring his *mise en scène* from ancient Rome – already of ill augury for the audiences of *Poetaster* and *Sejanus* – to modern Italy. For the Jacobeans Italy was the classic contemporary land of sensational evil-doing. Among Italian cities Venice, with Florence as the city of Machiavel, stood in the front rank for this sinister repute. Shylock was but one, and hardly the most consummate, of those whom the stage had shown plotting monstrous things by the Rialto. To make the Fox a Venetian grandee was thus to give him and his story the best chance of being at once piquant and plausible. English foibles do not indeed wholly escape the lash; but Sir Politick and his lady are introduced only as eccentric English visitors at the house of the Venetian grandee. If the scene, then, is laid in Venice, 'Venice' is no longer merely a transparent cloak for London, as the 'Florence' of the original *Every Man in His Humour* had been, and as the 'Rome' of the *Poetaster* in great part was. But neither does it mean precisely 'Venice' in the literal and realist sense which Jonson attached to 'London' in the revised play. There is no evidence or probability that Jonson had discovered

a Venetian Eucrates or Eumolpus. He had merely transferred
to a modern *milieu* a situation imagined in the spirit of
imperial Rome, and under the stimulus of the renewed and
close occupation with its historic records from which he had
but recently emerged. The element of scholarly and literary
reminiscence in Jonson's mind, so harmoniously allied with
his powerful realism in *Every Man in His Humour,* here gains
a decided predominance. The cunning slave and boastful
soldier of ancient comedy had done little more than give a cue
to the observant eye which elicited a Brainworm and a Boba-
dill from the Elizabethan throng. But Volpone bears the clear
stamp of his purely literary origin; the antique satiric stuff is
everywhere visible, and the intense intellectual elaboration it
has undergone has been carried out in comparative detachment from actualities. The result is work certainly wanting in
the fresh charm of the earlier piece; even repellent by reason
of the remote, abstruse, and at times scarcely human, types of
criminality among which we move. Yet for all its strangeness,
it attains, in the grip of Jonson's mind, an amazing imaginative veracity, which has made its sinister outlines only less in-
effaccable in the English memory than the more splendid and
passionate creations of Shakespeare.

If *Volpone* marks a wide departure from the realism he had
earlier enjoined upon the comic dramatist, it violates still more
strikingly his second demand, that comedy should 'sport with
human follies', not with 'crimes'. If Jonson ever 'sports' here,
it is in the sombre and lurid fashion of his own 'sporting Kyd'.
There is folly enough, to be sure; but it is the formidable and
menacing folly of men who have capacity and resource and
absolutely no scruples, and whether such men commit follies
or crimes is merely a question of occasion and circumstance.
All the principal persons are capable of any crime; they are
gamblers playing desperately for high stakes, and when they
see their advantage, Corbaccio plays his son's inheritance, and
Corvino his wife's honour. The moral repulsion, however, with
which they so powerfully affect us is less due to the actual

crimes and vices they perpetrate than to the impression of un-
limited possibilities of evil which they convey. The air is heavy
and fetid with moral disease; a passing breath of freshness and
purity just stirs it when Celia and Bonario go by, but the relief
is faint and ineffectual, and the total impression is not sensibly
mitigated even by the catastrophe which attests that 'there is
force in the decrees of Venice' to punish even these iniquities.

Never before had Jonson painted with so much power
humanity denuded of every germ of goodness. Of moralizing
there is not a trace, but the moral accent is none the less per-
vading and intense, like a continuous burden accompanying
all the variations of the music, never distinctly or separately
heard, but qualifying the value of every note. To this intensity
of moral accent neither Petronius nor Lucian, it need hardly
be said, contributed or could contribute anything whatever.
Juvenal, whose temper was kindred, contributed little more.
Jonson understood the lighter arts too, and was already win-
ning by his Masques – his *Masque of Blackness* had been produced but a few months before – a better title than any of his
literary contemporaries to be called the 'arbiter elegantiarum'
of the Court of James. But those gracious artifices of the
Christmas candlelight were only the *parerga* of a great and
strenuous artist, for whom his art was a weapon, and whose
writing, more than any other of his time, was inspired by the
indignation which makes silence hard. The indignation which
inspired *Volpone* was, it is true, not the purely ethical passion
of the Hebrew prophet, or even of Juvenal; it is, on the evi-
ence of his own eloquent Preface, stirred as much by the
degradation into which the glorious name of poetry had fallen,
as by the rampancy of vice. And that degradation was itself in
part purely literary; a matter of bad style, – 'such impropriety
of phrase, such plenty of *solœcismes*, such dearth of sense, so
bold *prolepse's*, so rackt *metaphor's*'; – and who shall say that
the stylistic audacities of *King Lear* and *Macbeth*, neither of
them many months old, were not in Jonson's mind when he
wrote these words? But the deeper ground of that degradation

and of his anger lay in the gross neglect by contemporary poets
of the lofty function prescribed for the poet by antiquity, to be
a moral educator of mankind; and in their imperviousness to
the high doctrine received from the same source, that no man
can become a 'good Poet, without first being a good man'.
'The too-much licence of *Poetasters*, in this time, hath much
deform'd their Mistris'; and, whatever we may think of the
critical perception which discerned, on the morrow of *Hamlet*
and *Othello*, no compensatory accesses of glory about her
'deformed' shape, *Volpone* remains a magnificent vindication,
among other things, of the office even of the 'comic' poet 'to
imitate iustice, and instruct to life', as Jonson understood
these things.

III

Happily, he understood them as a poet, and carried them out,
fundamentally, under the conditions of poetry. The desire to
hold up a terrifying example is subordinated to a passion,
hardly apparent before *Sejanus*, and even there far less rigorously carried out, for complex and intricate but perfectly
organic plot. The ground-work is laid with great care.

Volpone is no unknown foreign adventurer, like Petronius'
Eumolpus, but a grandee of Venice whose rank and position
are beyond dispute. He is not all impostor. He is really wealthy,
and really childless, as he professes. His imposture starts from
a foundation of assured respectability. The consideration he
enjoys facilitates his fraud and enables him to carry it to further lengths with impunity; it delays his detection, and when
detected, it softens the rigour of the law, in favour of one who
is 'by bloud, and ranke a gentleman' (v xii 117). In this case
at least, Jonson unhesitatingly blunted his 'moral' in order to
benefit his plot. On the other hand, he has perhaps given his
moral scorn for this 'Venetian gentleman' too free a rein to be
wholly true to the part. He has given him the highest degree of
the subtle craft, and the calculated cruelty, for which the

patrician government of Venice was famous; but nothing of
the high-bred courtesy in speech and manner which prevailed
in Venetian society, and which Shakespeare had just rendered
so excellently in *Othello*, and rather less excellently earlier in
The Merchant of Venice. Volpone is no mere amateur in
roguery, but a professional virtuoso exulting in his virtuosity.
The artist in him is even stronger than the wealth-hunter or
the voluptuary. He is not merely, like Overreach, a grasping
man of brains, who cheats with professional coolness for
definite practical ends; on the contrary, he takes a huge delight
in the tricks he plays for their own sake, glorying

> More in the cunning purchase of my wealth,
> Then in the glad possession,

and carries them out when he has everything to lose and
nothing to gain. His room, crowded with the costly offerings
of his dupes, is a sort of private box from which he watches
unobserved the sordid comedy of contending greeds. In the
intervals of these performances he finds diversion in another
yet more hideous spectacle, – the contortions of a dwarf, a
eunuch, a hermaphrodite, whose splayed or stunted ditties are
made, with horrible ingenuity, to reflect their several deformities. But Volpone is too inveterate an artist to be content with
the role of the looker-on. Like Nero, he leaps upon the stage,
recites, assumes characters, compels the plot to move as he
wishes. If Nero's colossal caprices have any parallel in literature, it is in the lurid imagery with which the brain of Volpone
invests his vices and his crimes. The morning hymn to gold,
with which he first opens his lips in our hearing, transfigures
avarice with the glamour of religion and idealism; the sordid
taint of usury, the prosaic associations of commerce, fall away
from this man who boasts :

> I wound no earth with plow-shares; fat no beasts
> To feede the shambles; . . .

I blow no subtill glasse; expose no ships
To threatnings of the furrow-faced sea;
I turne no moneys, in the publike banke. (ɪ i 34–9)

And when the supposed bedridden and impotent old man,
throwing off the mask, leaps from his couch before the hapless
Celia, he seems for a moment to have discarded with his
senility the grossness and brutality of his mind; he is not the
Faun gloating over his victim, but the young Antinoos whom
he once played

For entertainement of the great VALOYS,

ravishing his lady's ear with Catullian song and besieging her
imagination with visions of fabulous opulence and magnificence, –

A diamant, would haue bought LOLLIA PAVLINA,
When she came in, like star-light, hid with iewels,
That were the spoiles of prouinces; take these,
And weare, and loose 'hem : yet remaines an eare-ring
To purchase them againe, and this whole state. . . .
Thy bathes shall be the iuyce of iuly-flowres,
Spirit of roses, and of violets,
The milke of vnicornes, and panthers breath
Gather'd in bagges, and mixt with *cretan* wines.
(ɪɪɪ vii 195–216)

Volpone is a consummate actor; it is his misfortune that he is
liable to be carried away by the zest of his part. He owes his
final ruin less to rash and hasty unmaskings, such as this, than
to the audacious adventures he undertakes with the mask on.
His passion for taking part, as it were, in his own play, and
moving it on towards the consummation he desires, is the
mainspring by which the whole action is brought to the consummation he does not desire. The bent grows upon him
visibly, and is carried out to more and more extravagant

lengths. The monstrous jest of the commandatore (v v–ix) would be incredible had it not been preceded by the gay adventure of the mountebank, as that would be had it not been prepared for by the farce of the sick room. With each fresh success his temper grows more sanguine, his humour more wanton; he cannot bear his fortune soberly. 'I must ha' my crotchets! and my *conundrums*!' (v xi 16) . . . till at last he makes a snare for his own neck and runs his head into it wilfully. The dramatist Cumberland objected to this final mad freak of Volpone's as 'the weak part of the plot'. But this is to demand, as the eighteenth century was too prone to do, that the persons of a drama should never act contrary to a reasonable view of their own interests. The Elizabethans retained no such illusion; and Jonson had the peculiarly keen eye common in men of his vehement temperament and critical brain for the fatuities of the overweening. The collapse of Volpone's astuteness in the delirious joy of his wanton triumph is imagined with an irony yet more Greek than Elizabethan. While the supposed 'commandatore' is gaily mocking the victims he has disinherited, the spectator knows that Mosca, the pretended heir, is quietly preparing, behind the scenes, to ruin the pretended testator. And it is only by the desperate shift of stripping off his own mask that Volpone is able to checkmate the superior cunning of his formidable parasite, and send him to a doom yet sterner than his own.

IV

Neither this wonderfully contrived catastrophe nor the quondam ally whom he compels to share it owes much to any earlier model. The hideous sketch of Eumolpius, who at Croton acts as servant to Eumolpus, has but the vaguest resemblance to Mosca. Nor has he much affinity with the ordinary parasite of classic comedy. We must look for an analogy rather to that more potent and terrible 'parasite' of history, whose 'fall' had so recently occupied Jonson's imagination. With certain obvious qualifications, Mosca is a Sejanus of private life. In the history of Sejanus Jonson found the fundamental situation of his two greatest comedies. The league of two able villains, master and servant, ending in a deadly struggle between them, was a theme of immense dramatic possibilities new to the English stage. The finale of *Sejanus* by no means equals in constructive mastery the unsurpassed catastrophes of *Volpone* and *The Alchemist*; but this was not altogether Jonson's fault; and some of the most impressive effects of the two later plays are foreshadowed, within the limits imposed by the historic facts, in the earlier. Like the Letter of Tiberius, the final confession of Volpone abruptly closes the career and life of the quondam 'parasite' at the moment when his triumph seems complete. But Jonson was now free to 'punish vice', and bent upon punishing it, without reserve; the master therefore, unlike Tiberius, shares, with slight modification, the servant's doom. In *The Alchemist*, where this primitive zeal was allowed less ample scope, the issue of the duel was still further and more ingeniously varied; it being here the 'parasite' who gets the upper hand, by a yet more daring and unexpected stroke.

Mosca has thus hardly a closer relation than Sejanus to the parasite of classic comedy, though the title is expressly applied to both. Jonson felt this, and has adroitly forestalled criticism by making Mosca himself, in an incisive soliloquy, explain his points of superiority to the ordinary breeds of the creature. Volpone's all-powerful familiar will not be confounded with the hungry professional 'diners-out' who

> haue your bare towne-arte,
> To know, who's fit to feede 'hem;

and vend their scraps of news for a precarious invitation, to jest for a dinner, at the risk of summary expulsion if the jest should not please.[6] As little will he be mistaken for one of the low cringing companions –

With their court dog-tricks, that can fawne, and fleere,
Make their reuennue out of legs, and faces,
Echo my-Lord, and lick away a moath.

If his position and authority distinguish him from the vulgar
parasite in the literal sense, his brilliant capacity equally dis-
tinguishes him from the professional jester. His 'mystery' is a
liberal art, exacting great wits and worthy of them, the

> fine, elegant rascall, that can rise,
> And stoope (almost together) like an arrow;
> Shoot through the aire, as nimbly as a starre;
> Turne short, as doth a swallow; and be here,
> And there, and here, and yonder, all at once;
> Present to any humour, all occasion;
> And change a visor, swifter, then a thought!
> This is the creature, had the art borne with him;
> Toiles not to learne it, but doth practise it
> Out of most excellent nature : and such sparkes,
> Are the true Parasites, others but their *Zani's.* (III i)

Mosca, like his master, has something of the artist's joy in his
feats, and is carried away no less by the zest of the game. With
all his astuteness he falls, in the wantonness of success, into a
blunder which, in conjunction with Volpone's final escapade,
involves the final ruin of the fortunes of both.

> I feare, I shall begin to grow in loue
> With my deare selfe, and my most prosp'rous parts,
> They doe so spring, and burgeon; I can feele
> A whimsey i' my bloud : (I know not how)
> Successe hath made me wanton. I could skip
> Out of my skin, now, like a subtill snake,
> I am so limber.

It is in this reckless, 'limber' mood that, with obvious intention
on Jonson's part, he encounters Bonario, the son whom Corbaccio is about to disinherit in Volpone's favour. The amazing
audacity of his next move, the communication to Bonario of

his father's design, coupled with the fatal consequences for himself which actually accrue from it, has led some sober critics to accuse Jonson of having brought about a situation he required (Bonario's presence in the gallery when Celia is attacked), without troubling to provide a sufficient motive.[7] But it is in Mosca's character to take great risks; from first to last he is playing a dangerous game, and at this very moment he is elated by success. But he is not wantonly courting danger. He has a definite plan, and it is not the fruit of a sudden impulse on the appearance of Bonario. 'Who's this?' he says to himself on seeing him enter, 'The person I was bound to seeke' (III ii 1). Mosca's own subsequent explanations of his motives to Corbaccio and then to Voltore (III ix) are naturally seasoned to their palate. But it is not difficult to detect the real policy, now frustrated, which had dictated his act. Corbaccio was attached to his son, and corrupt as he is, had at first demurred to the project of disinheriting him. It is Mosca's cue to prevent any recurrence of these dangerous scruples, and he takes the course which he expects will promptly and violently alienate father and son. What he meant to happen is substantially what he tells Corbaccio *has* happened, with a climax which Corbaccio's tardy arrival prevented. Bonario was to break out in rage against his father and threaten his life; Mosca would then intervene to save him, securing thereby the gratitude and confidence of the old man for himself and the legacy for his chief.[8] There were several openings for failure in this calculation; as there were in the calculations of Iago and of Richard. But it was sufficiently well grounded to be adopted by an able and daring man; and the circumstance which upsets it, the premature arrival of Corvino and Celia, is provided with a motive admirably in keeping with Corvino's character, and yet so extravagant in its vileness that even the depraved imagination of Mosca could not be expected to foresee or reckon with it.[9]

V

The three dupes are drawn in less detail but with a no less
incisive and powerful hand. They stand clearly and unmistakably apart, but not because they differ a jot in the
quality or degree of their rapacity. Raven, crow, vulture, they
represent but a narrow class even among birds of prey. They
differ in their circumstances, not in their bent. Voltore, the
knowing advocate, is as blinded by greed and as easily gulled
as the dull and deaf Corbaccio, and executes volte-faces when
the cause requires it as shamefully as Corvino. Wonderfully as
the adventures of the three are invented and discriminated,
one cannot but contrast with the unrelieved monotone of their
decadent and criminal corruption the picturesque diversity of
the clients of Subtle and Face. Both the strong ethical bias
which animated Jonson in *Volpone*, and the comparative
absence of realistic stimulus and suggestion, contributed to this
effect. In no other of the comedies are the persons so sharply
distinguished as bad or good. The rank and uniform depravity
of the rogues and dupes is set off by the white innocence of
Celia and Bonario, who to tell the truth are, as characters,
almost as insipid as they are innocent. Even the *avocatori* fall
apart into two corresponding groups, – the three abstract and
colourless administrators of justice, and the 'fourth', who
seeks to temper its rigour to a possible son-in-law. Of the
proper and normal material of comedy, extravagancies and
absurdities, there is, in the main plot, nothing. Its nearest
approach to humour lies in the horrible simulations of the
ludicrous effected by the misshapen creatures of Volpone's
household.

One exception there is, however, to the otherwise unbroken
predominance of dull virtue and revolting vice – the by-plot
of Sir Politick Would-be. A breath of lighter and more wholesome air from the old Humour-comedies enters with this
quaintly refreshing personage and his associates; and it is

significant that Jonson recovers the normal temper of his
comedy precisely where he is reverting to his normal topics,
when he turns from the Venetians of his erudite invention to
the English of his familiar experience, the eccentrics whose
humours were to be studied from the life in Fleet Street and
Westminster. Sir Politick and his lady are, in truth, as alien to
the spirit of the play as they appear to be to the usages of
Venice; foreigners full of naïve curiosity and enterprise, who
thrust themselves into dangerous entanglement with an affair
which they do not in the least comprehend and on which they
have not the least effect. The peculiar humour of the picture
depends in large part on the contrast between their fussy and
officious interference and their irrelevance; humour which was
not to be had, if their absurd contortions had had any bearing
upon, or inner relation to, the main theme. Jonson had painted
in Puntarvolo the absurdities of English travellers at home; his
Venetian scene here provided an opening hard to resist for
exhibiting the fantastic tricks they played in the foreign cities
of their resort, and nowhere more extravagantly than in
Venice. Cumberland and others have demurred to their 'loose
connexion with the plot', and justly enough if perfect plot-
building means that every person contributes definitely to the
progress and evolution of the action. But in that case what
function remains in drama for the fussy, inefficient people who
only blunder round about the real business without affecting
it, important buzzing flies upon the engine wheel? A most
effective comic role would in that case have no legitimate
place in comedy. Jonson had from the first dealt largely in
pretentious inefficiencies, and the exposure of this kind of
comic irrelevance was in truth a part of his finished technique.
Master Stephen and Master Matthew may in a sense be said
to set the plot of *Every Man in His Humour* in motion, but
through its remaining course the humour of Stephen, in
particular, lies precisely in his uncomprehending irrelevance.
For the rest, without belonging to the highest rank of Jonson's
comic characters, Sir Politick is a pleasant variation of his

'projector' type, and Lady Would-be an admirable specimen
of the seventeenth-century bluestocking, more comic in herself
and employed to more genuinely comic purpose than the
Collegiate Ladies of the next play, which her merciless
loquacity at the expense of Volpone in another way anticipates.

SOURCE : C. H. Herford and Percy Simpson (eds),
Ben Jonson, II (1925) 47–63

NOTES

1. The allusions in II i to 'another' young lion 'whelped in the
Tower', 'three porcpisces seene, aboue the bridge', and 'a whale
discouer'd, in the riuer as high as *Woolwich*', are very explicit,
and the two latter, in any case, can only refer to the incidents
which Stow thought it worth while to record under January 19,
'and a few days later', 1606, in terms almost identical with
Jonson's. Peregrine, who reports these wonders, says that he left
London on the very day of the appearance of the whale, and
that this was 'seven weeks' before. We are not bound to take this
reckoning as exact, but it would be quite in the manner of
Jonson's realism to identify the supposed date of the action with
the actual date of the performance. In this case, the piece must
have been played about the middle of March (allowing a week
from January 19 for Stow's 'a few days later'); in any case before
the 25th, if we are to rely upon the date '1605' of the Quarto
title-page. See also Holt in *Modern Language Notes*, xx 6.
    2. The dedicatory epistle is dated in the Quarto : *'From my
house in the Black-Friars this* 11 *of February*, 1607.'
    3. e.g. Horace, *Epp.* I I. 77; Juvenal, III 129; Pliny, *Epp.* II
20; IV 2. 2.
    4. Cf. *Mod. Phil.* II 238 f.; *Modern Language Notes*, XXI
113 f.
    5. Lucian, Νεκρικοὶ διάλογοι, V–IX.
    6. Eupolis, Κόλακες, fr. 1 (ed. Meineke):
        εἶτ' ἐπὶ δεῖπνον ἐρχόμεσθ' ἄλλυδις ἄλλος ἡμῶν
        μᾶζαν ἐπ' ἀλλόφυλον, οὗ δεῖ χαρίεντα πολλὰ
        τὸν κόλακ' εὐθέως λέγειν, ἢ φέρεται θύραζε.
    7. J. A. Symonds, *Ben Jonson*, p. 86.

8. This seems more likely than to suppose, with M. Castelain (*Ben Jonson*, p. 303), that Mosca reckons on Bonario *killing* his father. For, warned as he was, it was probable that he would do this, if at all, before the old man had completed the transfer of his inheritance; and then where was Mosca's advantage?

9. III vii 4, 5 : '. . . did ere man haste so, for his hornes? A courtier would not ply it so, for a place.'

L. C. Knights

FROM *DRAMA AND SOCIETY IN THE AGE OF JONSON* (1937)

(*a*) From Chapter 6, 'Tradition and Ben Jonson'

Sejanus, like the other greater plays, is the product of a unique vision; but in stressing the uniqueness one has to avoid any suggestion of the idiosyncratic. It is not merely that the matter on which the poet works is provided by the passions, lusts and impulses of the actual world, the firmly defined individual spirit which moulds that matter springs from a rich traditional wisdom; it relies, that is to say, on something outside itself, and presupposes an active relationship with a particular audience.

The point can be made by examining a passage [in *Volpone*] that is commonly recognized as 'great poetry'.

> See, behold,
> What thou art queen of; not in expectation,
> As I feed others : but possess'd and crown'd.
> See, here, a rope of pearl : and each more orient
> Than that the brave Ægyptian queen caroused :
> Dissolve and drink them. See, a carbuncle,
> May put out both the eyes of our St Mark;
> A diamond, would have bought Lollia Paulina,
> When she came in like star-light, hid with jewels,
> That were the spoils of provinces; take these,
> And wear, and lose them : yet remains an ear-ring
> To purchase them again, and this whole state.
> A gem but worth a private patrimony,
> Is nothing : we will each such at a meal.
> The heads of parrots, tongues of nightingales,
> The brains of peacocks, and of estriches,
> Shall be our food : and, could we get the phœnix,
> Though nature lost her kind, she were our dish.
>
> (III vi; III 249)[1]

Mr Palmer, supporting a general thesis that Jonson 'wrote for a generation which had still an unbounded confidence in the senses and faculties of man. England had not yet accepted the great negation . . .', remarks: 'In the figure of Volpone Jonson presents the splendours of his theme. Was ever woman so magnificently wooed as the wife of Corvino?'² This is to miss the point completely. The poetic force of Volpone's wooing has two sources. There is indeed an exuberant description of luxury – 'Temptations are heaped upon temptations with a rapidity which almost outstrips the imagination' – and the excited movement seems to invite acceptance. But at the same time, without cancelling out the exuberance, the luxury is 'placed'. We have only to compare passages (from the early Keats, for example) in which the imagined gratification of sight, taste and touch is intended as an indulgence merely, to see how this placing is achieved. It is not merely that the lines quoted have a context of other swelling speeches (compare *Sejanus*), so that by the time we reach them the mode is established, the exaggeration, which reaches a climax at 'phœnix', is itself sufficient to suggest some qualification of Mr Palmer's 'splendours'. The verse demands the usual scrupulous inspection of each word – we are not allowed to lapse into an impression of generalized magnificence – and the splendours, in 'caroused', 'spoils of provinces', 'private patrimony', are presented clearly enough as waste. 'Though nature lost her kind', at least, implies a moral judgement; and the references to Lollia Paulina and Heliogabalus (Gifford quotes 'Comedit linguas pavonum et lusciniarum'), which would not be unfamiliar to an Elizabethan audience, are significant.

The manner of presentation (relying on a response which later criticism shows is neither obvious nor easy) suggests that the double aspect of the thing presented corresponds to a double attitude in the audience: a naïve delight in splendour is present *at the same time as* a clear-sighted recognition of its insignificance judged by fundamental human, or divine, standards. The strength of this attitude is realized if we com-

pare it with a puritanic disapproval of 'the world' on the one
hand, or a sensuous abandonment on the other. It is the possession of this attitude that makes Jonson 'classical', not his Greek
and Latin erudition. His classicism is an equanimity and
assurance that springs – here at home'[3] – from the strength of
a native tradition.

NOTES

1. The second reference in parentheses is to the volume and
   page of the Gifford–Cunningham edition of Jonson's *Works*
   (1875).
2. *Ben Jonson,* pp. x and 175.
3. And make my strengths, such as they are,
   Here in my bosom, and at home.
   (A Farewell to the World)

(b) From Chapter 7, 'Jonson and the Anti-Acquisitive Attitude'

I have tried to show that the vitality of Jonson's plays draws
on a popular source. However much he might flaunt 'the
vulgar' in his prologues and inter-means, his code formed part
of a healthy tradition which his audience helped to keep alive.
The most effective way of demonstrating the value of the
inherited standards of the period is to examine those masterpieces of Jonson's in which they are present as a living force.
More, of course, goes to the making of a great comedy than an
acceptable moral code. In *Volpone* and *The Alchemist* Jonson's general anti-acquisitive attitude combines with powerful
emotions, with subtle observation, with all those constituents
of value that are only susceptible to literary analysis. But here
I shall single out only a few strands of that rich combination.
Since they represent aspects of Jonson's art which have been
largely neglected, the emphasis may help to make possible a
more complete assimilation of his work.

In *Volpone*, Jonson's greatest comedy, played at the Globe

in 1606, the sardonically alert criticism of accumulation is so obvious as to need merely a brief illustration. Herford and Simpson show that Jonson found the theme of legacy-hunting in Lucian and Petronius, and proceed :

> In choosing such a subject as this Jonson, then, necessarily abandoned one of his surest holds upon the play-going public, his powerful presentment of the London life at their doors. In Jacobean London similar concoctions of greed, cunning, and credulity, were not perhaps much less rife than in imperial Rome; but this particular variety of them was not yet at home there. Yet the very unfamiliarity of this 'folly' touched the vein of a Jacobean audience at another point. If they enjoyed seeing London gallants and prentices, country simpletons and City wives, made sport of, they were at least as accessible to the romantic fascination of strange or exotic crime.[1]

'The romantic fascination of strange or exotic crime' is utterly beside the point. Whether 'fishing for testaments' was actually one of the contemporary forms of fortune-hunting or not, its significance here is solely as a manifestation of human greed, peculiarly appropriate in the era that was then beginning.

The general construction can be paralleled in most of Jonson's plays. The main theme is focused in a sharp, strong light. Behind it, as it were, there is, first, a representation of minor follies (the songs of Nano, etc., on the one hand, and Sir Politick and Lady Would-be on the other) – variations which help to shape our attitude towards the main theme; then the final sombre setting – 'When I am lost in blended dust' (i i; iii 178),

> So many cares, so many maladies,
> So many fears attending on old age
>
> (i i; iii 189)

With *Sejanus* in mind we can understand the sense in which *Volpone* represents 'the creation of a world'.[2] It draws potently enough upon the actual, but there is a similar exclusion, a similar concentration upon one dominant group of

impulses, 'a unity of inspiration that radiates into plot and
personages alike'.³

The nature of that inspiration I tried to make clear in my
analysis of 'See, behold, what thou art queen of . . .'. The
greed that forms the subject of *Volpone* includes both the
desire of sensuous pleasure as an end in itself, and the desire
for riches; and the expression of each makes similar demands
upon the reader.

> Good morning to the day; and next, my gold!
> Open the shrine, that I may see my saint.
> *(Mosca withdraws the curtain, and discovers piles of*
> *gold, plate, jewels, etc.)*
> Hail the world's soul, and mine! more glad than is
> The teeming earth to see the long'd for sun
> Peep through the horns of the celestial Ram,
> Am I, to view thy splendour darkening his;
> That lying here, amongst my other hoards,
> Shew'st like a flame by night, or like the day
> Struck out of chaos, when all darkness fled
> Unto the centre. O thou son of Sol,
> But brighter than thy father, let me kiss,
> With adoration, thee, and every relick
> Of sacred treasure in this blessed room. . . .
>   (ɪ i; ɪɪɪ 166)

There is no need to repeat the criticism of the previous chapter, but we may remark that this 'morning hymn to gold' does
not 'transfigure avarice with the glamour of religion and
idealism'.⁴ It brings the popular and religious tradition into
play, but that is a different matter; religion and the riches of
the teeming earth are there for the purpose of ironic contrast.
   Volpone himself may

>   glory
> More in the cunning purchase of my wealth,
> Than in the glad possession, (ɪ i; ɪɪɪ 167–8)

but the suitors are solely personifications of greed. 'Raven,

crow, vulture, they represent but a narrow class even among
birds of prey. They differ in their circumstances, not in their
bent.'⁵ And in order that the theme may be complete and
whole the four judges, the Avocatori, are made to represent
anything but justice. Their complacent fatuity is apparent in
their stilted and tautological comments. (The court scene, like
the meeting of the Senate in *Sejanus*, is highly stylized.)

> 1. *Avoc.* The like of this the senate never heard of.
> 2. *Avoc.* 'Twill come most strange to them when we
> report it. (IV ii; III 273)

They display a new-found politeness to Mosca when it seems
that he is the heir (v vi; III 309), and the Fourth Judge considers this 'proper man . . . a fit match for my daughter' (v
viii; III 314). As for Celia and Bonario, they are completely,
and intentionally, null, and there is no point in talking about
their 'white innocence'.⁶ The one mode is maintained consistently to the end.

> Why, your gold
> Is such another med'cine, it dries up
> All those offensive savours : it transforms
> The most deformed, and restores them lovely,
> As 'twere the strange poetical girdle. Jove
> Could not invent t'himself a shroud more subtle
> To pass Acrisius' guards. It is the thing
> Makes all the world her grace, her youth, her beauty.
> (v i; III 289)

Volpone is a work of art, a particular experience, and in
reading it we are concerned solely with those passions that
Jonson chooses to exhibit, and the particular way in which he
exhibits them. But it is worth noticing how many variations
are, at different points, explicitly related to the main themes.
The Third Act opens with Mosca's praise of his profession in
typical hyperbole :

> O ! your parasite
> Is a most precious thing, dropt from above,
> Not bred 'mongst clods and clodpoles, here on earth. . . .
> . . . And, yet,
> I mean not those that have your bare town-art,
> To know who's fit to feed them; have no house,
> No family, no care, and therefore mould
> Tales for men's ears, to bait that sense; or get
> Kitchen invention, and some stale receipts
> To please the belly and the groin; nor those,
> With their court-dog-tricks, that can fawn and fleer,
> Make their revenue out of legs and faces,
> Echo my lord, and lick away a moth :
> But your fine elegant rascal. . . .
>
> (iii i, iii 225)

All the forms of parasitism that Mosca does *not* mean are here brought within the scope of the same trend of feeling as that which is aroused towards Mosca himself.[7] There is a similar effect in the praise of Volpone's craft :

> *Volpone.*   I gain
> No common way; I use no trade, no venture;
> I wound no earth with plough-shares, fat no beasts,
> To feed the shambles; have no mills for iron,
> Oil, corn, or men, to grind them into powder :
> I blow no subtle glass, expose no ships
> To threat'nings of the furrow-faced sea;
> I turn no monies in the public bank,
> No usure private.
> *Mosca.*   No, sir, nor devour
> Soft prodigals. You shall have some will swallow
> A melting heir as glibly as your Dutch
> Will pills of butter, and ne'er purge for it;
> Tear forth the fathers of poor families
> Out of their beds, and coffin them alive
> In some kind clasping prison, where their bones
> May be forthcoming, when the flesh is rotten :
> But your sweet nature doth abhor these courses;
> You loathe the widow's or the orphan's tears

> Should wash your pavements, or their piteous cries
> Ring in your roofs, and beat the air for vengeance.
>
> (I i; III 168)

What we are forced to notice here is the magnificently adroit transition from the legitimate forms of gain (that Volpone neglects these reflects only on himself) to those which stand there for bitterly derisive contemplation. The change is marked in the fifth line

> ... have no mills for iron,
> Oil, corn, *or men*, to grind them into powder,

and in Mosca's rejoinder grim caricature is followed by the emphatic moral indignation of,

> Tear forth the fathers of poor families
> Out of their beds, and coffin them alive
> In some kind clasping prison.[8]

Mr Eliot says that 'the worlds created by artists like Jonson ... are not fancy, because they have a logic of their own; and this logic illuminates the actual world, because it gives us a new point of view from which to inspect it'.[9] Mr Eliot's essay is the finest criticism of Jonson that we have, but the connexion between Jonson's plays and 'the actual world' is very much closer than that sentence allows. The attitude expressed in the passage last quoted informs the whole of *Volpone*, and it is, strictly, a moral attitude. Great literature cannot be discussed in purely moral terms, for the reason that these, at best, are too broad and general. But literary analysis is the keenest instrument we possess for the exploration of human values, and *Volpone* – a masterpiece of literary art – serves to make the point on which other great artists, besides Jonson, have been emphatic: 'The essential function of art is moral. Not aesthetic, not decorative, not pastime and recreation, but moral.'[10] The comedy of *Volpone* is universal, but it would

be perverse not to relate it to the acquisitiveness of a particular
time and place.

SOURCE: *Drama and Society in the Age of Jonson* (1937)
pp. 185–8, 200–6

NOTES

1. C. H. Herford and Percy Simpson (eds), *Ben Jonson: The
Man and his Work*, II 53.
2. T. S. Eliot, *Elizabethan Essays*, p. 79.
3. Ibid., p. 77.
4. Herford and Simpson, II 58.
5. Ibid., II 63.
6. 'The rank and uniform depravity of the rogues and dupes
is set off by the white innocence of Celia and Bonario, who to tell
the truth are, as characters, almost as insipid as they are innocent' (ibid., II 63–4).
7. Compare W. Empson, *Seven Types of Ambiguity*, pp. 261–
2, where the examples, although very different from this, illustrate the affirmative possibilities of 'not'.
8. Compare Jonson's attitude towards enclosures as expressed
in *King James's Entertainment in Passing to his Coronation,*
1603 (VI 425):

> Now innocence shall cease to be the spoil
> Of ravenous greatness, or to steep the soil
> Of rased peasantry with tears and blood.

9. *Elizabethan Essays*, p. 79.
10. D. H. Lawrence, *Studies in Classic American Literature*,
p. 117. Compare Jonson on 'the impossibility of any man's being
the good poet, without first being a good man' (Dedication of
Volpone, III 156), and the Prologues and Inductions generally.

Harry Levin

JONSON'S METEMPSYCHOSIS (1943)

Ben Jonson often professed to be more concerned with men than with monsters.[1] Yet the chorus of *Volpone* is a trio of deformed servants – Nano, the dwarf, Castrone, the eunuch, and Androgyno, the hermaphrodite. If Mosca is Volpone's parasite, they are Mosca's 'Sub-parasites'. And their monstrous antics seem almost innocent, by comparison with the moral deformities of Voltore, Corbaccio, and Corvino. At intervals throughout the play, most spectacularly in the second act, they appear as the zanies of their mountebank master, and reduce his intrigues to their own level of absurdity. In the first act, after the expository monologue in praise of gold and before the introduction of the three fortune-hunters, they perform a limping jig, which only Volpone could find 'very, very pretty' and only Mosca could claim credit for inventing.[2] Out of hand it is easiest to consider this scene an excrescence; a French critic would even call for its suppression.[3] So painstaking a playwright as Jonson, however, deserves to have his intentions more sympathetically explored; more recent scholarship would look to this very episode for a statement of his theme.[4] In that case it must be admitted that the development is clearer than the theme, for the passage in question is undeniably obscure. I venture to suggest that this obscurity may be clarified by relating the subject of Mosca's interlude to the thought of Jonson's age – which was also Donne's.

Mosca's interlude has already been related to literary tradition. Jonson's commentators, always more sensitive to classical echoes than to vernacular allusions, have debated at length whether 'the false pase of the verse' should be classified as anapestic, spondaic, dactylic, or the *pes proceleusmaticus*.[5] Actually it is a four-stress doggerel couplet, which had been one of the commonest measures in the old English moralities, and was to be the meter of the Vice's speeches in *The Devil is an Ass*.[6] In the latter play it is a vehicle for bringing old-fashioned ideas of good and evil to bear upon the new commercial enterprises of the Jacobean period.[7] In *Volpone* too, though somewhat more deviously, the play-within-the-play presents the point of view from which the play itself is about to launch its satirical attack. The classics, as usual, supply the ammunition for Jonson's contemporary satire. It was Horace, in the fifth poem of his second book of satires, who first coupled the beast-fable of the fox and the crow with the *captatio*, the Roman practice of legacy-hunting.[8] It was Petronius, in the last surviving chapters of the *Satyricon*, who showed how this morbid pursuit might be organized into a series of swindling operations on a grand scale.[9] And it was Lucian, in several of his *Dialogues of the Dead*, who sketched out the motives and cross-plots of Jonson's *dramatis personae*.[10]

The Lucianic influence has penetrated to the core of the drama. With the exception of a few details, which seem to have been gathered from Diogenes Laertius,[11] Mosca's interlude is based on Lucian's *Gallus*, otherwise known as *The Dream*. But Jonson, who had great Latin and less Greek, was most familiar with this dialogue in the translation of Erasmus.[12] It was largely *The Praise of Folly*, as Professor Rea has pointed out, which served as the intermediary between *Volpone* and Jonson's classical sources. Thus Jonson's dedicatory epistle to the two universities borrows whole paragraphs from the *Epistola Apologetica* of Erasmus to Sir Thomas More.[13] The English comedy is more preoccupied with economic abuses; the Latin satire is more encyclopedic in its reduction of all would-be wisdom to the various forms of foolishness. Nevertheless Erasmus begins by making Folly the daughter of the god of riches, and ends by providing Jonson with instances of chicanery to adapt to his favorite formula of 'The Cheater Cheated'. Folly's most eloquent ironies, on the pleasures of

being a fool, find an English paraphrase in the song, 'Fooles,
they are the onely nation'.[14] The serious business which
follows is designed to exhibit what happens 'When wit waites
upon the foole'. The song completes the interlude because
Folly – before arguing that fools are happier than so-called
wise men – has argued that animals are happier than human
beings, and has taken Lucian's *Dream* as her example :

Proinde nunquam satis laudarim gallum illum Pythagoram,
qui cum unus omnia fuisset, philosophus, vir, mulier, rex,
privatus, piscis, equus, rana, opinor etiam spongia, tamen nullum
animal judicavit calamitosius homine, propterea quod caetera
omnia naturae finibus essent contenta, solus homo sortis suae
limites egredi conaretur.[15]

Jonson might have found in *The Dream* what Shakespeare
was finding in Lucian's *Timon*, an object-lesson in the bless-
ings of poverty and the corruptions of wealth. 'The Coblers
cock', by crowing at the wrong moment, arouses its indigent
master from his dream of a luxurious banquet, at which he
has been celebrating the inheritance of a vast fortune. In
response to the cobbler's surprise at hearing a bird speak, the
cock confesses that it harbors the reincarnate soul of Pythagoras, and offers an account of its successive transmigrations –
a series of Cynic jibes against the other philosophers.[16] This
has become a *locus classicus* on the subject of metempsychosis,
and is instanced by Robert Burton, along with a parallel
passage from Ovid's *Metamorphoses*, as a far-fetched proof of
the immortality of the soul.[17] Now the main theme of *Volpone*
is a comic distortion of a theme that is tragic in *Hamlet* and
tragicomic in *The Malcontent*, the pervasive Jacobean theme
of disinheritance. Volpone's suitors, cheated of their legacies
in the fifth act, are adumbrated in Lucian's cobbler, rudely
awakened from his illusory banquet. Here, then, is the connexion between the interlude and the play, but the connexion
has been left out of the interlude, which concentrates on
metempsychosis.[18] The cobbler has disappeared altogether,[19]

and Pythagoras has migrated from the cock to the epicene person of Androgyno, who seems to be both a fool and a hermaphrodite, and therefore an appropriately grotesque habitation for a soul that has already lodged in so many different men and monsters.[20]

Jonson has added one significant new stage to this protean career. The last incarnation has been spent as

> . . . a very strange beast, by some writers cal'd an asse;
> By others, a precise, pure, illuminate brother,
> Of those deuoure flesh, and sometimes one another :
> And will drop you forth a libell, or a sanctified lie,
> Betwixt euery spoonefull of a natiuitie-pie.[21]

In other words, as a Puritan. Fully endowed at this stage with all the gluttony and hypocrisy that Jonson associates with the type, he will eat a Christmas pie as readily as Zeal-of-the-Land Busy, but will refuse to call it by its popish name, just as Ananias later avoids mentioning the mass by speaking of 'Christ-tide'.[22] '*Pythagoreans* all!' as Truewit exclaims, exasperated by the rule of silence in the household of the puritanical Morose.[23] This intermixture of Puritanism and Pythagoreanism does not seem to have been peculiar to Jonson. Shakespeare himself, in a farcical scene, condemns Malvolio to imprisonment until such time as he shall hold the opinion of Pythagoras : 'That the soul of our grandam might happily inhabit a bird'.[24] But Jonson had his own reasons for accusing the Puritans of shifting their coats as often as the soul of Pythagoras changed its shape, and of 'Counting all old doctrine heresie'.[25] Jonson, 'in these dayes of reformation', was for twelve years a convert to Roman Catholicism.[26] *Volpone* was written at the height of this period, and in the immediate aftermath of the Gunpowder Plot. Sir Politick Would-be, with his genius for spying plots everywhere and his fear lest a tinder-box explode the Arsenale, is a caricature of the kind of suspicions from which Jonson must have been suffering.[27] His own relations with the chaplain to the Venetian ambassador may have suggested the locale of the play,[28] though Venice would seem to be an inevitable background for sharp mercantile practice and effete Italianate luxury.

The best chance of finding out anything about Jonson's personal preoccupations is to turn to his criticism of his fellow poets. In 1619, thirteen years after the composition of *Volpone*, he paid his publicized visit to Hawthornden. While there he frequently expressed, in his conversations with William Drummond, his fascination and exasperation with the poetry of John Donne. He went out of his way to explain a poem which has continued to perplex Donne's admirers and critics:

the Conceit of Dones transformation or μετεμψυχοσις was that he sought the soule of that Aple which Eva pulled, and thereafter made it the soule of a Bitch, then of a sheewolf & so of a woman. his generall purpose was to have brought in all the bodies of the Hereticks from ye soule of Cain & at last left it in ye body of Calvin. of this he never wrotte but one sheet, & now since he was made Doctor repenteth highlie & seeketh to destroy all his poems.[29]

Jonson's explanation does not quite fit the poem that has come down to us entitled *The Progress of the Soul* and dated 1601. 'This sullen Writ', though it remains a fragment, was the most ambitious poem that Donne had composed by that date. Its fifty-two ten-line stanzas could scarcely have been crowded into a single sheet. They specifically mention Mahomet and Luther, but not Calvin; instead, they darkly intimate that the soul's final destination is to be the body of Queen Elizabeth.[30] Small wonder that Donne left his project unfinished. A prefatory epistle, *obscurum per obscurius*, refers the reader to 'the Pithagorian doctrine', and pursues the subject back to a vegetable state, when it may have been served at some 'lascivious banquet'.[31] The poem itself, in picaresque fashion, traces the wandering spirit of heresy from the Garden of Eden through various flora and fauna as far as Cain's wife. Much discursive satire, Professor Grierson has noted, is directed against women

and courtiers – like the contemporaneous satire of *Hamlet*.[32]
Hamlet, it should also be noted, is obsessed with a perverse
notion of metempsychosis: his conceits follow the progress of
a king through the guts of a beggar, and dwell upon the metamorphoses of Alexander and Caesar.[33] Indeed, Hamlet's
cynical belief that 'there is nothing either good or bad but
thinking makes it so'[34] is the burden of Donne's abrupt
conclusion:

> Ther's nothing simply good, nor ill alone,
> Of every quality comparison,
> .The onely measure is, and judge, opinion.[35]

The Progress of the Soul bears all the stigmata of having
been written in what Donne's biographer calls 'a feverish
crisis of intellectual pride'.[36] Having lost the Catholic faith of
his fathers a few years before, he was not to find a haven in
the Anglican church until he had spent several years in spiritual limbo. The Essex *débâcle*, which moved Cyril Tourneur
to elaborate the tortuous allegory of *The Transformed Metamorphosis*, must have prompted Donne to express his profound sense of the transformation from one age to another.
The scheme of his poem was probably derived from Lucian's
Dream.[37] But in Donne's mind, the mind of a skeptical theo-
logian, Lucian's fantasy was only the point of departure for
his own explorations into the problem of evil. Rashly he
undertook to account for the maladies of the new age by
following them back, through a chain of being, to the original
fruit of the tree of knowledge. To reconcile the values of this
world with the ethics of traditional Christianity, or to justify
the ways of men to God – these were problems as insoluble as
to tell where all past years are, or who cleft the devil's foot.
The logical solution was an ethical relativism, which accepted
the Reformation as a necessary evil and regarded the aging
queen as neither good nor bad but great.[38] This was 'greatness' in Fielding's sense of the word, a greatness closely allied

to roguery. But it was not Donne's ultimate solution; from the pulpit of his later years we find him reverting to 'this trans-migration of sin'.[39] So Dr Faustus, having denied absolute sin, recognized its existence in his final outcry, and prayed to be reborn as a brutish beast : 'Ah *Pythagoras metemsucosis*'.[40]

Satire springs from some perception of the disparities between the real and the ideal. Hence the satirist's position is always shifting; sooner or later he must embrace one extreme or the other. Donne, in choosing religion, chose the idealistic extreme. Jonson chose realism, and *Volpone* marks this crucial phase of his development. Possibly Mosca's interlude was written before the rest of the play, like the puppet-show in *Bartholomew Fair*.[41] At all events, it is a product of the mood that produced *The Progress of the Soul*. That mood had not abated from 1601 to 1605, but Jonson's animus against the Puritans had extended to the professions of medicine and law, and to the whole world of finance. On the relations between early protestantism and modern business, which social historians have been calling to our attention,[42] he is a shrewd and voluble witness. In *Volpone* he is still willing to sacrifice comedy to morality; he is still embittered by the failure of the tragedy of *Sejanus* and the mood of the 'Comicall Satyres' – his three unsuccessful attempts to make the theatre an instrument of reform and put John Marston out of his humour. *Volpone* is Jonson's last experiment in poetic justice, and his own reservations about the final arraignment are confirmed by Dryden's criticism.[43] In his next play, *Epicœne*, the mood is relaxed; the earlier satire is burlesqued in a legalistic *dénouement*; and the scene is set, for the first time, in no 'fustian countrie' but on English soil. All that was needed, before the consummate realism of *Bartholomew Fair*, was to naturalize the Italian comic types of *Every Man in His Humour*, and to announce in the prologue to *The Alchemist* :

> Our *Scene* is *London*, 'cause we would make knowne,
> No countries mirth is better than our owne.

> No clime breeds better matter, for your whore,
>   Bawd, squire, impostor, many persons more,
>   Whose manners, now call'd humours, feed the stage.[44]

In some respects *The Alchemist* is a realistic version of *Volpone*. The germ of the mature comedy is the mountebank scene, where Sir Politick is gulled by Volpone's medicine-show, and Peregrine comments:

> But *Alchimy*,
> I neuer heard the like: or BROUGHTONS bookes.[45]

Here, reading between the lines, we can see the plot already hatching that will pit the jargon of the alchemists against the rival cant of the Puritans, and confuse everything – in the nick of time – with the ravings of the Reverend Hugh Broughton. The motive power of *The Alchemist*, the device of the philosophers' stone, may likewise have been furnished by Erasmus.[46] It is a greater hoax than Volpone's will, for the sinister magnificence of *Volpone* is supposed to be real, even though it is never inherited by the Venetian conspirators. Whereas the pretensions of *The Alchemist* are spurious from the start, and the London conspirators – delineated by a more tough-minded realist – are a familiar and threadbare pack of coney-catchers and gulls. Sir Epicure Mammon, perhaps, is a gull extraordinary. His very name is a compound of luxury and wealth. But the only fortune that he inherits is the legacy of Lucian's cobbler – the harsh reality that wakes him from his golden visions and epicurean banquets. He is a voluptuary, like Volpone, and he speaks the same magnificent language; but unlike Volpone, who is a great rogue, Mammon is a great fool. Yet Mammon is the more comic figure, and it may be argued that *The Alchemist* is the greater comedy. If folly and roguery are the two staples of Jonsonian comedy, then the follies of *Volpone* are too sinister, while the rogueries of *The Alchemist* are comparatively genial. By the time that he was ready to revise *Every Man in His Humour*, Jonson had learned that the true function of comedy is 'To sport with humane follies, not with crimes'.[47] As his powers of realistic depiction came into full play, he gradually relinquished his loudly proclaimed moral purposes. Vainly Face apologizes for the amoral ending of *The Alchemist*.[48] Shakespeare and Donne had discovered that good and evil, in this world, are matters of opinion. So, finally, had Jonson. Mankind was subdivided, it now seemed, not into good men and bad, but into rogues and fools. Consequently, the rôle of the comic playwright was not to judge but to observe. After *Volpone*, it may be said that Jonson's genius underwent a metempsychosis of its own and, having died with a stern satirist, was reborn in a genial observer.

SOURCE: *Philological Quarterly*, xxii (1943) 231–9

NOTES

1. See the epigraph from Martial on the title-page of *Sejanus*; the prologue to the Folio version of *Every Man in His Humour*, l. 30; the glance at *The Tempest* in the induction to *Bartholomew Fair*, ll. 127–32. Numerical references to Jonson's text are to the edition of C. H. Herford and Percy and Evelyn Simpson (Oxford, 1925–41).

2. *Volpone*, i ii 63–5.

3. Maurice Castelain, *Ben Jonson, l'homme et l'œuvre* (Paris, 1907) p. 301.

4. J. D. Rea (ed.), *Volpone, or the Fox*, Yale Studies in English, LIX (New Haven, 1919) pp. xxvii, 194.

5. John Upton, *Remarks on Three Plays of Ben Jonson* (London, 1749) pp. 8–10. Cf. William Gifford (ed.), *The Works of Ben Jonson* (London, 1816) iii 174–5 n.

6. e.g. *The Devil is an Ass*, i i 44–53.

7. Suggestive in this connexion is L. C. Knights, *Drama and Society in the Age of Jonson* (London, 1937).

8. Upton, op. cit., pp. 18, 19.

9. F. Holthausen, 'Die Quelle von Ben Jonsons *Volpone*', *Anglia*, xii (1890) 519–25.

10. J. Q. Adams, 'The Sources of Ben Jonson's *Volpone*', *Modern Philology*, ii (1904) 289–99.

11. W. Bang, 'Zu Jonsons Quellen für seinen *Volpone*', *Mélanges Godefroid Kurth* (Liège, 1908) II 351–5.

12. Rea, op. cit., pp. xvii–xix, 160, 161. See also C. R. Thompson, *The Translations of Lucian by Erasmus and St Thomas More* (Ithaca, 1940).

13. A phrase from this letter, which has not been pointed out, may well have suggested the character of Mosca. To justify his learned trifling Erasmus cites a number of literary burlesques, including two of Lucian's, *The Fly* and *The Parasite*. This association *('muscam et parasiticam Lucianus')* tends to support the view of Upton and Adams, questioned by Rea, that Mosca's eulogy of parasites at the beginning of the third act is also founded on Lucian. See I. B. Kan (ed.), *Stultitiae Laus* (The Hague, 1898) p. iv.

14. Rea, op. cit., pp. 161–3. By a curious coincidence, Machiavelli's *Mandragola* contains a similar song, as well as a plot which is similar to the Corvino–Celia subplot of *Volpone*. Cf. Domenico Guerri (ed.), *Le commedie* (Turin, 1932) p. 30 :

> Quanto felice sia ciascun sel vede,
> Chi nasce sciocco ed ogni cosa crede!

15. Kan, op. cit., p. 62. Further references to this dialogue occur on pp. 91, 159.

16. Jonson utilizes 'that stranger doctrine of PYTHAGORAS' as a poetic conceit in his epigram to Sir Henry Savile, and nicknames the juggler Banks 'our PYTHAGORAS' – presumably because he trained animals – in 'The Famous Voyage'. B. H. Newdigate (ed.), *The Poems of Ben Jonson* (Oxford, 1936) pp. 31, 55. Cf. also the stock allusion in *The Fortunate Isles*, ll. 255–9.

17. A. R. Shilleto (ed.), *The Anatomy of Melancholy* (London, 1893) I 186.

18. Elsewhere in the play *The Dream* is echoed in occasional *sententiae* on the power of gold. Rea, op. cit., pp. 152, 220, 221.

19. He appears, however, in Robert Wilson's *The Cobbler's Prophecy* (1594), which is based on the kindred theme of Alectryon, and may conceivably have influenced Jonson. The influence of another latter-day morality by Wilson, *The Three Lords and Three Ladies of London*, upon *Cynthia's Revels* has been demonstrated by C. R. Baskervill, *English Elements in Jonson's Early Comedy*, University of Texas Studies in English, I (Austin, 1911) pp. 253–6. It might be added that *Cynthia's Revels* owes something to Erasmus as well. 'The Fountayne of

selfe-Loue' takes the place of Folly's fountain, but Moria accompanies Philautia into Jonson's *dramatis personae,* and Hedon and Anaides are apparently the sons of Folly's ladies-in-waiting, 'Ήδονή and "Άνοια. Cf. Kan, op. cit., p. 12.

20. The Jacobean interest in hermaphroditism is attested by the Citizen's Wife in *The Knight of the Burning Pestle.* A. R. Waller (ed.), *The Works of Francis Beaumont and John Fletcher* (Cambridge, 1908) VI 201.

21. *Volpone,* I ii 42–6.

22. *The Alchemist,* III ii 43.

23. *Epicœne,* II ii 3.

24. *Twelfth Night,* IV ii 54–65.

25. *Volpone,* I ii 30–2.

26. *Ben Jonson's Conversations with William Drummond of Hawthornden,* Herford and Simpson, op. cit., I 139.

27. Professor Rea (pp. xxx–xliii) has made out an ingenious case for identifying this character with Sir Henry Wotton, then English ambassador to Venice. But, since there is no external evidence on Jonson's side, the argument – like all such identifications – becomes a *petitio principii.* Certainly it is hard to imagine Jonson paying to the original of Sir Politick the high tribute of memorizing his verses; see Herford and Simpson, I 135.

28. See Jonson's letter to Lord Salisbury, ibid., I 202.

29. Ibid., I 136.

30. H. J. C. Grierson (ed.), *The Poems of John Donne* (Oxford, 1912) I 297.

31. Ibid., I 294.

32. Ibid., II 219.

33. *Hamlet,* IV iii 32–3; V i 224–39.

34. Ibid., II ii 255–7.

35. Grierson, op. cit., I 316.

36. Edmund Gosse, *The Life and Letters of John Donne* (London, 1899) I 141.

37. This is the view of the most conscientious student of Donne's reading. Miss M. P. Ramsay, *Les doctrines médiévales chez Donne* (Oxford, 1917) p. 58.

38. For the relation of this position to other aspects of his thought, see C. M. Coffin, *John Donne and the New Philosophy* (New York, 1937) p. 252.

39. Henry Alford (ed.), *The Works of John Donne* (London, 1837) III 611.

40. C. F. T. Brooke (ed.), *The Works of Christopher Marlowe* (Oxford, 1910) p. 193.

41. Gifford, op. cit., iv 509 n.
42. Notably R. H. Tawney, *Religion and the Rise of Capitalism* (London, 1926).
43. W. P. Ker (ed.), *Essays of John Dryden* (Oxford, 1926) i 73.
44. *The Alchemist,* Prologue, ll. 5–9.
45. *Volpone,* ii ii 117–18.
46. Gifford, op. cit., iv 118 n.
47. *Every Man in His Humour,* Prologue, l. 24.
48. *The Alchemist,* v v 157–65.

Jonas A. Barish

THE DOUBLE PLOT IN *VOLPONE* (1953)

For more than two centuries literary critics have been satisfied
to dismiss the subplot of *Volpone* as irrelevant and discordant,
because of its lack of overt connection with the main plot.
Jonson's most sympathetic admirers have been unable to
account for the presence of Sir Politic Would-be, Lady Would-
be, and Peregrine any more satisfactorily than by styling them
a 'makeweight' or a kind of comic relief to offset the 'sustained
gloom' of the chief action.[1] Without questioning the orthodox
opinion that the links of intrigue between the two plots are
frail, one may nevertheless protest against a view of drama
which criticizes a play exclusively in terms of physical action.
What appears peripheral on the level of intrigue may conceal
other kinds of relevance. And it is on the thematic level that
the presence of the Would-be's can be justified and their
peculiar antics related to the major motifs of the play.

John D. Rea, in his edition of *Volpone*, seems to have been
the first to notice that Sir Politic Would-be, like the characters
of the main plot, has his niche in the common beast fable:[2]
he is Sir Pol, the chattering poll parrot, and his wife is a
deadlier specimen of the same species. Rea's accurate insistence
on the loquaciousness of the parrot, however, must be supplemented by recalling that parrots not only habitually chatter,
they mimic. This banal but important little item of bird lore
offers a thread whereby we may find our way through the
complex thematic structure of the play. For Sir Politic and
Lady Would-be function to a large extent precisely as mimics.
They imitate their environment, and without knowing it they
travesty the actions of the main characters. In so doing, they
perform the function of burlesque traditional to comic sub-
plots in English drama, and they make possible the added

density and complexity of vision to which the device of the burlesque subplot lends itself.

His effort to Italianize himself takes the form, with Sir Politic, of an obsession with plots, secrets of state, and Machiavellian intrigue. His wife, on the other hand, apes the local styles in dress and cosmetics, reads the Italian poets, and tries to rival the lascivious Venetians in their own game of seduction.

Further, and more specifically, however, Sir Politic and Lady Would-be caricature the actors of the main plot. Sir Pol figures as a comic distortion of Volpone. As his name implies, he is the would-be politician, the speculator *manqué*, the unsuccessful enterpriser. Volpone, by contrast, is the real politician, the successful enterpriser, whose every stratagem succeeds almost beyond expectation. Sir Pol, like Volpone, is infatuated with his own ingenuity, and like Volpone he nurses his get-rich-quick schemes; but none of these ever progresses beyond the talking stage. While Volpone continues to load his coffers with the treasures that pour in from his dupes, Sir Pol continues to haggle over vegetables in the market and to annotate the purchase of toothpicks.

Lady Would-be, for her part, joins the dizzy game of legacy-hunting. Her antics caricature the more sinister gestures of Corvino, Voltore, and Corbaccio. She is jealous, like Corvino, as meaninglessly and perversely erudite as Voltore, and like Corbaccio, she makes compromising proposals to Mosca which leave her at the mercy of his blackmail. But, like her husband, Lady Would-be is incapable of doing anything to the purpose, and when she plays into Mosca's hands in the fourth act, she becomes the most egregious of the dupes because she is the blindest.

We do not learn of the existence of the Would-be's until the close of the first act,[3] and then only in a scrap of dialogue between Mosca and Volpone. Mosca's panegyric on Celia, following his sarcasms about Lady Would-be, serves to initiate a contrast which prevails throughout the play, between the

households of Corvino and Sir Politic. If Corvino's besetting
vice is jealousy, that of Sir Pol is uxoriousness, and the contrast enlarges itself into a difference between the brutal, obses-
sive passions of Italy and the milder eccentricities, the acquired
follies or humors, of England. The contrast continues to un-
fold in the opening scene of Act II, where Sir Politic talks to
his new acquaintance, Peregrine. Peregrine, it should be mentioned, probably belongs to the beast fable himself, as the
pilgrim falcon. A case for this possibility would have to be
based on the habits of hawks, commonly trained to hunt other
birds. One then might find propriety in the fact of the falcon's
hunting the parrot in the play. In Jonson's Epigram LXXXV
(Herford and Simpson, VIII 55), the hawk is described as a
bird sacred to Apollo, since it pursues the truth, strikes at
ignorance, and makes the fool its quarry. All these activities
are performed by Peregrine vis-à-vis Sir Politic.

In the initial scene between them, three chief ideas are
developed, all of cardinal importance to the play and all inter-
related. The first is the notion of monstrosity. Monstrosity has
already made its spectacular appearance in the person of
Androgyno and in the passage on Volpone's misbegotten offspring. We are, thereby, already familiar with the moral
abnormality of Venice and its inhabitants. The present
passage, with its reports of strange marvels sighted in England
– a lion whelping in the Tower, a whale discovered in the
Thames, porpoises above the bridge – introduces us to an
order of monsters more comic than those to be met with in
Venice, but to monsters nonetheless, in the proper sense of the
word. Sir Pol's prodigies are distant echoes of the moral earthquake rocking Venice, a looking glass for England whereby
that country is warned to heed the lesson of the Italian state
lest its own follies turn to vices and destroy it.

The enactment of the interlude in the first act, by placing
the soul of the fool in the body of the hermaphrodite, has
already established an identification between folly and monstrosity.[4] Appropriately enough, then, having discussed mon-

sters, Peregrine and Sir Pol turn to speak of the death of a
famous fool, thus reinforcing the link between the two ideas.
Sir Pol's excessive reaction to the event prompts Peregrine to
inquire maliciously into a possible parentage between the two,
and his companion innocently to deny it. The joke here, that
Sir Pol is kin to the dead fool through their mutual folly if not
through family, merges into a larger reflection on the ubiquity
of folly, picking up that suggestion by ricochet, as it were, from
the interlude in Act I. When Peregrine asks, 'I hope/You
thought him not immortall?' (Act II, scene i, lines 55–6), the
question implies its own Jonsonian answer: Master Stone, the
fool, is not immortal, but his folly lives on incarnate in hun-
dreds of fools like Sir Politic, much as the soul of Pythagoras,
in the interlude, invested the body of one fool after another for
thousands of years, only to reach its final and most fitting
avatar in the person of Androgyno.

The colloquy concerning the Mamuluchi introduces the
third chief motif of the scene, that of mimicry. This passage,
where baboons are described in various quasi-human postures,[5] acquires added irony from the fact that it is recited by
the parrot, the imitative animal par excellence, and also from
the fact that the activities of the baboons, like those of Master
Stone, the fool, consist chiefly of spying and intriguing and
therefore differ so little from the way Sir Pol himself attempts
to imitate the Italians.

The arrival of Volpone disguised as a mountebank produces the expected confrontation between the archknave and
the complete gull, the latter hopelessly hypnotized by the
eloquence of the former. Volpone commences by disdaining
certain imputations that have been cast on him by professional
rivals. By way of counter-attack, he accuses them of not knowing their trade, of being mere 'ground *Ciarlitani*', or spurious
mountebanks. If there is any doubt about the application of
the passage to Sir Politic, it is settled by that individual's cry
of admiration: 'Note but his bearing, and contempt of these'
(II ii 58). Sir Politic thus plays charlatan to Volpone's

mountebank as, within the larger frame of the play, he plays
parrot to Volpone's fox. But Volpone has brought along his
own misshapen child, the dwarf Nano, as an accredited imitator. Nano, who fills the role of Zan Fritada, the zany, is the
domesticated mimic, the conscious mimic, as Androgyno is the
conscious fool, while Sir Pol remains the unconscious mimic
and the unconscious fool.

Volpone, pursuing his attack on imitators, assails them for
trying to copy his elixir: 'Indeed, very many haue assay'd,
like apes in imitation of that, which is really and essentially in
mee, to make of this oyle' (II ii 149–50). What is 'really and
essentially' in Volpone we know already to be monstrosity, so
that to imitate Volpone (as Sir Politic does) is to imitate the
unnatural, and therefore, in a sense, to place one's self at two
removes from nature. But Volpone believes himself, not without justification, to be inimitable. The wretched practitioners
who try to duplicate his ointment end in disaster. 'Poore
wretches!' he concludes, 'I rather pittie their folly, and indis-
cretion, then their losse of time, and money; for those may be
recouered by industrie: but to bee a foole borne, is a disease
incurable' (II ii 157–9). At this moment all that would be
needed to drive home the application of Volpone's *sententia*
would be a pause on his part, followed by a significant look
from Peregrine to Sir Pol.[6] But the situation conceals a further
irony. Volpone's aphorism applies to himself. Before long, he,
the archknave, will have proved the greatest fool, and this
despite the versatility which enables him to transcend for the
moment his own preferences, in order to cater to the prejudices
of the public. Paradoxically, in this scene, speaking out of
character, Volpone utters truths which reverse the premises of
his former behavior. In Act I, gold, the great goddess, served
him as sovereign remedy and omnipotent healer. For the
saltimbanco Scoto of Mantua, peddling his fraudulent elixir,
newer and relatively truer axioms celebrate the treasure of
health: 'O, health! health! the blessing of the rich! the riches
of the poore!' (II ii 84–5). But with the application of this

facile maxim, error descends again. The new truth proves to
be only a distorted half-truth. In place of gold, Volpone offers
only his humbug ointment as the 'most soueraigne, and
approued remedie' (II ii 103–4). The real point, and he has
made it himself, escapes him : to be a fool born is a disease
incurable, and it is this disease to which he himself is destined
to succumb.

The 'little remembrance' which Volpone now presents to
Celia proves to be a cosmetic powder with virtues more miraculous than those of the *oglio* itself. It is the powder 'That
made VENVS a goddesse (giuen her by APOLLO) that kept her
perpetually yong, clear'd her wrincles, firm'd her gummes,
fill'd her skin, colour'd her haire; from her, deriu'd to HELEN,
and at the sack of *Troy* (vnfortunately) lost : till now, in this
our age, it was as happily recouer'd, by a studious Antiquarie
. . . who sent a moyetie of it, to the court of *France* . . . wherewith the ladies there, now, colour theire haire' (II ii 235–43).
Thus the history of the powder parallels the metempsychoses
of Pythagoras. Like Pythagoras' soul, the powder began its
career as a gift from Apollo, and in its transmigrations
through the goddess of love, the whore of Sparta, and the court
ladies of France, it serves to underline the ancient lineage
of vanity as a special case of the folly rehearsed in the interlude.

Mosca's opening soliloquy in Act III shows that this excellent counterfeiter is himself, like his master, obsessed by the
notion of imitators. His contempt for ordinary parasites suggests that there is a hierarchy of counterfeits, ranging from
those who are deeply and essentially false (like himself) to
those who practice falsity out of mere affectation, who are, so
to speak, falsely false and therefore, again, at two removes
from nature. The shift of scene back to Volpone's house produces still another variation on the theme of mimicry. In order
to beguile their master from his boredom, the trio of grotesques
stage an impromptu interlude, dominated by Nano, who
claims that the dwarf can please a rich man better than the

eunuch or the hermaphrodite. The dwarf, explains Nano, is little, and pretty :

> Else, why doe men say to a creature of my shape,
> So soone as they see him, it's a pritty little ape?
> And, why a pritty ape? but for pleasing imitation
> Of greater mens action, in a ridiculous fashion
>
> (III iii 11–14)

The first interlude, it may be recalled again, established an identification between folly and the unnatural. The present fragment confirms a further identity between mimicry and deformity, already hinted at in the mountebank scene where Nano appeared as the zany, or mimic, to Volpone's Scoto. At this point one may represent some of the relationships in the play diagrammatically as follows :

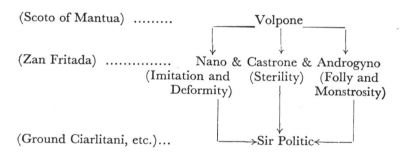

(Scoto of Mantua) ....   _____Volpone_____

(Zan Fritada) ....   Nano & Castrone & Androgyno
                               (Imitation and (Sterility) (Folly and
                                 Deformity)   Monstrosity)

(Ground Ciarlitani, etc.)...   └──→Sir Politic←──┘

Since Volpone has (presumptively at least) sired both Nano and Androgyno, and since Sir Pol combines the chief attributes of both, one may, with the aid of the diagram, infer what is already emerging plainly in context, that mimicry itself is something monstrous and abnormal. It is unnatural for baboons and apes and parrots to counterfeit human behavior. It is equally unnatural for men to imitate beasts. It argues a perversion of their essential humanity. It is not for nothing, then, that the chief characters of the play fit into one zoölogical classification or another. As men, they duplicate the habits of beasts; as beasts, they brutishly travesty humanity. They belong to the genus *monster* – half man, half brute – that order of fabulous creatures whose common denominator is their unnaturalness, their lack of adherence to whatever category of being nature has assigned them.

The arrival of Lady Would-be, fuming and fussing over her toilet, and snapping at her servingwomen, provides still a further object-lesson in falsity. Here, as so often in Jonson, face physic symbolizes the painted surface hiding the rotten inside; the cosmetic care of the face signifies the neglect of the soul. It signifies equally an attachment to appearances, an incapacity to look beyond the superficies of life or truth. The powder which Volpone offered to Celia and which Celia did not need, since her beauty was of the platonic sort that revealed the purity of her soul, might with more justice have been given to Lady Would-be, and it is Lady Would-be who deserves the epithet of 'lady *vanitie*' (II v 21) with which Corvino, in his jealous tantrum, has stigmatized Celia.

The scene between Lady Would-be and Volpone serves partly as a burlesque of the parallel scenes in Act I between Volpone and the other *captatores*. All the essential ingredients of those scenes reappear, but scrambled and topsy-turvy. Once again Volpone feigns sickness, but this time it is in self-defense against the terrible oratory of Lady Would-be. Once again remedies are prescribed, but these are neither Corbaccio's deadly opiate nor his *aurum palpabile* offered as pump-priming, but the fantastic assortment of old wives' restoratives dredged up from Lady Would-be's infernal memory. She rains down the hailstones of her learning on the helpless Volpone, until the archrogue, anticipating the judgment to be rendered on him in Act v, cries out in despair: 'Before I fayn'd diseases, now I haue one' (III iv 62). The whole episode is a rich application of the principle of comic justice. If in the final denouement Volpone suffers the penalty of vice, here he reaps the more ludicrous reward of his own folly. Trapped by Lady Would-be's rhetoric, itself a consequence of his own scheming, he is finally driven to pronounce himself cured. But the talking machine grinds on, and only Mosca's happy notion of exciting her jealousy, as he has previously aroused Corvino's, and for the same purpose, succeeds in getting rid of her. As her contribution to Volpone's coffers, she leaves behind a wrought cap of her own making; this forms a suitably ridiculous contrast to the treasures earlier offered by Corvino, Corbaccio, and Voltore.

The same scene serves as introduction and comic distortion of the scene immediately to follow between Volpone and Celia. Celia's unearthly purity is made to seem even more unearthly by its contrast to Lady Would-be's lecherousness, this latter apparent in the lady's addiction to cosmetics, in her slips of the tongue, and in her barely disguised sexual overtures. Lady Would-be's attempted seduction of Volpone having been thwarted, the stage is set for Volpone's attempted seduction of Celia. Volpone commences his wooing with a characteristic boast: 'I, before/I would haue left my practice, for thy loue,' he swears, 'In varying figures, I would haue contended/With the blue PROTEVS, or the horned *Floud*' (III vii 150–3). Justifiably proud of his powers of disguise, Volpone emphasizes them further by citing a past occasion on which he masqueraded in the ambiguous role of Antinous, Nero's favorite. Embarking on an enumeration of the exotic splendors in store for Celia, he reserves as his final inducement the promise that she will participate, with him, in transmutations without end: 'Whil'st we, in changed shapes, act OVIDS tales' (the *Metamorphoses*, of course),

> Thou, like EVROPA now, and I like IOVE,
> Then I like MARS, and thou like ERYCINE,
> So, of the rest, till we haue quite run through
> And weary'd all the fables of the gods.
> Then will I haue thee in more moderne formes,
> Attired like some sprightly dame of *France*,
> Braue *Tuscan* lady, or proud *Spanish* beauty
>   (III vii 221–8)

We have already witnessed, in the first interlude, the metempsychosis of folly and, in the powder offered to Celia in Act II, the transmigrations of vanity. Now, as a climax to his eloquence, Volpone rehearses the metamorphoses of lust. Jonson thus endows his central themes with vertical depth in time as well as horizontal extension in space. Folly, vanity, lust, have been, are, will be. At any given moment their practitioners are legion, and often interchangeable.

It is at this point that Celia's refusal crystallizes into a repudiation of folly, vanity, and lust combined and that her behavior contrasts most sharply with that of Lady Would-be. The recollection of Lady Would-be lacquering her face and making indecent advances to Volpone brings into sharper focus Celia's sudden horror at her own beauty, and her plea that her face be flayed or smeared with poison, in order to undo the lust she has aroused. If, for Lady Would-be, the cosmetic art is a necessary preliminary to sexual conquest, its opposite, the disfigurement of the face, becomes for Celia the badge of chastity. Where Lady Would-be strives to adopt Italian vices for her own, Celia's gestures as well as her name demonstrate her alienation from the moral and spiritual province of Venice.

Act IV carries us back into the open street, where Sir Pol, ignorant of the plot developing at Volpone's house, continues babbling of plots in terms which ordinarily have one meaning for him and another for the audience. After a patronizing recital of 'instructions' to Peregrine on methods of deportment in Venice, he confides suddenly that his money-making projects need only the assistance of one trusty henchman in order to be put into instant execution. Evidently he is hinting that Peregrine undertake that assignment and thus play Mosca to his Volpone. But Peregrine contents himself with inquiring into the particulars of the plots. The most elaborate of these proves to be a way to protect Venice from the plague by using onions as an index to the state of infection on ships entering the harbor. This mad scheme, with its echo of Volpone's claim

to have distributed his *oglio* under official patent to all the
commonwealths of Christendom, serves chiefly to remind us
again of the moral plague prevailing in Venice and of the
incomprehension of that fact on the part of those characters
who prattle most about disease and cure.

The ensuing scene parodies the episode in Act II where
Corvino discovers his wife in conversation with the mounte-
bank. Just as Corvino interrupts Volpone while the latter is
advertising his medicine, so Lady Would-be bursts in on Sir
Politic as the knight is dilating on his schemes and projects. As
Corvino babbles jealously of lechers and satyrs, so Lady
Would-be jabbers of land sirens, lewd harlots, and fricatrices.
Corvino beats away the mountebank. Lady Would-be rails at
Peregrine. Both harp on 'honor', and both discard that term
as soon as it becomes an inconvenience, Corvino when it
becomes an obstacle to his plan of inheritance, Lady Would-be
when she discovers that Peregrine is no harlot in disguise, but
a young gentleman. As for Sir Politic, though he too plays his
part in the little impromptu from the *commedia dell'arte*, he
remains, unlike Volpone, quite oblivious to the fact. Actually,
Sir Pol reenacts not the role of 'Signior FLAMINIO', the lover
in disguise – that part, however reluctantly assumed, belongs
to Peregrine – but the female role, the 'FRANCISCINA',
guarded by a jealous 'PANTALONE *di besogniosi*' (II iii 3–8).
The confusion of sexes symbolized in Androgyno, in the indis-
criminate journeyings of the soul of Pythagoras, in Volpone's
masquerade as Antinous, in Lady Would-be's error, as well as
in the reversed masculine–feminine roles of Sir Pol and Lady
Would-be, contributes its own kind of abnormality to the
deformity of the moral atmosphere chiefly figured by the metamorphoses of beasts into men. And if one regards Sir Politic's
uxoriousness as a kind of metaphoric emasculation, one may
then equate him with Castrone, as he has already been equated
with Nano and Androgyno, to make the pattern of mimicry
complete.[7]

The fourth-act trial starts with justice and concludes with a perversion of it. The monsters begotten by Volpone, the prodigies and portents that exercised such a hypnotic effect on Sir Pol, now make a lavish and climactic reappearance in the language of the scene. First they designate their proper objects. But as Voltore begins to exercise his baleful rhetoric, the parlance of unnaturalness, appropriate to the guilty, begins to turn against the innocent. Corbaccio disavows his son for 'the meere portent of nature'; he is 'an vtter stranger' to his loins, a 'Monster of men, swine, goate, wolfe, parricide' (iv v 109–11). Finally Lady Would-be arrives, the eternal parrot, to give testimony which virtually clinches the case against Celia:

> Out, thou *chameleon* harlot; now, thine eies
> Vie teares with the *hyaena*. (iv vi 2–3)

The beast characters in the play display an unerring faculty for describing the innocent as beasts. Corvino has already called Celia a crocodile, referring to that animal's notorious ability to imitate human tears, and Lady Would-be, though she has her unnatural natural history somewhat confused, invokes another creature famous for its powers of mimicry, the hyena, as well as the even more versatile chameleon.

The juxtaposition of the hyena and the chameleon reminds one that there is a point at which the ideas of metamorphosis and mimicry coalesce. The chameleon, shifting its colors to blend itself with its environment, indulges in a highly developed form of protective mimicry. Volpone carries the principle a step further. He goes through his restless series of transformations not as a shield but in order to prey on his own kind, to satisfy something in his unnatural nature which demands incessant changing of shape and form. But knavery and credulity, mimicry and metamorphosis, alike reflect aspects of one basic folly: the folly of becoming, or trying to become, what one is not, the cardinal sin of losing one's nature. Only Bonario and Celia, of all the creatures in the play, never ape others, never change their shapes, never act contrary to their essential natures. And in the unnatural state of Venice it is chiefly they, the unchanging ones, who are attacked as hyenas and chameleons.

Volpone, in short, may be read as a comic restatement of a theme familiar in Shakespeare's plays of the same period, the theme of disorder. Order figures here not as social balance or political hierarchy, but as a principle of differentiation in nature whereby each species, each sex, maintains its separate identity. With the loss of clear-cut divisions between man and beast, between beast and beast, between male and female, all creatures become monsters. The basic structure of nature is violated. The astronomical portents discussed earlier by Sir Pol and Peregrine in connection with animal prodigies reflect the upheaval of the cosmos itself following the degeneracy of man.

But by this time, justice has become as monstrous as its participants, and the *avvocatori* close the session piously intoning their horror at the unnaturalness of Celia and Bonario. Volpone's last and greatest hoax is destined to set the balance of nature right again. It starts, however, with one more act of unnaturalness. Volpone, a monster, who therefore occupies no fixed place in the order of created beings, feigns death and thus symbolically demonstrates his lack of status. One by one the inheritors file in for the legacy, only to find that they have been duped by Mosca.

The first to receive her dismissal is Lady Would-be. Having made overtures to both Mosca and Volpone, she is in a position to be summarily blackmailed. 'Goe home,' advises Mosca, 'and vse the poore sir POL, your knight, well;/For feare I tell some riddles: go, be melancholique' (v iii 44–5). Thus the learned lady who knew so many bizarre ways of curing Volpone's melancholy now has the opportunity to treat herself for the same ailment, and so do her colleagues. The value of this scene consists partly in its inflicting comic justice on the legacy-hunters before the *avvocatori* render their sterner legal judgments, just as Volpone has already, in Lady Would-be, met a comic foretaste of the retribution which overtakes him at the *Scrutineo*. But since the parrot, for all its shrillness, remains less venal than the crow or vulture, the untrussing of Lady Would-be goes no further. In the realm of the severer truths, vice and folly may appear as different aspects of a similar spiritual malaise. In the realm of poetic justice, however, a distinction continues to be practiced. Vice, which is criminal and attacks others, must suffer public correction, whereas folly, a disease essentially self-destructive, may be dealt with in private and without the assistance of constituted authority. For Lady Would-be it is sufficient that, awakened to some sense of her own folly, she vows to quit Venice and take to sea 'for physick'.

And so with her preposterous knight, Sir Politic, whom we now encounter for the last time, the victim of a private plot which performs the same service of mortification for him that the final trial scene does for Volpone. The *mercatori* enlisted by Peregrine perform the office of the *avvocatori* who pronounce sentence on Volpone, and the divulging of the pathetic notebook, with its scraps from playbooks, becomes the burlesque substitute for the exposure of Volpone's will, in bringing on the disaster. Peregrine, echoing Voltore's suggestion that Volpone be tested on the strappado, warns Sir Pol that his persecutors will put him to the rack. Whereupon the knight remembers an 'engine' he has designed against just such emergencies, a tortoise shell. And to the disgust of three hundred years of literary critics he climbs into the ungainly object, playing possum after the fashion of his model, Volpone, who has feigned death in the foregoing scene. The arrival of the merchants brings on the catastrophe :

> *Mer.* 1. What
> Are you, sir? *Per.* I' am a merchant, that
> came heere
> To looke vpon this tortoyse. *Mer.* 3. How?
> *Mer.* 1. St MARKE !
> What beast is this? *Per.* It is a fish. *Mer.* 2.
> Come out, here.

> *Per.* Nay, you may strike him, sir, and tread
>   vpon him :
> Hee'll beare a cart. (v iv 62–7)

Eventually, by stamping and poking, they goad Sir Politic out
of his exoskeleton. The scene thus rephrases in a vein of
broadest tomfoolery the essential question of the play : 'What
kind of creatures are these?' Throughout the action one has
seen beasts aping men and men imitating beasts on the moral
and psychological levels. Here the theme of mimicry reaches
its literal climax in an episode of farce, where the most imitative of the characters puts on the physical integument of an
animal and the hired pranksters stand about debating its probable zoölogical classification. The final unshelling of the tortoise, a parallel to the uncasing of the fox in the last scene,
arouses further comment from the merchants :

> *Mer.* 1. 'Twere a rare motion, to be seene, in *Fleet-street* !
> *Mer.* 2. I, i'the terme. *Mer.* 1. Or *Smithfield,* in the faire.
>   (v iv 77–8)

Sir Politic, thus, so inquisitive about prodigies, has finally
become one himself, a specimen fit to be housed among the
freaks of Smithfield or amid the half-natural, half-artificial
curiosities of Fleet Street. With the knowledge that he is
destined to become a victim of the kind of curiosity he himself
has exhibited, his disillusionment is complete and his chastise-
ment effected. He and Lady Would-be, the only survivors, in
this play, of Jonson's earlier humor characters, are now 'out
of their humor', purged of their imitative folly by the strong
medicine of ridicule.

Public punishment, however, awaits the actors of the main
plot. Jonson is not sporting here with human follies like those
of the Would-be's, but dealing grimly with inhuman crimes.
The names of fabulous monsters, basilisks and chimeras, con-
tinue to echo in our ears as the catastrophe approaches, fasten-
ing themselves at last onto their proper objects, the conspirators

in the game of *captatio*. Voltore's spurious fit spells out in concrete theatrical terms his unnatural status and the lesson pointed by the *avvocatori* : 'These possesse wealth, as sicke men possesse feuers,/Which, trulyer, may be said to possese them' (v xii 101–2). The delivery of Volpone's substance to the *Incurabili* places a final and proper valuation on the medicinal powers of gold. The imprisonment of Volpone is specifically designed to give him the opportunity to acquire in reality the diseases he has mimicked and the leisure to ponder the accuracy of his own text : to be a fool born is a disease incurable. Voltore and Corbaccio are henceforth to be secluded from their fellow-men like the unnatural specimens they are, while Corvino's animality is to be the object of a public display more devastating than Sir Politic's brief masquerade as a tortoise.

Thus on successive levels of low comedy and high justice, the monsters of folly and the monsters of vice suffer purgation, exposed as the sort of misshapen marvels they themselves have chattered about so freely. The relative harmlessness of Sir Pol's downfall serves to differentiate his folly from the viciousness of the Venetians, but the many parallels between his catastrophe and theirs warn us that his kind of folly is sufficiently virulent after all, is closely related to graver sins, and, if it persists in imitating them, must ultimately fall under the same condemnation.

If these observations are accurate, it should be clear in what sense the subplot of the Would-be's is relevant to the total structure of *Volpone*. Starting from a contrast between Italian vice and English folly, Jonson personifies the latter in two brainless English travelers, makes their folly consist chiefly in mimicry of Italian vice, and Italian vice itself, in its purest form, consist of the more comprehensive form of mimicry we have termed 'metamorphosis', thus bringing the two aspects of evil together into the same moral universe and under a common moral judgment; with the use of the beast fable he binds the two together dramatically, and by the distribution of poetic justice he preserves the distinction between them. Each of the episodes involving the Would-be's, including the much despised incident of the tortoise, thus serves a definite dramatic purpose, and one may conclude, then, that the subplot adds a fresh dimension and a profounder insight without which *Volpone*, though it might be a neater play, would also be a poorer and a thinner one.

SOURCE: *Modern Philology*, LI (1953) 83–92

NOTES

1. The quoted phrases are from George Saintsbury, *A History of Elizabethan Literature* (New York, 1912) p. 181. For substantially the same view see John Addington Symonds, *Ben Jonson*, 'English Worthies' series (New York, 1886) p. 86; Maurice Castelain, *Ben Jonson* (Paris, 1907) p. 301; G. Gregory Smith, *Ben Jonson*, 'English Men of Letters' series (London, 1919) p. 111; C. H. Herford and Percy Simpson (eds), *Ben Jonson* (Oxford, 1925–50) II 64; and Arthur Sale (ed.), *Volpone* (London, 1951) pp. vii, 176. Recent studies of Jonson by Townsend, Sackton, and others intimate some uneasiness about the canonical view of the subplot in *Volpone* but do not seriously challenge it.

2. (New Haven, 1919) p. xxxiii. The further possibility, advanced by Rea (pp. xxx–xliii) and sharply challenged by the Simpsons (IX 680–2), that Sir Politic was intended as a caricature of Sir Henry Wotton need not be dealt with here. The identification is by no means certain, and if it were, it would not materially affect the present analysis of Sir Politic, whose role transcends mere personal satire.

3. For the sake of brevity, this discussion will confine itself as closely as possible to the scenes actually involving the Would-be's. Jonson's sources, which are legion for this play, have been assembled both by Rea and by Herford and Simpson in their editions but will not be considered here. All citations to *Volpone* will be from Herford and Simpson, vol. v.

4. For an analysis of the first interlude and its importance to the play as a whole see Harry Levin, 'Jonson's Metempsychosis', *Philological Quarterly*, XXII (1943) 231–9.

5. Rea quotes from Edward Topsel's chapter 'Of the Cyno-cephale, or Baboun' in *The Historie of Four-footed Beastes* (1607) : 'It is the error of vulgar people to think that *Babouns* are men, differing only in the face or visage. . . . They will imitate all humane actions, loving wonderfully to wear garments . . . they are as lustful and venerous as Goats, attempting to defile all sorts of women' (Rea, p. 178).

6. A proper staging of the scene would involve, I think, placing Sir Pol fairly close to Volpone, so that the two stare each other in the face, the one collecting with ardor every flower of rhetoric that falls from the other. At this moment, Volpone him-self might stop to gaze into the infatuated countenance before him : by now Sir Pol's credulity is as apparent to him as it is to Peregrine.

7. Actually, Florio's *Worlde of Wordes* (1598) defines *Cas-trone* not only as 'a gelded man', but as 'a noddie, a meacocke, a cuckold, a ninnie, a gull' (quoted in Rea, p. 144). Any of these will serve as accurate epithets for Sir Pol, with the possible exception of 'cuckold', and if that designation does not fit it is not owing to any lack of effort on Lady Would-be's part.

S. Musgrove

TRAGICAL MIRTH: *KING LEAR* AND *VOLPONE* (1957)

In my first lecture I tried to show that a good case can be made out for thinking that Shakespeare and Jonson enjoyed a closer companionship, as friends and as playwrights, than is often supposed. Today I wish to consider two plays which seem to show the effects of such an association, though at first sight they are widely dissimilar: *King Lear* and *Volpone*. *Volpone* was performed in 1605, and *Lear* belongs either to that same year, or to a date very close to it. In comparing these two plays I am not, in the main, looking for literary borrowings of a direct kind, nor for verbal indebtedness: but for larger likenesses of theme and imaginative intention. If we can legitimately suppose that Shakespeare and Jonson talked over what they were writing, argued about subject, treatment and problems, as writers will, it could very well happen that two plays, very unlike each other, but written about the same time, might show a profound and essential similarity beneath their obvious differences. There is, I believe, such a similarity between these two plays, even when every allowance has been made for coincidence and common ground.

The subject of *Volpone*, in the most obvious sense, is money – or rather, greed, and the corruption which greed works in the human soul. In recent years much work has been done – for instance, by L. C. Knights – on the presentation of this theme in Jacobean drama, and scholars have been inclined to connect its frequent appearance with the consciousness of the breakdown of one form of society, or of social cohesion, and the birth of another: the birth, in fact, of something that we can call capitalism. In other words, the dramatists had become aware that the older system of social unity, a system depending on mutual service and loyalty, and in its origin feudal and mediaeval, had given way to a newer form of social obligation, dependent on money, or credit, on what has been called the 'cash-nexus'. They were not interested in, and certainly did not understand, the economics of this change. What concerned them was its morality – the way in which an ancient set of beliefs about what was right and wrong between man and man had to yield, or to adapt itself, to a 'bond' of a new kind – of Shylock's kind. And, on the whole, they did not like what they saw.

This phenomenon is too well known to make it necessary for me to go over such well-trodden ground again, but it is certain that Jonson was vitally interested in it, and that *Volpone* is an important document in its dramatic history. I am concerned here only to point out that at least one play by Shakespeare was written directly and centrally on this theme – or on part of it : *Timon of Athens,* which belongs to 1607. *Timon* is, if you like, a Jonsonian play : a fiercely moral denunciation of the human passion of greed, presented through a set of characters much more like 'humours' than those of Shakespeare's other plays. It is also a failure. Despite passages of almost unbearable intensity, of insight so bitter and yet so true, even if only imperfectly true, as to make one hate human kind, it does not cohere either in structure or, completely, in theme. It has even been suggested, though I doubt whether the suggestion is necessary, that Shakespeare was emotionally unable to finish it – that he suffered, under the pressure of human ugliness of act and motive, some sort of crisis or breakdown which led him to abandon it in its present unsatisfactory state. Whether this be true or not, it is obvious enough that he could not write a 'Jonsonian' play, any more than Jonson could write *Hamlet.* All I wish to establish here is that Shakespeare was, at a date not very far from that of *Volpone,* deeply interested in the same kind of subject as *Jonson* had in mind in that play. We need not, therefore, be surprised, if a similar theme emerges in other plays of approximately the same date; and, in fact, if

Timon and *Lear* are compared, it is possible to point to many details, both verbal and thematic, which are closely akin.

Direct evidence that Jonson had read *King Lear* (apart from what is contained within *Volpone* itself) is less easy to come by; curiously enough, there are almost no contemporary references to *King Lear* anywhere in the Jacobean period. It does not seem to have been nearly so popular as *Hamlet*, though the history of its publication suggests that it was performed fairly frequently. It is however interesting that several important phrases from *King Lear* have found their way into a masque written by Jonson in 1606 – *Hymenaei*, composed for the marriage, soon to be a source of scandal and murder, between the Earl of Essex and Frances Howard. One occurs in a speech uttered by Hymen, when certain masquers, representing the irrational emotions, burst in and interrupt the ceremonies :

> If there be
> A power, like Reason, left in that huge body
> Or little world of man from whence these came,
> Look forth . . .

The 'little world of man' here refers to a 'globe figuring a man' from which the masquers have stepped; but it is the same phrase, used to refer to man himself, which is applied to Lear in III i. He is out in the storm, and a gentleman describes him thus :

> Strives in his little world of man to out-scorn
> The to-and-fro-conflicting wind and rain.

The idea of course is common enough – that the constitution of man is a small analogue of the constitution of the universe – but the phrase itself is not; and it may well have remained in Jonson's mind from seeing or talking about *King Lear* itself. In the same masque, too, some of the 'lords' are dressed in a garment which is described as 'Persic', reminding one of Lear's

piteous description of Edgar's torn and threadbare blanket in
III vi :

> . . . I do not like the fashion of your garments; you will
>   say,
> they are Persian attire; but let them be changed . . .

Perhaps, too, the mysterious 'sea-monster' to which Lear compares the ingratitude of his daughters (I iv) has something to
do with the 'six huge sea-monsters, varied in their shapes and
dispositions' which appear in the *Masque of Blackness.*

These however are small points, which prove only what we
have already considered probable enough – that odd phrases
and ideas from Shakespeare's plays tend to find their way into
Jonson's memory, and to stick there. To these we may add one
small external link. It is highly probable that Shakespeare, in
seeking material for *King Lear,* read (perhaps before publication) Camden's little collection of historical essays and anti-
quarian annotations called *Remaines,* which was published in
1605. This book was certainly known to Jonson; Camden was
his early patron and friend, and it could have been he who
drew Shakespeare's attention to it. It is however more reward-
ing to turn from such trivia to the larger issue and the deeper
likeness between *Lear* and *Volpone.* Before we enter upon any
details, it is perhaps necessary to say that there should be no
occasion for surprise in finding similarities between the most
pessimistic and terrible of Shakespeare's tragedies, and a
comedy of contemporary life. Jonson's aim, in his great satirical comedies, is deeply serious : he is moved by a stern passion
of moral indignation at the crimes and follies of men, and his
laughter is curative and purgative, not frivolous or accom-
modating. *Volpone* is introduced by a long critical dedication,
offered to the two universities, which contains a justification of
the dignity and prestige of great drama. The aim of the comic
poet is no less than Justice itself, and, as Jonson sees it, comedy
on this great scale merits the approval and applause of both
moralist and scholar. The play itself is conceived in the same

spirit. It is sometimes described as possessing as large a share of the tragic as of the comic spirit; and though Jonson would not have accepted that terminology, the phrase makes its point to our modern ears. Neither *Volpone* nor *King Lear* is meant to send its audience home in a spirit of happy acceptance of things as they are; both, in Macmillan Brown's phrase, contemplate a possible 'victory of evil' in the world.

It may be useful by way of preface to recall the plot of *Volpone* to those not familiar with it. Volpone, the Fox, aided by his parasite Mosca, has laid a trap for the greedy citizens of Venice. He pretends to be desperately ill and at the point of death, and gives it out that he is looking for an heir to whom he may leave his considerable wealth. Into this trap fall Voltore, Corvino and Corbaccio, who are induced by Mosca to offer sundry valuable gifts in order to gain the favour of the dying man. The plot, under Jonson's brilliant control, grows more and more complex as the dupes are drawn further into the mire. Corbaccio disinherits his son Bonario and names Volpone as his heir, in the hope of reaching a reciprocal arrangement with him. Corvino offers to prostitute his wife Celia to Volpone, on Mosca's assurance that this is medically desirable. Bonario rescues Celia from Volpone's clutches, whereupon Bonario and Celia find themselves accused in court of adultery and of plotting the murder of Bonario's father. At this point the plot is so closely woven that no summary can do it justice : it must suffice to say that Voltore's nerve breaks in court, and that by a complicated series of plots and counter-plots, involving Volpone's supposed death and the naming of Mosca as his heir, and after a dizzying series of turns and returns on the part of the 'fox', the mathematically satisfying solution is reached whereby Volpone can keep his mouth shut and be ruined, or open it and be ruined. He chooses the latter course, the guilty are all condignly punished, and the innocent waved briefly away. Entwined round this central strand is a secondary plot involving a pair of minor English fools, Sir Politic Would-be – the traveller who always has the inside

story on foreign politics, and always the wrong one – and his
wife, who is an awful example of the terrible effects that education may have upon a woman. She has read everything, and
understands nothing. These two are in turn victimised by an
agreeable English rogue, Peregrine. Such a summary, of
course, is the merest skeleton, and gives no idea of the essential
force of the play, which depends for its effect on the author's
sense of moral outrage and its exhibition of the self-destructive
nature of the human passions.

I said at the beginning of this lecture that the subject of
Volpone was greed, and the corruption which greed works on
the human soul. This is also the subject of *Lear*, as expressed
in one set of terms : once the bonds of human love are broken,
there is nothing to stand between man and his naked appetites.
In both plays this theme is worked out on a universal scale :
both portray, of deliberate intention, a state of affairs in which
one passion is dominant over the rest and over reason itself, in
which dog eats dog, and a whole group of human beings goes
down before its own instinct to cannibalism. Both plays make
their thematic point explicitly. Lear's well-known meditations
on the nature of human 'need' are on this subject; but more
directly, Albany says

> It will come,
> Humanity must perforce prey on itself
> Like monsters of the deep.

Mosca, likewise, meditates on the high mystery of parasitism,
and comes to the conclusion that

> All the wise world is little else, in nature,
> But parasites or sub-parasites –

a theme which Shakespeare works out at length in *Timon* also,
more particularly in Timon's speech in iv iii, which lays it
down that the universe is peopled by thieves. Both moon and
sun are by nature thieves, and

> the earth's a thief
> That feeds and breeds by a composture stolen
> From general excrement, each thing's a thief.

Both plays, in their different ways, postulate a vision of things in which nature is assaulted and corrupted by this monstrous power of greed.

The two words 'nature' (taken from Mosca's lines) and 'monstrous' (taken from Albany's 'monsters') are key words. It is a commonplace of criticism that in *King Lear* these two words sound through the play like the tolling of a bell, and contain within themselves the central message of the play. Indeed, the master idea of all Elizabethan tragedy, as we now read it, is the fracture of 'nature', of a natural, divinely ordained and rational order of things, by universal evil, which is properly called 'monstrous' because it is a contradiction of nature, a distortion and abuse of her proper lineaments and proportions, as a physical monster is a sort of blasphemy on humanity. Thus Cordelia's fault is in Lear's eyes a 'thing . . . monstrous', and she herself

> a wretch whom Nature is asham'd
> Almost to acknowledge hers,

Edmund preaches his paradoxical sermon on the two concepts of nature, Edgar is misunderstood by his father as a 'monster', Goneril and Regan are 'unnatural hags' and typified by the 'sea-monster', and so on, time and time again throughout the play.

It is less well known that Jonson chooses precisely these two words to describe the relationships of Bonario and his father Corbaccio. (It will be remembered that Bonario is falsely accused of plotting to murder his father, who disinherits him.) In III ii, Bonario, in conversation with Mosca, says:

> I know not how to lend it any thought
> My father should be so unnatural,

and Mosca, in his slimy way, condoles with him in suffering a 'wrong' so 'monstrous and abhorred'. A little later Mosca is telling Corbaccio that his son, in seeking to kill him,

> Sought for you, call'd you wretch, unnatural –

words almost identical with those applied by Lear to Cordelia, even to the word 'wretch'. As a consequence, Corbaccio disowns his son, using the word 'portent' which is a variant upon the more usual term 'monster' :

> The mere portent of nature !
> He is an utter stranger to my loins.

This is precisely parallel to Lear's disowning of Cordelia for her 'monstrous' fault :

> Here I disclaim all my paternal care,
> Propinquity and property of blood,
> And as a stranger to my heart and me,
> Hold thee from this for ever . . .

The two words crop up commonly in other sections of *Volpone*, most obviously in the trial scenes, where they are applied, not merely to the relations of Corbaccio and his son, but to the 'unnatural' and 'monstrous' behaviour of Corvino towards his wife : another example of the fracture of the natural order. To any Elizabethan ear the significance of these words would come home with the same force of moral suggestion as they possessed in *Lear*.

The implications contained within them, however, can be extended further still. The ultimate breach of nature, as between father and son, is the killing of the father – the destruction of one's own source of life; and therefore the ultimate in horror attaches to the word 'parricide' which is used for the attempted as well as for the achieved deed. This term is applied both to Bonario (III ii, in the mouth of Voltore and of Corbaccio, Bonario's father) and to Edgar, the disinherited son in *King Lear*, where it is uttered from the mouth of his brother Edmund. Both Edgar and Bonario are victims of a similar plot : each is innocent, and each is accused of attempting the death of his father. Even the same trick is used by the two plotters : both Mosca and Edmund exhibit a slight wound, which they allege has been made by the 'parricide' in an attempt to kill them, as they loyally resist his horrid intentions (III ii and II i). There is yet one more connection between the two characters. One of the crucial 'natural' relationships in *Lear* is that of the bastard Edmund to his legitimate brother Edgar. Edmund's long speech on the two concepts of nature, as represented by legitimacy and bastardy, is at the heart of the play : in practice, his whole efforts are directed towards taking his brother's place – towards replacing the claims of his legitimate brother by the claims of his own bastardy. This same threat is used against Bonario – his father, according to Mosca, threatens not merely to disinherit him, but to proclaim him bastard :

> Hear yourself written bastard, and profest
> The common issue of the earth.

It cannot be emphasised too strongly that these relationships of father and child are not secondary and trifling matters, but essential and central to the theme and structure of both plays. The breakdown of the universe which is shown in *Lear*, and of the moral world which is the subject of *Volpone*, are both fractures of nature : and both are figured in little, as it were, in these parent–child relationships, which to an Elizabethan are not merely social relationships, but inherent and vital parts of the whole universal system. It is for this reason that the incident from which *Lear* takes its origin, the disinheritance of Cordelia for 'unnatural' reasons, is not trivial or frivolous as it may seem to us, but a criminal and irrational offence against nature, exaggerated and laden with a more tragic burden because the chief participant is a king. Now *Volpone* is also about inheritance and disinheritance. We have already noticed that the disinheriting of Bonario is parallel to the disinheriting of Cordelia : except that it is only a secondary element in the play. But the mainspring of the action in *Volpone* is of the same kind : the trick played by Volpone, by which he raises money by promising to make the greedy sharks his heirs, is a sort of paradoxical disinheritance. It too is unnatural : wealth is being diverted from its proper and useful ends to the service of mere greed, by reversing the usual relationships of heritance. It is not so heinous a fault as Lear's, for this is a comedy (if a grim one) and moves therefore in the moral rather than the metaphysical world; but it is of the same kind, especially in the relationship of the aged Corbaccio to Volpone. Corbaccio is almost on the point of death himself, but none the less hopes to inherit from Volpone, who is very much alive and still in the prime of life. Finally, of course, all these unnatural 'heirs' are disinherited, and an even more unnatural one put in their place : the parasite of parasites, Mosca, who of all the characters of the play has the least claim to the fortune which has acted as bait to them all.

We have already noticed that the word 'unnatural' is applied in *Volpone* to another relationship : that between Corvino and his wife Celia. He is portrayed as being pathologically jealous of her (so jealous, that he will have her bricked up for life merely for looking out of the window), but none the less persuades himself to prostitute her to Volpone's lust in order to gain his fortune – and, by a supreme example of Jonsonian irony, he is persuaded that there is no 'shame' in this, that his 'honour' is safe. There is no close parallel to this situation in *King Lear*, though the theme of lust plays its part in Edmund's reception by Goneril and Regan; but there is certainly a general resemblance in the temper of mind towards women and their love exhibited by Corvino and by Lear in his madness. Some of the most terrible passages in *Lear* are those in Act IV where he denounces the 'burning, scalding, stench, consumption' of women's love: it is a denunciation of life itself, which seems to him corrupt at its very source, befouling the whole business of living in the world. The same vileness inspires Corvino's speeches to Celia, more particularly in the punishments which he envisages for her when she refuses to obey him, as Lear has envisaged sundry hellish torments for his ungrateful daughters. We may select one as a specimen:

> Death! I will buy some slave
> Whom I will kill, and bind thee to him, alive!
> And at my window hang you forth, devising
> Some monstrous crime, which I, in capital letters,
> Will eat into thy flesh with aquafortis,
> And burning corsives, on this stubborn breast . . .

(Anticipating the verbal echoes which we must look at later, we may note, in this speech, how Lear boasted near his pitiful end, 'I killed the slave that was a-hanging thee'.) The same phrase is used in both plays – to 'do the act' – in describing sexual relationships. Jonson almost goes out of his way to make the point that Corvino's attitude to his wife is as unnatural as a similar attitude would be from father to daughter. When Mosca is persuading Corvino to hand Celia over to Volpone, he points out that one of the consulting physicians, Signor Lupo, has offered Volpone his virgin daughter. Corvino thinks it all over, and decides that this is precedent enough: for, as he says,

> The cases are all one of wife and daughter.

I do not suggest that Jonson is here deliberately nudging his reader to make him remember *Lear*; he is making the more general point, that any rupture of the natural relationship, whether between father and daughter or husband and wife, is in itself evil. We may also think, though I would not press this point, that there is some significance in the name Celia. Jonson usually gives his audience a hint of how his characters are to be taken by their nomenclature; thus Bonario is obviously derived from *bonus*, meaning 'good'. The name Celia means 'heavenly one', and certainly represents her innocence. Cordelia, likewise, has been interpreted by many critics, especially those who are attached to the game of 'hunt the symbol', as representing the principle of divine and redeeming Grace in the play, like Beatrice in Dante. This interpretation is in itself arguable, and we need not press the parallel too far; but at least we can say that the functions of the two women are alike in their common innocence and ineffectual goodness.

Another major theme which is common to the two plays is that of corrupt justice. True justice, once again, is part of the natural order of things, and one result of the fracture of that order is the collapse of justice itself. This point is made at least twice in *Lear* : once in certain speeches by Lear himself in Act IV, in which he denounces the 'great image of authority', a dog in office. The Beadle who whips the whore at the cart's tail, 'hotly lusts to use her in that kind for which he whips her'; and when a judge sentences a prisoner, 'the usurer hangs the cozener'. In Act III also we have the terrible parody of human justice in which Lear, the fool, and Poor Tom – that is, a madman, a zany, and a man pretending to be mad – stand as a type of human justice, judging Lear's daughters in the shape of a stool. *Volpone* ends in the traditional *iudicium* – the bringing of knaves to the bar of justice – which is a standard element in moral comedy; but the essence of this court is that it is as corrupt as the people it professes to judge. The lawyer who pleads before it is Voltore, one of the three sharks who would inherit Volpone's wealth. His speech is totally compounded of lies; the witnesses lie; and the judges themselves are so infected with the prevailing disease that before the case is over they are quietly planning to marry off a spare daughter to Mosca, now that he has inherited Volpone's wealth. It is true that in the end all the villains receive their deserts, but no thanks go to the court for this. The rogues are betrayed by their own roguery and by their quarrels with each other; the court's function in the final disposition of the spoil is mechanical. In fact, both in *Lear* and *Volpone*, goodness gets short shrift : Cordelia is killed, Lear dies, Kent is soon to follow him, and though there is a sort of perfunctory assurance at the end that Albany will restore the state to health, we cannot feel that 'justice' has in any sense 'triumphed'. Similarly, in *Volpone*, Bonario and Celia are dismissed from the play with a casual wave of the hand : Bonario is given his father's wealth, and Celia sent back to her parents, but nobody really cares. In both plays the dramatist's eye is centred on evil rather than on good.

The last general resemblance which I wish to mention lies in the role of the fool or fools in the two plays. The fool is a type of monstrosity – something on the edge of nature which he serves to emphasise by the contrast he poses. This role, which is a standard one in Elizabethan drama, is made more pointed and obvious in *Volpone* by the fact that the three fools are literally monsters – dwarf, eunuch and hermaphrodite. It is a commonplace of criticism that the fool has a central role in *Lear*; he is contrast, chorus, Lear's conscience, the general subconscious, the running commentary made by suppressed and disguised truth upon a state of things where truth is forbidden to speak openly and without disguise. It is less frequently observed that the fools in *Volpone* have an equally real function to perform. On stage their roles are often cut, for obvious reasons, and in fact Jonson has not built them into the play quite so firmly as he could have done. Nevertheless they have their part, not merely in the general thematic sense of being physical prefigurements of the process of folly and monstrosity which we are witnessing. They touch the business of the play in two vital points : first, in that Mosca tells us that they are the children of Volpone himself. Whether we are to suppose this to be factually true or not, it is symbolically true : these are the monstrous offspring which are born of the sort of life the play presents. Secondly, it is the fools who bring Mosca down in the end. Overconfident of his success, he begins his reign as heir by turning them out of doors, and this action and no other first opens Volpone's eyes to Mosca's intentions (Act v iii and vii). In the same way, it is the fool (or the fool and the disguised madman, Poor Tom) who with less success endeavour to make Lear see the truth of his daughter's intentions. In one sense, the truest insight in both plays remains with the fools, so that Jonson's fools can sing

> Fools they are the only nation,
> Worth men's envy or admiration . . .
> When wit waits upon the fool.
>   O who would not be
> He, he, he?

In the same way Lear's fool is constantly emphasising the interchange of roles compelled by the fracture of nature, by which fool and wise man change places: 'when a wise man gives thee better counsel, give me mine again' – and

> Fools had ne'er less grace in a year,
> For wise men are grown foppish,
> And know not how their wits to wear . . .

The case I have been presenting is essentially a simple one: not that Jonson was directly 'influenced' by Shakespeare in writing *Volpone*, or Shakespeare 'indebted' to Jonson in writing *Lear*, but that certain common ideas exist in the two plays; and I have suggested that these might well have come from the friendship of the two men. Jonson's play, on his own testimony in the prologue, took but five weeks to write, and was composed without help from anyone else. But the two men were working on the two plays about the same time. They may have talked them over; they may have read each other's work in manuscript; they may have seen them in rehearsal as well

as on the stage; whatever the means, there is evidence enough
of two great minds moving upon and handling similar ideas
presented in two very different forms. . . .

SOURCE: *Auckland University College Bulletin,*
no. 51 (1957) 21–32

John J. Enck

FROM *JONSON AND THE COMIC TRUTH* (1957)

. . . The imagery of *Volpone* is precise, and boundaries define its limits exactly. Like *Sejanus* it relies upon animals, but for a different effect. *Sejanus* implied a contrast : men, who should have better natures, unfortunately behaved like animals. Here, the men are animals. Their names, of course, merely use Italian words for beasts and birds : Volpone, fox; Mosca, fly; Voltore, Corvino, and Corbaccio, vulture, crow, and raven respectively. Sir Politic Would-be is Sir Pol, that is, a parrot, and Peregrine, the single sound person in the play, surely is the peregrine falcon, the pilgrim hawk. If this nomenclature were advanced by itself as an initial trick, it could be swiftly dismissed, but the connection extends more deeply. In both the quarto and the folio the running-title is *The Fox*, and the play was commonly referred to by this name throughout the century. Volpone himself mentions the association early in the action.

> Now, now, my clients
> Beginne their visitation ! vulture, kite,
> Rauen, and gor-crow, all my birds of prey,
> That thinke me turning carcasse, now they come. . . .
> (I ii 87–90)

The complementary view follows at once :

> *Vol.* Good ! and not a foxe
> Stretch'd on the earth, with fine delusiue sleights,
> Mocking a gaping crow? ha, Mosca? (I ii 94–6)

A statement so unequivocal at the outset allows a wide range of freedom for innuendo during the course of the struggle itself; not too insistent verbal parallels need be projected to define Volpone as a fox. Also, like an animal, he wears furs, and the dialogue tells that stage business between him and Mosca prolongs the process of dressing the fox in his skins to receive the birds of prey. When losing ground during the final trial scene, Volpone repeatedly refers to his totem animal, as though he sought a reassurance in the bare image. The three clients exhibit less than human traits: Corbaccio's glasses twist into 'his foure eyes' (v iii 63), and his cane becomes a part of 'that filthy couetous wretch,/With the three legges . . .' (v iii 67–8). Moreover, other animals, as comparisons or in names used for expletives, keep their natures constantly before the audience through one rhetorical guise or another.

The profuse indications in the dialogue that none of the characters walks like a man make the intention sharper than inserted stage directions could. They prance, skip, creep, or slither, more closely resembling beasts or maimed men than any upright human beings. As Jonson noted in *Timber*, 'Looke upon an effeminate person : his very gate confesseth him. If a man be fiery, his motion is so : if angry, 'tis troubled, and violent' (H. & S., viii 592–3). Actual animals spill over from the figurative descriptions. They leap forth as portents, but whereas in *Sejanus* supernatural appearances presaged fatal events, here the inept Sir Pol twists natural phenomena into dire warnings. A fantastic creature supposedly flies from Corvino during the trial, similar to the words which leave Crispinus in *Poetaster*, but here it is imaginary. Finally, poor Sir Pol becomes literally a reptile on stage when he takes refuge under his shell and Peregrine deliberately mistakes him for a turtle. The bouncing swing of this imagery has a grim elation, like a barbaric or medieval frieze in which the human and the bestial wantonly mingle. No implicit judgment blames men or animals, except that both are equally vicious. Their natures reinforce without hesitation the bases of the rationale. Animals denote not only a depth of cunning but also a height of luxury. Volpone during his frantic wooing of Celia plans an exquisite banquet on the brains of peacocks and ostriches, concluding with, if possible, the phoenix. Elsewhere, too, animals stand for the softest taste and sensuality, as well as the complementary side of these excesses, the crudest vulgarity and frenzy. The place is Venice; the people recognizable types; the time the late Renaissance; and the language serviceable English : yet, the whole offers startling vistas and nearly creates, transcending these, 'a new element with creatures indigenous thereto, their costumes and cuisines',[1] a feat supposedly beyond the reach of the imagination.

Throughout *Volpone* Jonson has mastered his poetry for swollen visions which are strikingly rich, if a trifle askew. With impeccable authority he names an object, then another, then another, and another without asserting their binding quality until through this progression the lines themselves clarify the complexity. This style ranges at random, and by its variations it unites everything from Volpone's vaunting declarations to Lady Pol's inane twaddle. The blank verse satisfies all occasions with two deliberate exceptions, the songs of the deformed trio and Volpone's mountebank salesmanship. These two provide revealing contrasts by their different idioms. Except for these excursions, it is Jonson's first comedy entirely in blank verse and in his mature style. Part of the effectiveness derives from another rhetorical device which might be termed the negative catalogue. This scheme lists attributes not possessed by the object or situation under discussion. Such items do not range across whatever happens to lie at hand but are carefully formed into a commentary on possibilities which might be, but are not. The contrast by negation presents no desirable values but evils which may be realized and happen, for the moment, to lack prominence. The temptation to quote long passages proves nearly irresistible, although any illustrations distort the tone. The verse always requires its context; the two reinforce each other, and both almost demand the stage for which Jonson designed them. The setting must give them life.

Some commentators have withheld approval from the long scene where Volpone goes out disguised as a mountebank to glimpse Celia because it contributes little to the play and because it may have been composed independently. Both charges look justified only after an imperfect reading. They undervalue the importance of the passage in relation to the structure. Volpone transcends being a simple hoarder, although, like Jaques, he buries his gold, granted that both the hiding places become profane shrines. For every penny he pinches, Volpone lavishes another upon an extravagance. The deceptions spun for his clients please him; while he performs for them, he watches them acting for him. For being happy and successful in his profitable business he is one of the most well-adjusted characters in literature. More than a mere cadaver, he does not ineffectually depend upon his accomplished parasite; far from inactive wits have already carried him high in the financial world. Thus, when he quits his room to act the mountebank, a convincing demonstration of his abilities dramatizes his prowess before a double audience : the one in the theater and the one on the stage. The resulting performance leaves no doubt about his talents for salesmanship. Among his admirers stands the rapt Sir Pol, who instructs an undeceived Peregrine; the scene further binds the two plots. The speech develops as a marvel of English prose, especially for this period. It moves with firm logic, wholly false, of course, and by the errors underscores misapplied knowledge and criticizes pseudo learning which perverts rhetoric to subservient ends by a crude ingenuity. Here the prose, which allows a greater semblance of this dishonesty within order, functions at each maneuver. As a set piece it has enough merit almost to justify its inclusion, even were it at the expense of the story. Perhaps this excellence in itself has contributed to its being misunderstood; it achieves its own ends so brilliantly that its essential ramifications have been neglected.

Throughout, the rhetorical devices which formerly expressed the humours now reach to different ends. Whereas the humours flowed on and on beyond the control of those afflicted, here the inventiveness, the elaboration of a single concept, provides Volpone and Mosca with the trappings of an ability as agile as it is mischievous and their dupes with the fixations of an immoderation which has but one goal in view. The comparison with the humours may introduce a misleading clue. The theory behind the humour comedies can scarcely be stretched to enclose a group as conniving as these men are.

For measuring the wide differences between *Volpone* and the earlier plays, a contrast of how they end will indicate the growth of Jonson's talents. A correction, of different degrees of severity, removed people from their humours, after which they were free to go their ways, no longer having much kinship with the beings they appeared during the affliction. If they had no afterlife to speak of beyond the final epilogue, this lack does not matter because their essence is that they must perish and that one does not care if they do. They might turn into almost anything. No cure exists for Volpone and his intriguing circle. Their punishment reveals them for what they are, and their follies, to the Venetian justices, are crimes. A momentary quirk will fall to the blandishments of common sense. A humour, by implication, sprang forth from idleness, where lack of restrictions allowed an accepted force to distend itself into futility. In *Volpone* the term describes an irrational deviation from the behavior which an individual exhibits generally; thus the primary meaning reverts back to its original status in the scornful comedies. The image of a stream subsides to an aside: 'his sonnes ills/Growing to that strange floud . . .' (IV v 57–8). Time and again Jonson tests his own assumptions of ridicule by ridicule, particularly when about to abandon them, at least deprive them of their force. Lady Would-be, still borne along on the old stream of humour, does not fit in with the rest and seems to bear a label 'Not Wanted on Voyage', while she forges out over the play as a contrast with, not continuation of, the ruling passions of the other figures. Her primary trait consists of hopping from one correct observation to another without being able to hold any within a necessary connection. Superficiality is her chief attribute. She jumbles accurate and absurd literary judgments with so little notion of what she means that all may as well be wrong. Similarly, her opinions and observations about the humours and sickness are not so much wrong as wrongheaded. Her proffered diagnoses would nearly be a remedy in the earlier plays. Here, through Lady Pol, the prescriptions become a pompous mess, rendered more ludicrous when wished on Volpone who does not want to listen, who has long passed beyond a belief in sweetness and light, who is not ill anyhow, and who, should he wish the salvation almost any improvement would require, could not possibly achieve it.

If the reliance on a theory of humours falls into abeyance, sickness becomes more closely physical, although bound up in the psychological. Rhetorical figures keep up a running commentary. Volpone himself, pretending to be stricken, brings the embodied disease to the stage, and the clients' suggested cures, doubly ironic because they are gratuitous and because no one wants him to recover, swell the language. Further, to reinforce this point, gold and sickness are allied. The treasures the greedy offer represent an admission charged to watch a dying man, and Volpone obligingly stays ill as long as his box office puts out its S.R.O. sign. The contagion spreads as he infects the innocent Celia and Bonario when they come in contact with him. At the end his punishment fixes on him permanently the deformities he has been feigning. The objection that Zweig's adaptation is superior because it supplies a kind of release in squandering the evil money[2] instead of having it confiscated puts modern sociology and economics before Elizabethan dramaturgy. The gold must be condemned as a positive danger, not a neutral substance misapplied in the hands of its possessors as it appeared in *The Case Is Altered*. To have this plague showered down upon the unsuspecting poor is strangely gross sadism, if one understands the values in the play. Were the seized treasures tossed into the Grand

Canal, that gesture might satisfy equally Jonson, *Volpone*, Elizabethan stagecraft, and modern critics, but not, surely, seventeenth-century Venice.

There can be no correction because no standard exists in the city. Any explicit disapproval of Venetian lasciviousness must be read into *Volpone* from the implicit condemnation in every line of the verse. After the enlightened despot Cynthia, the implacable Augustus, and the unredeemable duplicity of Tiberius, the justices and courts of Venice are refreshingly familiar: they know only what they are told, accept bribes, assume that a good reputation must hide an evil man, and can be molded by a lawyer's bombast. On the other hand, they do represent the forces of the law; when aroused they perceive the truth, rather later than anyone else, and mete out punishments. The state and its laws, consequently, cannot be guaranteed to deal fairly with their subjects, although there is as favorable a chance that they will as that they will not: scarcely a cynical view. Jonson preserved a fine balance between this newer mode and his older ones. The concluding punishment of Volpone is not too stern; he might have escaped entirely. The moral at this level does not preach the currently popular cliché that crime does not pay, but rather that crime does not pay indefinitely because it leads to success which can no longer contain itself within any limits and will, therefore, split apart. In terms of psychology and the law the fifth act fulfills all requirements: to carry any situation out to its bitter end, when not against the wishes of those indulging themselves, results in comedy. A corollary of this theory, that virtue does not pay indefinitely because it too reaches a limit so that eventually the good man becomes a victim results usually in tragedy. In both, the function of justice does not require it to investigate and uncover but to punish the uncontainable when enormities, from whatever violence, break laws.

Venetian justice, then, is not blind but purblind. A similar condition marks all the characters as well. *The Case Is Altered* championed the easy belief that the desire to see what the truth is will conjure its immediate emergence. The outlook has shifted gradually until here approximately a quarter-turn has been made. No one bears the qualifications to recognize what is true nor to appreciate it. The basis of disguise remains clothes, as Volpone, the master of deceits, concedes. Nevertheless, not alone by stagecraft – by the furs of the fox; by setting, the bed which commands the most prominent position; by make-up, the dissipation, which the squandering of money brings on and which in turn pays dividends; by direction, the placing of clients in Volpone's room; or by press agentry, Mosca's proddings – are the aspiring heirs taken in. Volpone is not a tyro like the humour characters who hopefully study one pose and trust this will suffice them until they become what they pretend. Rather, he throws himself into creating his role with the ardor of one of Stanislavsky's disciples.

> 'Tis well, my pillow now, and let him enter.
> Now, my fain'd cough, my phthisick, and my gout,
> My apoplexie, palsie, and catarrhes,
> Helpe, with your forced functions, this my posture,
> Wherein, this three yeere, I haue milk'd their hopes.
> He comes, I heare him (vh, vh, vh, vh) ô. (1 ii 123–8)

The invalid, although his stellar part, does not exhaust his material; his mountebank disguise maintains a fine balance between convincing one that a mountebank speaks in this way and that Volpone as a mountebank would express himself in precisely this style. He later selects Proteus for an imaginary rival and recalls he acted in the form most dependent on metamorphosis, the masque. His declaration of lust to Celia mounts a finer repertoire for disguises than had beguiled the empty reveries of the static women in *Cynthia's Revels* while he recounts through how many masquerades he and Celia will amuse themselves in loving. The end finds him still pretending, this time as an official of the court about to unmask him.

This duplicity of appearance, as the action proceeds, twists all surfaces to whatever frenzy dictates; most ludicrous is Lady

Pol's assumption that Peregrine is a woman in man's clothes, and, most shocking, the conspiracy of falsehood at the first trial. The innocent, but naïve, are accused of machinations falling beyond their abilities, interests, or understanding, though perfectly within the scope of their accusers. Celia is

> This lewd woman
> (That wants no artificiall lookes, or teares,
> To helpe the visor, she has now put on)
> Hath long beene knowne a close adulteresse,
> To that lasciuious youth there ; not suspected,
> I say, but knowne ; and taken, in the act ;
> With him. . . . (IV v 34–40)

Before Voltore's rhetoric, Bonario's reputation melts away. Mosca, once again linking with Musco of *Every Man in His Humour*, has an identical function, that of keeping the action in motion. This time, however, not he himself but Volpone wears the disguises. In this society the parasite plies his trade without apology and achieves more rewards and amusement than his forebears did for all their multiple changes of costume. That he frankly recognizes himself and boasts about his position provides a likeness with Musco, but Mosca's temperament is treacherous and bent more on profit than on pleasure. He analyzes accurately the shortcomings of the clients and, incidentally, himself.

> *Mos.* True, they will not see't.
> Too much light blinds 'hem, I thinke. Each of 'hem
> Is so possest, and stuft with his owne hopes,
> That any thing, vnto the contrary,
> Neuer so true, or neuer so apparent,
> Neuer so palpable, they will resist it –
> *Volp.* Like a temptation of the diuell. (V ii 22–8)

Like Thorello's exposition of similar failings, this knowledge discloses the means of justifying further indulgences. At the end he is caught or, rather, catches himself. Everyone in *Volpone* shows the paranoiac's trait of rushing onward to the conclusion no matter how inevitable the defeat.

In *Sejanus* and *Catiline* night falls as the dimming of human insight before tragedy. Here the approach of dark becomes an accentuation in the comic pattern. It represents how an inevitable process catches up the deluded. Mistakes, close to unforgivable error, create a tragedy; in petty individuality and in choosing false standards lies the ridiculous. If one prefers hearing the still, sad music of humanity, the classical tempo in *Volpone* may sound repugnant, but this predilection merely tells one that audiences remain somewhat behind Jonson as connoisseurs of comedians. With disguise so convincingly pervasive, the eye cannot guide one, but this shift occurs because of the change in defining personality. Despite an undeniable cleverness, the clients are so obsessed that they see only what they wish, and, since it nearly amounts to the same thing, what Volpone wants them to. The voice continues to mislead when shaped by the rhetoric of Volpone and Voltore. There is, then, no accountable force to deliver moralizing speeches and to round off all corners nicely. Viewed in this way, the rationale of the play must be accepted as largely negative; judgments have to be brought from outside the dramatic frame by the audience roused through what the stage denies them.

Except as pure comedy, *Volpone* contains little of a positive nature. *Sejanus* substituted the broad effects of chaos for individual fates; here, the limited chaos within individuals permits a diminution of the enveloping social forces. *Sejanus* looks so long and uncompromisingly upon the cancer of evil that the tone must, because it is honest, occasionally be sardonic. *Volpone* keeps its attitudes focused on the protuberances of folly so steadily that its tone must, if it is equally honest, be wholly sardonic. The device of comedy generally composes a frame within which events are sometimes – and how infrequently depends upon the writer's skill – moved from what would appear a predestined end; a completed pattern emerges after a dexterous reliance upon what may be taken as logic not wholly predictable because of an ambiguously worded postulate. Obviously Dryden had some such formulation in mind for his famous examination of *Epicene*. In *Volpone* nothing is accidental and, at the same time, nothing forgivable. In this sense, that a clarity pervades every moment, it becomes one of the rare hermetic comedies in English and probably the only thoroughly successful one. The majority of them, even the best Wycherley and Congreve, demand that at a few, or many, points the audience take on faith the goodness of a few, or many, characters in a milieu which does not on the evidence of preponderant stress engender such virtues. By introducing this positive force for the inexplicable the comedy grows soft and untruthful; it no longer plays the game by its own rules. The humours, after all, no matter how fully bolstered, harbor this weakness. Their angry streams ravage a pretty landscape until, at the end, more like water from a closed faucet, they abate and send a munificent rainbow over everything, an effect as incongruous as this metaphor. *Volpone* remains resolutely true to its negatives; everyone is either a fool or a knave, neither condition necessarily better than the other. . . .

The strength of the play derives partially from its tensions which are fully comprehended not in isolation but as segments of the total structure. Nothing in the great comedies is idle; there are frills in neither detail nor design. Most comedy relies on improvisation, as, indeed, does some lesser tragedy. In the latter, however, drawing as it must upon hidden forces and motivation, the unforeseeable can be encompassed as nearly in the scheme of things, whether the fall of princes on an imagined Fortune's wheel or the keenest irony of a mind's self-discovery. At the core of tragedy lies a mystery of personality, inexplicable within the world of the particular play and at least partially vexing outside of it. For effective comedy this impenetrability must be eschewed. The great comedies of

Jonson revel in the probable, if no longer the simply mechanical. The banana skin, the pratfall, the custard pie, and the double take are all irresistible after they have been planted. How to bring them into the plot poses the problem. Nothing limits their numbers and effects except the string of episodes itself. Jonson's design includes much more than skits and blackouts. *Volpone*'s story begins where most others leave off, as the five main characters, already inured in their traits, clash against one another with misdirected cunning. When they devise ways for preying on one another, in the process they plant each effect until the climax. The trial which establishes Volpone's innocence in the fourth act, especially, points up how no momentary triumph can satisfy him or Mosca.

Perhaps an illustration will help pin down these generalizations, for example, the implications of the game Truth or Consequences. Basically, it is play, that is, it mimics lightly an activity and has no ostensible end except its own completion. If, however, the demanded consequences, upon the failure of truth, get out of hand, they may exceed the limits of amusement. Comedy is true because it is likewise inconsequential. Nothing follows from it; the final applause collapses the puppets, and the cast marches off or the curtain falls. Its very simplicity bestows its truth; one has enjoyed the illusion of having witnessed one world and its laws. Tragedy, in partial opposition, entails consequences. It cannot limit the qualities of its created world, and its ramifications point outside itself. In this sense no tragedy can embrace one truth, although it may hint at many. It depends upon a private spiritual mystery, the continuation in life of its theatrical game. The circus and vaudeville embody the nearly ideal comic forms because they correspond to nothing one knows except their own performances in a universe where legerdemain and prestidigitation rule. If the aerialist falls, one's sympathy extends beyond the act; the show itself is spoiled. The tightrope dancer is true to her art as long as she keeps her balance.

Some definitions by insisting that society sets the norm for

comedy reduce the scope and exclude too much. Throughout
every comic number there runs the sense that a standard is
being upheld, the more fragile, the more interesting. In drama
this code can most readily refer to social norms, as it does when
exorcising the humours. Because the major part of comedy
defies – without, however, breaking – laws (whether the law
of gravity in trapeze acts, the law of cause and effect in magic,
the laws of etiquette in farce, or the civil laws in *Volpone*) no
rule can be taken seriously. In a word, true comedy must know
that everything is relative and nothing fixed, but in the face of
this awareness it pretends that absolutes exist. For the great
Jonsonian pieces society cannot set punishments, and thus the
Venetian justices are quite as corrupt as the people they try.
The principle recurs in any memorable comedy : the Keystone
cops chase ineffectually across the screen, and Chaplin must
wander down a glowing road into another world at the end
of his tales. In this light, the interpretation of justice in *Volpone* suits the *données* of the comic. Volpone ignores society
and the laws, but until his uncasing no Venetian citizen criticizes him. Again, by keeping the comedy negative, its standards
grow absolute; by defying the codified rules, it honors its own
codes.

No one supposes that acrobats suspend the law of gravity
while they cavort in the air. Their livelihood depends upon
incisively grasping principles of weights and balances. With
this special information they may in a measure of safety risk
what for anyone else would be disaster. Beyond their moment
of delight and astonishment, however, these performances
cannot endure. They stay in a sense imperishable because one
forgets them readily. Every circus act appears *sui generis*; one
carries in active memory slight tokens for comparison. An
awareness of this impermanence haunted Jonson; fortunately
it prompted him to publish his writings so that they might
'last beyond Marble' (H. & S., IV, facing p. 348). Unfortunately, this drive toward the enduring beguiled him too often
into tacking on voices of authority which draw their incongru-

ously social moralizing from antisocial material. For *Volpone*
he allowed the comedy to exist in its own right except for some
inadequate didacticism at the end. . . .

Volpone and his dupes observe the surfaces, and from
these they try to deduce all. The mere sight of Volpone in his
bed convinces everyone about his sickness; because all want to
believe, and can believe, but one thing, no further investigation is required. The whole process of becoming his heirs,
unlikely as it may sound at the outset, once taken for granted
weighs upon their senses so heavily that it allows them to see
only what they wish to, subject, of course, to a precautious
correction by the wit which launches their scheming in the
first place. These men pursue their singular desires as though
all lay within easy reach; Mosca, as well, must finally play the
comedy out to its end, aware though he may be of the stupidity
of others. Their monstrous faith in the monster Volpone is not
wholly misplaced. They are, after all, less deceived than Sir
Pol, whose propensities lead him to see all as what it is not. He
delves constantly beneath surfaces to emerge with the most
unlikely set of conjectures, whereas the dupes require the
prodding of Volpone's professional flashiness for their confu-
sions. Sir Pol everywhere detects spies, portents, agents, and
wonders. For him nothing is what it appears, but only what
it might conceal. His wife, as has been observed, survives
weakly from the humour comedies. She volunteers discon-
nected observations on nearly any subject, always in the
manner of the humourists and always incorrectly. For her
nothing exists but her own erratic universe. The sole character
to regard the scene with detachment is Peregrine. His stability
renders him powerless to turn aside the headlong plunge of
stupidity. His standing to one side provides a weak counter-
balance to the strong self-dramatizing centers. If he assumes
the function of removing Sir Pol from his witch-hunting
mania, this does not mean he could ensure any general
improvement. Sir Pol is permitted, after his disgrace, to
return home to England to try to reform. Like the second plot

of *The Case Is Altered*, the auxiliary business here picks up, in reversed fashion, the concerns of the chief one.[3]

Yeats's opinion to the contrary notwithstanding, Celia and Bonario scarcely count in this welter of cheating. They neither know nor understand what they are doing, nor, indeed, much of what happens to them. Their virtue, such as it is, must be taken for granted, but it has affinities with nothing in *Volpone* itself. . . .

Every now and then a trio stumbles onto the scene to amuse Volpone, rather than to be entertained by him. This final aspect of the play consists of the dwarf, eunuch, and her-maphrodite. They may be Volpone's bastards; wherever they come from, they make external his inner defects. Their parti-cular function, especially with their songs which Mosca writes and which inordinately amuse Volpone, suggests many over-tones, most of which have already been well set forth else-where.[4] Their presence itself contributes a certain force. They keep before the audience the excesses of folly when carried to a second generation and help sustain the distortions which must at each point inform the drama. Their verses are jang-ling rhymes, quite at variance with the firmness of the blank verse itself. This crude expression comments adequately upon itself, for, as the main action of the drama demonstrates how desire can inflate itself by vanity, these three underline the level to which thought sinks by total surrender to deformity: Pythagoras is merely 'that iuggler diuine' (i ii 7). Theirs is the negation of everything, a reduction to babbling imbecility. Volpone's final question to them, when Mosca has turned them out of the house, might, in addition to that of the fox and the crow, be designated the second emblem for the play : 'How now! who let you loose? whither goe you, now?/ What? to buy ginger-bread? or to drowne kitlings?' (v xi 8–9). To the deformed, both pastimes would be equally agree-able. In the play itself values reverse to the extent that pleasure may give pain, and pain pleasure, and both are weighed on the same scales. It is the destruction of values, but, because the

characters themselves are held absolutely true to their deformity, the whole is wonderfully, if terrifyingly, comic. Jonson's
control soars to such heights that it seems he adopted as his
own goal the advice Volpone gives Mosca, 'Play the artificer
now . . .' (v ii 111). In its manipulation of each nuance *Volpone*, in addition to all its other appeals, delights as a sheer
marvel close to prestidigitation, the matrix of all comedy. In
the respect that its qualities rest solidly on material luxuries
and, somehow, tower into the heights of delicacy, *Volpone*
resembles a description of Venice itself.

A commercial people who lived solely for gain – how could
they create a city of fantasy, lovely as a dream or a fairy-tale? . . .
There is no contradiction, once you stop to think what images of
beauty arise from fairy tales. They are images of money. Gold,
caskets of gold, caskets of silver, the miller's daughter spinning
gold all night long. . . .
A wholly materialist city is nothing but a dream incarnate.
Venice is the world's unconscious : a miser's glittering hoard,
guarded by a Beast whose eyes are made of white agate, and by
a saint who is really a prince who has just slain a dragon.[5]

After such an uncompromising demonstration of technique
and subject, one should be satisfied by the competence itself.
If anything more is demanded, it must be sought, and perhaps
gratefully, not in the grandeurs of this Venice and its Volpone
but back in the imprecisions of the merely living.

SOURCE : *Jonson and the Comic Truth* (1957) chap. v,
'The Artificer' – pp. 111–31 (extracts)

NOTES

1. Wallace Stevens, *The Necessary Angel* (New York, 1951)
p. 74.
2. Edmund Wilson, *The Triple Thinkers* (rev. ed., New York,
1948) p. 227, makes this point.

3. Jonas A. Barish, 'The Double Plot in *Volpone*', *Modern Philology*, LI (1953) 83–92, treats this topic thoroughly.

4. Harry Levin, 'Jonson's Metempsychosis', *Philological Quarterly*, XXII (1943) 231–9.

5. Mary McCarthy, *Venice Observed* (New York, 1956) p. 50.

Edward B. Partridge

FROM *THE BROKEN COMPASS* (1958)

The final lines of the play sum up and comment on the meaning of the animal imagery. The First Avocatore, who seems to have more sense than the others, says, 'Mischiefes feed/Like beasts, till they be fat, and then they bleed.' And it is this natural fattening and natural bleeding which restores the order of things. The principal mischiefs, the fox and the fly, fatten themselves on the birds of prey, and, by their own over-reaching, bleed themselves. Volpone 'must be merry, with a mischiefe to me!' (v xi 14). Mosca, the 'flesh-flie' who had so long lived off the flesh of another, began 'to grow in loue/ With my deare selfe', felt 'a whimsey i' my bloud' and sought to set himself up (III i 1–4). The beasts, not the law, restore the order.

The first half of the play tended to revolve around Volpone's bed; the second half around the court. The true function of both has been perverted. Normally, a bed is an age-old symbol of rest, sex, and conception, and secondarily, of birth, death, and sickness. But in *Volpone* it has become symbolic of pretence and falsity. The sickness is false; the death is false; the rest is false. Volpone is more vigorous and active than anyone except Mosca. Even the sex is false, for Volpone finds gulling fools more pleasurable than making love to women. Since the normal function of the bed has been so perverted, Volpone's punishment is symbolically just :

> And, since the most was gotten by imposture,
> By faining lame, gout, palsey, and such diseases,
> Thou art to lie in prison, crampt with irons,
> Till thou bee'st sicke, and lame indeed. (v xii 121–4)

He had fattened himself up to this fate for some time. Early in the play he was wise enough to see what a 'rare punishment' avarice is to itself (i iv 142–3). Then, after his first hearing at court, he begins to 'bleed'. His left leg has the cramp, and some power has struck him with a 'dead palsey' (v i 5–7). Volpone, who was a 'sharp disease' to others, has become one to himself.

But the power that strikes him with a 'dead palsey' is brought on by himself, not the court. The knot is undone by 'miracle', according to the First Avocatore. Nothing could be less true, because the Fox, refusing to be gulled, uncases himself. Judicial sanity has been so lost by the court that it, like the Third Avocatore, is at one time 'turn'd a stone' (iv v 154) and, at another, has 'an earthquake in me' (iv vi 58). Magnificent in dealing out punishment, the court is inept at finding the guilty. 'Miracle' implies a Christian providence which has as ineffectual a voice in the court as in the bedroom. Thus:

> *Corv. Volt.*   We beg fauor,
> *Cel.*   And mercy.
> *Avoc.* 1. You hurt your innocence, suing for the guilty.
> > (v xii 105–6)

Celia, the heavenly one, whose first word was 'patience' and whose last word is 'mercy', is unheeded in both pleas.

The final lines of the play – 'Mischiefes feed/Like beasts, till they be fat, and then they bleed' – also sum up the imagery of feeding which has cut across the artificial lines drawn in this analysis. Feeding might be said to symbolize the double theme of greed for riches and lust for sensuous pleasures.[1] One might call it the central image of the play because it is the core of many other images. It is at the heart of the animal imagery; the birds of prey are always 'pecking for carrion' or 'gaping'; Volpone constantly thinks in terms of feeding others or himself. He feeds others in expectation (iii vii 188–9), but not Celia: she shall have the phoenix and other rare delicacies.

Both Volpone and Mosca think of hope as something to eat. Mosca says,

> Your hopes, sir, are like happie blossomes, faire,
> And promise timely fruit, if you will stay
> But the maturing; (III v 30–2)

Later he says that the gulls could not sense that they were being tricked because each is 'stuft with his owne hopes' (v ii 23–4). Hopes are 'milk'd' (I ii 127), and hope itself 'Is such a bait, it couers any hooke' (I iv 134–5).

How many things in the Volpone world are eaten! Celia is 'a wench/O' the first yeere! a beautie, ripe, as haruest!' (I v 108–9). That would make her a lamb or grain. 'All her lookes are sweet,/As the first grapes, or cherries' (I v 120–1). Laughter becomes something eaten, as Volpone indicates when he is anticipating the scurvy treatment of the gulls: 'O, 'twill afford me a rare meale of laughter' (v ii 87). Or, once eaten, it is something purged. Mosca counsels his master to contain 'Your fluxe of laughter, sir' (I iv 134). Flux, in the physiological sense, meant an 'abnormally copious flowing of blood, excrement, etc., from the bowels or other organs' (*OED*). The scurvy treatment itself is thought of by Volpone as a 'feast' (v iii 108–9).

Gold is drink: 'Our drinke', Volpone tells Celia, 'shall be prepared gold, and amber' (III vii 217). Characteristically, Jonson builds imaginatively on what was actually so: *aurum potabile* (drinkable gold) was thought of as a remedy of great efficacy. But Volpone's drinking gold seems like a parody of the Communion: he must drink the blood of his dumb god, riches. Mosca works on this belief in the efficacy of *aurum potabile* early in the play when he tells Corbaccio that the gold he has brought is 'true physick', 'sacred medicine', 'great elixir' (I iv 71–2). The medicinal qualities of gold were also the subject of another image already analysed (v ii 98 ff.). But gold is not simply something to be drunk. Note the extraordinary figure which Mosca uses in asking Voltore to remember him.

> When you doe come to swim, in golden lard,
> Vp to the armes, in honny, that your chin
> Is borne vp stiffe, with fatnesse of the floud, (I iii 70–2)

Gold becomes both a bath and a meal.

But the ultimate reach of feeding is beyond gold, hope, woman as a sexual object, or laughter. The final food is man. This is implied in more than one place. Early in the play when Volpone says that he will not earn money by usury, Mosca adds,

> No, sir, nor deuoure
> Soft prodigalls. You shall ha' some will swallow
> A melting heire, as glibly, as your *Dutch*
> Will pills of butter, and ne're purge for't; (I i 40–3)

Volpone will not feed so; but the implication is that someone in his hideous world will. Just before this, as though to foreshadow this last image, Volpone says that he will

> fat no beasts
> To feede the shambles; haue no mills for yron,
> Oyle, corne, or men, to grinde 'hem into poulder;
>   (I i 34–6)

Volpone will not grind corn or man into a powder; that is the 'common way' to gain. The definition of a Puritan by Androgyno is another glance at the feeding of man on man : 'Of those deuoure flesh, and sometimes one another' (I ii 44). The next statement of this is as casual as the others. Volpone, in congratulating himself on his morning's 'purchase', says,

> Why, this is better then rob churches, yet :
> Or fat, by eating (once a mon'th) a man. (I v 91–2)

When Volpone, in his last words, refers to his lying in chains as 'mortifying', he apparently thinks of himself as food for others. 'Mortifying', as Percy Simpson points out, probably plays on the cookery term, which means making meat tender by hanging it up after it has been killed. These images of man being ground at a mill, of a prodigal being devoured, of Puritans sometimes eating one another, give the bite to the last lines in which 'Mischiefes feed/Like beasts, till they be fat. . .'. For mischiefs feed on men.

This picture of the world is universalized in one of the most remarkable speeches in the whole play – Mosca's soliloquy in Act III, scene i.

> I feare, I shall begin to grow in loue
> With my deare selfe, and my most prosp'rous parts,
> They doe so spring, and burgeon; I can feele
> A whimsey i' my bloud : . . .
>   I could skip
> Out of my skin, now, like a subtill snake,
> I am so limber. O ! Your Parasite
> Is a most precious thing, dropt from aboue,
> Not bred 'mong'st clods, and clot-poules, here on earth.
> I muse, the mysterie was not made a science,
> It is so liberally profest ! almost
> All the wise world is little else, in nature,
> But Parasites, or Sub-parasites. (III i 1–13)

Mosca's 'mysterie', that is, his art or profession, has not been made a specialized science, known only to few, because almost everyone is a parasite or a sub-parasite. The literal meaning of parasite – one who eats at the table of another – remains. To that has been added the biological meaning : an animal or plant which lives on or upon another organism. The qualifications to this universal picture – 'almost' and 'in nature' – are important because they give enough freedom of choice to save man from being only a beast. There can be more to life than this parasitic feeding of one man on another. But, though 'in nature' implies a way out, it defines even more sharply how natural such feeding is. Thus, Mosca widens the references of

this parasitism, even as Volpone did in Act I, by showing what
the common parasite is.

> I meane not those, that haue your bare towne-arte,
> To know, who's fit to feede 'hem; . . .
>   . . . or get
> Kitchin-inuention, and some stale receipts
> To please the belly, and the groine; nor those
> With their court-dog-tricks, that can fawne, and fleere,
>   (III i 14–20)

Mosca, like his master, is an aristocrat among parasites.

> But your fine, elegant rascall, that can rise,
> And stoope (almost together) like an arrow;
> Shoot through the aire, as nimbly as a starre;
> Turne short, as doth a swallow; and be here,
> And there, and here, and yonder, all at once;
> Present to any humour, all occasion;
> And change a visor, swifter, then a thought!
> This is the creature, had the art borne with him;
> Toiles not to learne it, but doth practise it
> Out of most excellent nature: and such sparkes,
> Are the true Parasites, others but their *Zani's*.
>   (III i 23–33)

The images of the arrow, the star, and the swallow show that
Mosca, like Volpone, thinks himself above the 'earth-fed'
parasites. The true parasite feeds on man continually, not
intermittently as the ones with either 'bare towne-arte' or
'court-dog-tricks' do. Such a fine rascal is 'Present to any
humour, all occasion', and able to exploit anyone any time:
in short, the perfect entrepreneur of human nature. His
ability to 'change a visor [an expression of the face which conceals the real feeling], swifter, then a thought' implies that
abuse of reason which all his plots and counter-plots demonstrate. The last lines reveal the other side of 'nature'. If 'nature'
as previously used implies a certain freedom on the part of a
man who will conquer his animal nature, here 'nature' seems

to mean natural endowment, intellectual as well as animal. The true parasite is one who uses his natural endowment as a man to feed on others. The others are only buffoons who mimic his tricks.

Feeding, then, is the great symbolic act of the play, the one gross act which dramatizes man's insatiable greed. Bird feeds on fox, fox on bird, and fly on both : that is nature. In so far as man plays the part of a bird of prey, a fox, or a fly by living off another man, he abuses the very quality that makes him a man – his reason. And he breaks the fundamental Christian law which Paul, with imagery similar to *Volpone*'s, explained in his epistle to the Galatians, v. 14–15 : 'For all the law is fulfilled in one word, *even* in this, Thou shalt love thy neighbour as thyself. But if ye bite and devour one another, take heed that ye be not consumed one of another.'

This Volpone world in which man feeds on man, and possessor is pursued with an animal-like ferocity, might be looked on, by a critic willing to do some violence to the play, as a prophetic vision of the society which capitalism, even in Jonson's day, was creating. One can easily interpret the scenes of Volpone worshipping his gold as extravagant caricatures of that idolatry of wealth which, according to R. H. Tawney, is 'the practical religion of capitalist society', and see in the animal and feeding imagery a horrifying picture of an economic system divided into possessors and pursuers.[2] Or one can claim, as L. C. Knights does, that in *Volpone* and *The Alchemist* Jonson is drawing on the anti-acquisitive tradition inherited from the Middle Ages.[3] A reading of *Volpone* based on either of these views makes sense. Yet neither one exhausts the meaning of the play, which is large enough to contain both a medieval tradition and a modern criticism of capitalism. It is precisely this universality that seems to me impressive – but its universality as an artistic structure, not simply as an economic tract.

SOURCE : *The Broken Compass* (1958) pp. 104–11

NOTES

1. J. D. Rea claims that the theme is not greed, but folly in all its phases. Rea (ed.), *Volpone* (New Haven, 1919) p. xxvii. But that seems to me a misreading of the play, possibly resulting from his discovery that Jonson used Erasmus's *Praise of Folly* as one of the principal sources.

2. R. H. Tawney, *Religion and the Rise of Capitalism* (New York, 1947) pp. 234–5.

3. Knights, *Drama and Society in the Age of Jonson*, p. 190.

S. L. Goldberg

FOLLY INTO CRIME: THE CATASTROPHE OF *VOLPONE* (1959)

The catastrophe that befalls the protagonists of *Volpone* has worried critics as it evidently worried Jonson himself. Jonson's editor only echoes common opinion when he judges it too grim for comedy and compares it, as he compares the whole play, to the tragedy of *Sejanus*.[1] And in his dedicatory Epistle, Jonson admits the problem, even while he defends his own solution of it:

> And though my *catastrophe* may, in the strict rigour of *comick* law, meet with censure, as turning back to my promise; I desire the learned, and charitable critick to haue so much faith in me, to thinke it was done off industrie: For, with what ease I could haue varied it, neerer his scale (but that I feare to boast my owne faculty) I could here insert. But my speciall ayme being to put the snaffle in their mouths, that crie out, we neuer punish vice in our *enterludes,* &c. I tooke the more liberty; though not without some lines of example, drawne euen in the ancients themselues, the goings out of whose *comœdies* are not alwaies ioyfull, but oft-times, the bawdes, the seruants, the riuals, yea, and the masters are mulcted: and fitly, it being the office of a *comick-Poet*, to imitate iustice, and instruct to life, as well as puritie of language, or stirre vp gentle affections.

On the other hand, two recent critics have defended the ending on rather different grounds. The first points out that, since *Volpone* is after all a comedy, the ending is not to be taken too seriously: it is 'not the necessary culmination of a severe and gloomy play, but rather a concession to the Puritans and one which might easily be withdrawn'. The other, remembering perhaps that so conscious and sophisticated an artist as Jonson would hardly have made concessions to his enemies in a matter of this kind, offers a more convincing explanation in terms of the play itself. Its theme, he argues, is Folly; its characteristic method is irony; and its natural conclusion is the revelation of folly in Volpone and Mosca themselves.[2] But despite the greater subtlety of these interpretations of the play compared to Herford's, they seem to me to ignore one quality of it – more particularly, one quality of the verse – to which Herford obviously responded and which goes some way toward justifying his and Jonson's doubts about the catastrophe.

If, despite Herford's objections, we take Folly to be the central theme of the play, it must be in an older and wider sense of the word. What is involved is not mere borrowing from *The Praise of Folly*, but rather the imaginative realization of a whole range of related moral attitudes.[3] At the lowest level, it is the simple folly of Sir Politic Would-be with his absurd pretensions to worldly wisdom; at the next level, it is the folly of the suitors for Volpone's wealth, whose pretensions to cleverness are also exposed as absurd; at the next, the folly of Volpone and Mosca, who are deceived by their own cleverness; and finally, in Celia (and Bonario) we see perhaps a distant reminiscence of the 'folly' of Lear's Fool, which is the unworldly wisdom of the simple and innocent.[4]

More than that, Folly, in its widest Renaissance sense of a false estimation of reality or the Nature of Things, is the object of the moral satire. All the moral perversions in the play, from Volpone's sensual naturalism to the miserable avarice of the suitors, from the brilliant Machiavellism of Mosca to its farcical parody in Sir Politic, from Scoto's quackery to Corvino's jealousy, are the outcome and the dramatic expression of fundamental delusion. Folly must be understood as Erasmus or More or Pope understood it, or as Swift understood madness: it is 'the perpetual possession of being well deceived'. In fact, the play explores the question presented in the brilliant first scene :

Fooles, they are the onely nation
Worth mens enuy, or admiration;
Free from care, or sorrow-taking,
Selues, and others merry-making :
All they speake, or doe, is sterling.

. . . . .

    O, who would not bee
      Hee, hee, hee? (i ii 66 ff.)

The most important element in this exploration is the curious double-edged irony some critics have noted, the way in which Volpone and Mosca are used by Jonson to direct his satire at the others' vices and yet are themselves the unconscious objects of their own attack. Their irony at the expense of the suitors cuts back, as it were, producing a second irony beyond. Moreover, as L. C. Knights and D. J. Enright have observed, if Volpone and Mosca serve to 'place' the others, they are themselves morally 'placed' by the exaggeration and blasphemy implicit in their language; to perceive the nature of the poetry they speak is to perceive the nature of their outlook.

In the opening scene of the play, for example, Volpone's moral corruption emerges unmistakably from the blasphemous, unrestful imagery and tone of the poetry, just as, in the scene most crucially revealing of the moral theme, his seductive speeches to Celia expose in their oversensual, overexcited tone the essential 'folly' of his values.[5] But placing their emphasis so heavily on the critical effect of the poetry, both Knights and Enright tend to underrate the dynamics of the play, the controlling significance of the plot. The result is that they overlook the problem of the catastrophe. That Volpone should himself be caught in Mosca's 'fox-trap', and Mosca, by the last twist of the theme, find himself unable to carry his schemes through, is clearly the proper issue of the action. Their deceptions are a symbol of moral delusions, including their own, and Jonson's plot points the self-frustrating, suicidal instability of a world based on such values. But that they should fall catastrophically into the merciless hands of the Venetian state, appropriate as it may seem didactically, is another matter.

It may well strike the reader as rather too drastic a collapse, too external and striking a punishment, for the tone and mood of the play. Nor is it simply a matter of Jonson's didactic intent being imposed on the play at the last moment, an inorganic addition that could easily be 'withdrawn'. One of the most interesting aspects of the catastrophe is that it arises naturally from the rest of the play and reflects in its ambiguous resolution the necessary ambiguity of Jonson's satirical technique.

If we agree that the main effect of Volpone's and Mosca's poetry is self-critical, we must be careful not to regard it as merely critical. Their attitudes possess a menace in their very perversion, which is demonstrated by the play itself; but they also possess a menace in that we, the audience, are involved in them too. Indeed, this is what transforms *Volpone* from a moral fable into a poetic satire. Jonson's poetic and dramatic realization of the fundamental perversities in Volpone and Mosca is designed to draw our sympathies (or perhaps 'empathies' is a more accurate term) toward the specious and false. Only on this condition can satire work its moral catharsis.[6]

This is the necessary qualification to the comment often made that we remain quite detached from Jonson's characters and their world. We do remain detached or critical, but not completely detached from what they represent. Although we do not regard Volpone and Mosca as 'sympathetic characters' in the usual sense, we are forced to participate in many of their feelings and hence in some of their outlook; without that, we should not, as one critic puts it, be 'forced to doubt [our] own moral position'.[7] The judgment that criticizes the corruption is our own. In the last analysis, the object of the satire is not external to us, but within ourselves, and the force of the satire lies in the more permanent judgment the satirist directs, and helps us to direct, on our temporary disease. Volpone and Mosca are instruments in Jonson's hands to plague us, for it is our vision of a world where Folly is the end of man that he wishes to create, and create in such a way that we reject it even as we possess it. Were we not tempted, our rejection would have no significance.

Perhaps this is only another way of saying that great satire seems to delight in the very object of its attack. When Pope, for example, portrays the heroine of the *Rape of the Lock* at her dressing-table in terms obviously critical of 'the sacred rites of pride', he does so in such a way that we also imaginatively enjoy, even participate in, the wonders of her toilet at the same time as we 'place' them. Similarly, as F. R. Leavis has pointed out, Pope's 'pleasure *with*' the objects of his satire in *The Dunciad* is a crucial part of the whole effect.[8] It is more than a detached imaginative liveliness; it is an imaginative life at the heart of the satirist's moral attitude, guaranteeing, as it were, the validity of the criticism.

Jonson's presentation of Volpone and Mosca is analogous to Pope's presentation of Belinda. The blasphemy and exaggeration of Volpone's opening speech, for instance, betray him to our moral judgment, just as the hint of blasphemy betrays Belinda :

> Good morning to the day; and, next, my gold :
> Open the shrine, that I may see my *saint*.
> Haile the worlds soule, and mine. More glad then is
> The teeming earth, to see the long'd-for sunne
> Peepe through the hornes of the celestiall *ram*,
> Am I, to view thy splendor, darkening his :
> That, lying here, amongst my other hoords,
> Shew'st like a flame, by night; or like the day
> Strooke out of *chaos*, when all darkenesse fled
> Vnto the center. O, thou sonne of SOL,
> (But brighter then thy father) let me kisse,
> With adoration, thee, and euery relique
> Of sacred treasure, in this blessed roome.
> Well did wise Poets, by thy glorious name,

Title that age, which they would haue the best;
Thou being the best of things : and far transcending
All stile of ioy, in children, parents, friends,
Or any other waking dreame on earth.
Thy lookes, when they to Venvs did ascribe,
They should haue giu'n her twentie thousand Cvpids;
Such are thy beauties, and our loues! Deare *saint.* . . .
(1 i 1–21)

But when Herford, apparently missing this irony, says of the
verse that it 'transfigures avarice with the glamour of religion
and idealism',[9] he is not quite as misguided as later critics
have made out. Or when another critic,[10] overlooking the
moral corruption expressed in the verse itself, describes Volpone's language to Celia in the seduction scene –

                    See, behold,
What thou art queene of; not in expectation,
As I feed others : but possess'd, and crown'd.
See, here, a rope of pearle; and each, more orient
Then that the braue *Ægyptian* queene carrous'd :
Dissolue, and drinke 'hem. See, a carbuncle,
May put out both the eyes of our St Marke;
A diamant, would haue bought Lollia Pavlina,
When she came in, like star-light, hid with iewels,
That were the spoiles of prouinces; take these,
And weare, and loose 'hem : yet remaines an eare-ring
To purchase them againe, and this whole state.
A gem, but worth a priuate patrimony,
Is nothing : we will eate such at a meale.
The heads of parrats, tongues of nightingales,
The braines of peacoks, and of estriches
Shall be our food : and, could we get the phœnix,
(Though nature lost her kind) shee were our dish.
(III vii 188–205)

– as 'magnificent imagery . . . [rolling] in wave after wave of
voluptuous grandeur', however limited an account of the effect
this is, it is not totally absurd. In both cases the apparently
naïve critic has responded to a quality that may be overlooked

in too concentrated an awareness of the moral issues at stake –
the imaginative delight, the expansiveness, the generosity
almost, in the poetry Volpone speaks. We are, and we are
surely meant to be, attracted.[11]

The function of this attraction is not merely to reveal the
suitors' 'utter poverty of spirit' in contrast with Mosca's
'intelligence' and Volpone's 'romantic exuberance and joy in
living',[12] nor merely to lead us into identifying ourselves with
their explicit criticism of the others. More fundamentally, it
serves Jonson's didactic intent. Our enjoyment of Mosca's self-
delighting Machiavellian roguery, for example, is demanded
by the poetry he utters :

> I Feare, I shall begin to grow in loue
> With my deare selfe, and my most prosp'rous parts,
> They doe so spring, and burgeon; I can feele
> A whimsey i' my bloud : (I know not how)
> Successe hath made me wanton. I could skip
> Out of my skin, now, like a subtill snake,
> I am so limber. O ! Your Parasite
> Is a most precious thing, dropt from aboue,
> Not bred 'mong'st clods, and clot-poules, here on earth.
>
> (III i 1–9)

But our delight makes us, if only partially and temporarily,
Mosca's accomplices. We are *hypocrites lecteurs*; our response
is compromised by its ambiguity. To correct it, or rather to
enable us to correct it, Jonson administers the shocks of his
action.

The same process, incidentally, may be observed in *The
Alchemist*. We are largely brought inside the world of Face and
Subtle, delighting in the efficiency, the ingenuity, the justice of
their deceptions, even while we remain sufficiently detached
to be critical of the values they represent. Consequently, our
view of Sir Epicure Mammon is significantly different from
our view of the comparable outlook embodied in Volpone.
Mammon is already placed for our critical judgment when

he appears at the beginning of Act II; we already know him
to be the greatest gull of all – 'if his dreame last, hee'll turne
the age, to gold' (I iv 29). His speeches, however like Volpone's in attitude, therefore, are very different in dramatic
tone and effect – the magnetic attraction is missing.[13]

> *Volpone* : Thy bathes shall be the iuyce of iuly-flowres,
>   Spirit of roses, and of violets,
>   The milke of vnicornes, and panthers breath
>   Gather'd in bagges, and mixt with *cretan* wines.
>   Our drinke shall be prepared gold, and amber;
>   Which we will take, vntill my roofe whirle round
>   With the *vertigo* : and my dwarfe shall dance,
>   My eunuch sing, my foole make vp the antique.
>   Whil'st, we, in changed shapes, act OVIDS tales,
>   Thou, like EVROPA now, and I like IOVE,
>   Then I like MARS, and thou like ERYCINE,
>   So, of the rest, till we haue quite run through
>   And weary'd all the fables of the gods. (III vii 213–25)

> *Mammon* : I will haue all my beds, blowne vp; not stuft :
>   Downe is too hard. And then, mine oual roome,
>   Fill'd with such pictures, as TIBERIVS tooke
>   From ELEPHANTIS : and dull ARETINE
>   But coldly imitated. Then, my glasses,
>   Cut in more subtill angles, to disperse,
>   And multiply the figures, as I walke
>   Naked betweene my *succubæ*. My mists
>   I'le haue of perfume, vapor'd 'bout the roome,
>   To loose our selues in; and my baths, like pits
>   To fall into : from whence, we will come forth,
>   And rowle vs drie in gossamour, and roses. (II ii 41–52)

All this has a direct bearing on the catastrophe of *Volpone*.
To appreciate and assent to the justice done to the protagonists, we must be detached from them. But although our
'feelings-with' Volpone have been qualified from the start by
our perception of his inner corruption, by our perception of
Mosca's superior cunning, and by such intermittent revela-

tions as the attempted rape of Celia, and although our
'feelings-with' Mosca have been qualified in the same way (if
to a lesser degree), we still retain some by the end of Act v –
enough, at any rate, to find the catastrophe too severe a moral
catharsis. Our judgment may assent, but our feelings are still
lagging. The necessary ambiguity of our response to the two
villains, in fact, prevents any easy resolution of the action.

Nor, given his theme, is it easy to see how Jonson could have
avoided the problem. After the end of Act III, Volpone's and
Mosca's schemes involve a shift from a private to public Folly,
a further projection of the theme on to the larger screen of
political Justice. The development is signaled by Sir Politic
Would-be – 'I told you, sir, it was a plot' – and although he is
(foolishly) wrong, he is (ironically) right. His references to
Machiavelli and Bodin, the Renaissance spokesmen of political
naturalism, are no accident. In the subsequent court scene,
the trial of Celia and Bonario is accompanied by the perversion of family love, of innocence, modesty, and honest witness;
the individual conscience is shown powerless against the power
of the state; and as Voltore points out, ironically enough, the
perversion of Justice is a threat to the whole order of society :

> O, my most equall hearers, if these deedes,
> Acts, of this bold, and most exorbitant straine,
> May passe with sufferance, what one citizen,
> But owes the forfeit of his life, yea fame,
> To him that dares traduce him? which of you
> Are safe, my honour'd fathers? I would aske
> (With leaue of your graue father-hoods) if their plot
> Haue any face, or colour like to truth? (IV vi 38–45)

The villains produce their own order, 'so rare a musique out
of discordes' (v ii 18), but it is an inversion of the proper and
natural order. No Renaissance audience needed to be told that
such perversions of the natural order ordained by God were
incompatible with the survival of the community, were, indeed,
in the long run impossible. In Act v, Jonson portrays it break-

ing down from its own internal incompatibilities and incon-
sistencies.

Nevertheless, although the didactic point is established by
that breakdown, Jonson has necessarily involved the power of
the state as one of the actors. The question is now not merely
one of 'poetic justice' but also of civil Justice(Moral folly has
become judicial crime. And crime, as crime, must receive our
total repudiation) We may sympathize with the criminal, or
his motives, we may perhaps enjoy the excitement of his
criminal career, we may even think his crimes not 'really
crimes, but if we do see his deeds as willfully and seriously
destructive of laws necessary to society, then as social animals
· we inevitably reject them completely and wholeheartedly.
Comedy about crime is possible only if it inhibits the perception of the moral significance of the crime – as *Kind Hearts
and Coronets* shows, we can even laugh at multiple murder so
long as we never see it as really murder.)

There was good reason in Jonson's decision to 'sport with
humane follies, not with crimes'.[14] With the punishment of
Celia and Bonario in Act IV of *Volpone*, the problem of our
divided feelings is not acute, especially since it is clearly not
final. But with the catastrophe in Act v, our feelings are finally
and overwhelmingly directed against Volpone and Mosca.
The earlier dynamic interplay of 'feelings-with' and 'feelings-
against' is drastically resolved.

We feel this as drastic, I believe, because the final judgment
uses our earlier enjoyment of the villains' corruption – its force
as a judgment depends upon it, in fact – but it does not
account for the enjoyment. For example, the catastrophe cuts
Volpone and Mosca to the same level as the suitors, despite
our earlier sense that they were, at least in some respects,
better. On consideration, of course, we see that the Advocate's
judgment is just. The trouble is, we have to consider. The play
itself does not both distill and at the same time purge our
ambiguous attraction in dramatic terms. To put it another
way, the moral judgment offered is appropriate, but it is not

quite adequate to our total response to the play : the situation had seemed, or felt, more complex. The result is that we are not ready for the necessary simplification when it is demanded, and our detachment is forced instead of arising naturally and freely.

To say that Jonson's didacticism conflicted with his aesthetic purposes is too simple. His aesthetic purposes were themselves didactic, if we mean by that the dramatic expression of a deeply moral imagination; and the catastrophe does arise organically from the theme of the play. The problem that faced him was how to enforce a proper judgment on the most fundamental moral perversions while still retaining the effects of comedy – a problem that faced him only in *Volpone* and in *The Alchemist*. His solution in the former is, in fact, a surrender, or at best a technical trick. The concluding speech of the Advocate is as appropriate to a morality, or even some Elizabethan tragedies, as to a comedy :

> Now, you begin,
> When crimes are done, and past, and to be punish'd,
> To thinke what your crimes are : away with them.
> Let all, that see these vices thus rewarded,
> Take heart, and loue to study 'hem. Mischiefes feed
> Like beasts, till they be fat, and then they bleed.
> (v xii 146–51)

But as if he realized that the tone has become too dark, our feelings too heavily wrenched against Volpone and Mosca, Jonson restores the grounds of detachment. 'Volpone' steps completely out of the play and addresses us directly :

> The seasoning of a play is the applause.
> Now, though the Fox be punish'd by the lawes,
> He, yet, doth hope there is no suffring due,
> For any fact, which he hath done 'gainst you ;
> If there be, censure him : here he, doubtfull, stands.
> If not, fare iouially, and clap your hands.

After all, it is only a play; we need feel no concern. Considered in its poetic effect, this final speech indicates unmistakably the difficulty it is designed to overcome. It is no mere formal epilogue, as the similar speech in *The Alchemist* very largely is. Without it, *Volpone* lacks a note necessary to its harmonic resolution; but in order to provide it Jonson has had to step outside his action.

The last act of *The Alchemist* also suggests that Jonson recognized the problem and this time determined to meet it in dramatic terms. Whether he succeeded or not is at least rather more difficult to decide than with the earlier play. Certainly, *The Alchemist* as a whole does not probe to the depth of *Volpone*. And one small reason for this may well be the way Jonson presents the moral judgment in Act v. At the end of the previous act, Lovewit returns to the house the rogues are abusing, with the suddenness of a divine judge :

> *Dol.* Yes, but another is come,
>   You little look'd for !
> *Face.* Who's that?
> *Dol.* Your master :
>   The master of the house. . . .
> *Face.* We are vndone, and taken.
> *Dol.* Lost, I'am afraid. (iv vii 107 ff.)

> *Face.*   bethinke you,
>   Of some course sodainely to scape the dock :
>   For thether you'll come else. Harke you, thunder.
>   (v iv 135–7)

In the last act, Lovewit does execute the necessary judgment by stripping and dismissing the gulls with the appropriate moral comment. On the other hand, Jonson manages to preserve to the end the comic mood so largely dependent on our partial sympathy with the vitality of the rogues. Subtle and Dol are allowed to escape by the skin of their teeth, and Face is pardoned. It appears at first sight a solution to the problem raised by Volpone. Yet the cost is very high.

There is something of a *deus ex machina* about Lovewit.[15] His judgment is only partial in that it spares Face. What is more, his pardon of Face seems contingent on acquiring the material spoils – including the ripe, rich widow. His symbolic judgment is qualified by a suspicion about his motives. In the theater this would probably pass, and the epilogue spoken by Face reminds the audience, explicitly but effectively enough, of its own engagement in the follies enacted. Nevertheless, the ambiguities of Lovewit's role do leave a doubt whether Jonson quite succeeded even here in realizing his deepest moral convictions in the dramatic terms of comedy.

SOURCE: *Modern Language Quarterly,* xx (1959) 233–42

NOTES

1. *Ben Jonson,* ed. C. H. Herford and Percy Simpson (Oxford, 1925–52) II 49–50, 60. All quotations are from this edition.

2. Ralph Nash, 'The Comic Intent of *Volpone*', *Studies in Philology,* XLIV (1947) 30; John S. Weld, 'Christian Comedy : *Volpone*', ibid., LI (1954) 172–93.

3. Thus Jonas A. Barish, 'The Double Plot in *Volpone*', *Modern Philology,* LI (1953) 83–92, makes an illuminating exploration of the connections between Folly and the various distortions of nature in the play. For Herford's objections, see IX 678–9; and for those of a more recent critic, see Edward B. Partridge, *The Broken Compass* (London, 1958) p. 105 and note. Despite these objections, however, I still believe Folly a better term than 'greed' or 'feeding' to suggest the unity of the play.

4. I agree with Wallace A. Bacon, 'The Magnetic Field : The Structure of Jonson's Comedies', *Huntington Library Quarterly,* XIX (1956) 137–8, that there is a certain irony in the treatment of Celia and Bonario, though not altogether with the reason he gives for this. May not the source of the irony lie in the nature of their 'folly' and its relation to that of the other characters?

5. L. C. Knights, *Drama and Society in the Age of Jonson* (London, 1937) chap. 6; D. J. Enright, 'Poetic Satire and Satire in Verse', *Scrutiny,* XVIII (1951) 211–23. This point is repeated in greater detail by Partridge, chap. v.

6. For a closely similar point, see H. R. Hays, 'Satire and Identification : An Introduction to Ben Jonson', *Kenyon Review,* XIX (1957) 271.

7. Alexander H. Sackton, *Rhetoric as a Dramatic Language in Ben Jonson* (New York, 1948) p. 138.

8. F. R. Leavis, *Revaluation* (London, 1949) pp. 94 f.

9. Herford and Simpson, II 58. Cf. the remarks of U. M. Ellis-Fermor, *The Jacobean Drama* (London, 1936) pp. 113–15.

10. Helena Watts Baum, *The Satiric and the Didactic in Ben Jonson's Comedy* (Chapel Hill, 1947) pp. 98–9, cited by Weld, p. 189.

11. He is continually presented, we should notice, as a *magnifico,* a prince of his world of desire and sensual pleasure. Moreover, in his attempted seduction of Celia, he presents the moral problem Shakespeare's Tarquin had presented. He refuses to recognize Celia's appeal to religion, while her repudiation of nature ('that vnhappy crime of nature, / Which you miscal my beauty') is as equally irrelevant as Lucrece's. After all, beauty is not a crime of nature; nature has its proper uses. The scene could only be concluded by Volpone taking his position to its logical conclusion in rape; but since Jonson has made his point, he can afford to break the tension with Bonario's melodramatic rescue. I suspect this scene should be played with the touch of irony at Bonario's expense that the writing seems to suggest. Cf. Bacon, p. 137.

12. Enright, p. 213.

13. This, I believe, is a necessary qualification to Harry Levin's view in 'Jonson's Metempsychosis', *Philological Quarterly,* XXII (1943) 238–9, that the two characters 'speak the same magnificent language'. In his chapter on *Volpone,* Partridge occasionally notes the vitality and attraction of which I have been speaking : see, for example, p. 83 (on the importance of the characters being human, not figures in a bestiary); p. 92 (on Volpone's love-song to Celia); and pp. 94 and 97 (on the erotic vision Volpone presents). But he does not take any consistent account of their effect in the dynamic of the play, being concerned rather with tracing the theme of moral perversion especially as it appears in the 'imagery'. In effect, he almost ignores the action of the second half of the play.

14. *Every Man in His Humour,* Prologue (1616) line 24. It is most probable that this was written for the revised version, i.e. after *Volpone* (see Herford and Simpson, I 333–4, and IX 343–4),

in which case it may represent Jonson's maturer judgment on the problem discussed in this essay.

15. See Bacon, p. 145. Partridge, pp. 152–6, argues, however, that Lovewit is himself one of the objects of Jonson's ironic satire, and that Face's epilogue is an (unconsciously) self-betraying judgment on the rogues. True though this may be, it hardly meets all the issues involved.

Alvin B. Kernan

FROM INTRODUCTION TO *VOLPONE* (1962)

The crucial action of *Volpone* occurs in the first twenty-seven lines of the play, Volpone's celebration of his gold. He first elevates – as the host is raised in the mass – a round gold coin, and the shining, yellow piece of metal, the 'son of Sol', in that instant replaces the sun which has for ages past brought life to the 'teeming earth' and which on the first day of creation was 'struck out of chaos', driving the primal darkness to the lowest place in all creation, the center of the earth. Gold is the new center of the Volpone universe, the unmoved mover,[1] the still point, around which all existence now circles and from which it must draw its life. Having completed his new cosmology, Volpone hastens on to construct his new religion, his new history, his new society, and his new man. The high priest of the new cult, Volpone kisses 'with adoration' the 'relics of sacred treasure' and bursts into rapturous praise of his 'dear saint' (22–3):

> Riches, the dumb god that giv'st all men tongues,
> That canst do nought, and yet mak'st men do all things.

Where the traditional view of history held that mankind had degenerated from an innocent, simple way of life distinguished by a lack of precious metals, Volpone as economic historian redefines human history by making it a movement controlled by man's search for material prosperity beginning in an age of riches, the 'Golden Age' (14–15):

> Well did wise poets by thy glorious name
> Title that age which they would have the best . . .

As sociologist he substitutes hard cash for the forces of blood, piety, friendship, and love which have in the past bound men together (16–21):

> Thou [gold] being the best of things, and far
> transcending
> All style of joy in children, parents, friends,
> Or any other waking dream on earth.
> Thy looks when they to Venus did ascribe,
> They should have giv'n her twenty thousand cupids,
> Such are thy beauties and our loves!

As philosopher-psychologist he quickly defines man as a seeker of gold, who when he attains it achieves at one stroke all the goals for which men in the past have struggled so confusedly and painfully (25–7):

> Thou [gold] art virtue, fame,
> Honour, and all things else. Who can get thee,
> He shall be noble, valiant, honest, wise –

Volpone, an apostle indeed blessed by his 'dumb god' with the gift of tongues, is announcing in the opening lines a new act of creation; and as we watch the play we are watching this new gold-centered world coming into being. The brave new world begins in the house of Volpone, where life is given over to voluptuousness, freedom, and cunning; and these values create a new type of household. Here there is no wife, child, parent, ally, or servant, only grotesque relationships based on gold. Master and servant are confederated to cheat the world, and one another if possible; dwarf, eunuch, and hermaphrodite are said to be the unacknowledged bastards of the householder, begotten only for pleasure and used only for entertainment. To this house come 'friends' mouthing concern for the supposedly sick Volpone but in reality longing only for his death and willing to hasten it with poison or suffocation, so they may inherit his fortune. For Volpone these friends and fellow Venetians are no more than fools who can be coined 'into profit'.

From this golden center the infection spreads outward, recreating the world beyond. In hope of fortune Corbaccio disinherits his son, Corvino is willing to whore his wife, Lady Would-be offers her virtue, and Voltore, who for a few pennies would 'plead against his Maker', dishonours his profession. Judges in a court of law change their attitude towards men when they learn that they are rich; with money learning becomes possible, for you need only, as Mosca says, 'hood an ass with reverend purple . . . and he shall pass for a cathedral doctor'; gold becomes a 'sacred medicine' and physicians practice only for their fees, flaying a man before they kill him. Not only are individuals, professions, and social institutions remade by the power of gold, but the yellow metal ultimately becomes the standard by which all things material and spiritual are measured. Celia's beauty can find no greater praise in Mosca's mouth than to be styled 'Bright as your gold, and lovely as your gold'; and her concern for her virtue when she resists bedding with Volpone can be discredited by her husband's conclusive argument, 'What, is my gold the worse for touching?' In the world of *Volpone* gold, like grace in a Christian world, appears finally to have no limits to its miraculous power :

> Why, your gold
> Is such another med'cine, it dries up
> All those offensive savours! It transforms
> The most deformed, and restores 'em lovely . . .
> .   .   .   .
> It is the thing
> Makes all the world her grace, her youth, her beauty.
>   (v ii 98–105)

This gold-centered world is, of course, a grotesque image of the materialistic culture of the Renaissance, and Jonson constantly reminds us of the width of his satire by frequent reference to contemporary professions and practices : the courtiers who 'ply it so for a place' at court; the usurers who coffin men alive for debt; the mill owners who grind 'oil, corn, or men' into powder; the doctors who 'kill with as much licence as a judge'; the Puritans who sometimes 'devour flesh, and sometimes one another'; the projectors – i.e. entrepreneurs – with such fantastic commercial schemes as 'waterworks in perpetual motion'. . . .

I have spoken of the *Volpone* world as crudely materialistic and gold-centered, but Volpone and Mosca, despite the fact that they are the resident deities of this world, seem to transcend mere miserliness. They adore gold with a passion usually reserved for religion or love, but they treat it not as something possessed for its own sake, the attitude of the miser, but rather as an instrument used to purchase other delights, or as a symbol of their genius. Early in the play Volpone tells us that he glories 'more in the cunning purchase of . . . wealth,/Than in the glad possession' (1 i 31–2). And farther on he explains that the proper way for a man to live is to 'cocker up [his] genius and live free/To all delights . . . fortune calls [him] to . . .'. The word 'genius' is not used here in the restricted modern sense of 'extraordinary ability', but in the Latin sense of 'essential spirit' or 'that fundamental quality which makes a thing what it is', i.e. soul. For Volpone, the essence of man is, then, the exercise of cunning in order to gain wealth, and the proper life for a man is to nurture, 'cocker up',[2] this essential power.

Most immediately this means that Mosca and Volpone put all their minds and energies into bilking the fools and enjoying those pleasures of the senses and the mind which fortune calls them to. But the particular form their cunning takes is of central importance in the play. They are above all else master actors; not the kind of actors who learn their lines beforehand and move according to a pre-established plot, but improvisers like the *commedia dell' arte* players – referred to in the text in several places – who extemporize their lines and action and make up their plot as they go along. Volpone is an unusually impressive actor. He plays a sick and dying man to perfection, coughing at the right moment, seeming to recover slightly when necessary, moving his hands weakly or lying perfectly immobile as the situation requires. When stirred by lust for Celia, he typically solves the problem of how to see her by assuming another disguise, of mountebank, which he plays so well that the mountebank himself could not have been sure, as Mosca tells him, that he was an impostor. After Bonario interrupts his attempted rape of Celia, Volpone is called on to play his most difficult part, an absolutely impotent and dying old man. Despite the stringent requirements of the role – that he lie absolutely still and *look* as if he were on the verge of death – he delivers a magnificent performance. Mosca, with all the professional perfectionism of a Stanislavsky, accuses him of sweating while he lay there; but it is nevertheless an excellent piece of work. And finally, in order to torment even more the fortune hunters who already have been cheated of their money, Volpone puts on the costume of a sergeant of the court and plays an excellent clown, an ironic Dogberry.

But as excellent an actor as Volpone is, he is surpassed by Mosca, who can, he exults, 'change a visor swifter than a thought'. His great dramatic forte is flexibility. Where Volpone once having assumed a role continues to play it without much change, Mosca shifts roles from moment to moment. He can in swift succession be the humble servant of the legacy hunters, the crying friend of virtue who advises Bonario that his father is about to disinherit him, the smiling pander, the modest but stern inheritor of Volpone's fortune, the impressive and sober *magnifico*. There seems no end to his resources, and all that he plays he plays superbly. He is what he chooses to be. But even beyond the range of his acting, we must not forget that with such rare exceptions as the soliloquy at the beginning of Act III, he is playing two roles simultaneously: to Volpone he plays the subtle and obsequious servant; to the fools he plays whatever the occasion requires him to be; but underneath he remains the clever opportunist simply waiting for a chance to bilk his master.

Mosca has other theatrical talents as well. He is an excellent make-up man who carefully anoints Volpone's eyes to appear like those of a dying man; and he sees to it that they are kept sufficiently dulled. As costumer he arranges Volpone's fur robes on the 'sick' man, and later finds the uniform of a sergeant for him. As producer he oversees the erection of the mountebank's platform stage in Act II. As a director he truly excels. In the first four acts of the play, Mosca arranges the scenes of all the little plays within the play. In the sick-room play of Acts I and III he prepares Volpone for his role, directs him when to enter the bed, coaches him on how to act, and then opens and closes the curtains of Volpone's bed-stage at the proper moments.

His masterwork is, however, the court-room play of Act IV. Here he takes a variety of actors of widely differing capabilities and interests – Volpone, Voltore, Corbaccio, Corvino, and Lady Would-be – and creates a smoothly working ensemble. First, he passes among them, distributing their parts, i.e. making sure they know the lies they will tell. The lead is assigned to Voltore the lawyer, who is, as befits his profession, a considerable actor, able to speak

> To every cause, and things mere contraries,
> Till . . . hoarse again, yet all be law;
> That, with most quick agility, could turn,
> And re-turn; make knots, and undo them . . .
>
> (I iii 54–7)

After Voltore struts about and delivers his rather old-fashioned speech, accompanied by elaborate gestures, the witnesses are smoothly introduced to play their stock parts: Corbaccio, the kind old father cruelly treated by his son; Corvino, the gentle, forgiving husband taken advantage of by his lewd wife; Lady Would-be, an innocent, outraged wife. When Corbaccio or Corvino have doubts or hesitate, Mosca is there to prompt and reassure them. At just the right moment the apparently dying Volpone is carried into court.

So well-designed and smooth-running is Mosca's theatrical machinery that the innocents Bonario and Celia, despite their own efforts to state the truth, are drawn into Mosca's plot and designated the villains of the piece.

It is no wonder that Mosca considers this his 'masterwork', and Volpone is forced to agree that Mosca has 'played [the] prize' (v ii 15). But Volpone is not content to let the deceptions rest here, and he insists on directing two more plays himself, both of which lead to disaster. The first is the scene in which he retires, as director and audience, behind a 'traverse' curtain while Mosca pretends to be the heir to the fortune and drives away each of the fortune hunters in turn. The second is his pretense of being a sergeant. Both plays, while amusing for Volpone, are failures by the theatrical standards set up within the larger play. All of Mosca's plays present the fools with flattering images of themselves, persuade them that they are handsome, generous, noble, dignified, and, above all, full of promise for the future. The results are most gratifying: gold, plate, and jewels find their way into Mosca's hand and Volpone's treasure chest. So long as Mosca directs, illusions remain unshattered; but Volpone has a savage, satiric streak in him, and the two plays he arranges in Act v expose the inheritance seekers for the arrant fools and corrupt beings they essentially are. The result is disaster for Volpone's plans. The fools strike back in revenge, and all is at last uncovered.

As *Volpone* proceeds, the acting theme is strengthened by the knaves' constant use of the language of the theater: plot, forced posture, epilogue, scene, feign, mask, zany, action, Pantalone; we begin to have the odd feeling that we are watching a play within a play or – as the levels of deception multiply – a play within a play within a play. At times the theatrical quality present in language and action is fully realized on stage, and we are presented openly with a theater within a theater. The grotesque interlude presented by Nano and Androgyno in Act i, scene ii, and the performance of Volpone as mountebank on the platform stage erected on the

real stage are clear-cut instances, like 'The Murder of Gon-
zago' in *Hamlet*, of smaller performances within the larger.
But Volpone's huge bed with its movable curtains and acting
space on which he plays out his sickness is also a small stage –
an 'inner stage' – and in Act v, scene ii, Volpone and Mosca,
using a traverse, construct a second theater in which Mosca
plays out the comedy of driving each of the fortune hunters
out of his humor, stripping him of his hopes and of his pretenses. The court room with its performers and its spectators
also reproduces the physical arrangements of the theater.

Just as the theatrical metaphor which is woven into every
scene becomes manifest in a number of small theaters within
the real theater, so does the idea of acting. Volpone and
Mosca are nearly always acting, but from time to time they
retire to the wings, where, like the professionals they are, they
discuss the fine points of their art and congratulate each other
on their performances. Mosca, as I have mentioned, can be
hypercritical and refer maliciously to the fact that Volpone
broke out with sweat under the strain of acting a dying man
in court, but at other times he can generously praise a fine
performance. After Voltore has twisted truth to falsehood in
court with a ringing voice, fine gestures ('action'), and
beautiful pacing, Mosca can exclaim admiringly, 'I'd have
your tongue, sir, tipped with gold for this'. When Volpone
after his masterful impersonation of the mountebank Scoto
worries that his make-up may not have been sufficient ('Is not
the colour of my beard and eyebrows to make me known?'),
Mosca assures him that 'Scoto himself could hardly have distinguished'. Volpone then smugly exclaims, 'I did it well'.
Volpone, equally appreciative of Mosca's abilities, is always
bursting with admiration and praise for the particularly skill-
ful ways in which Mosca acts his parts for the fortune hunters.

The idea of 'playing' is the central theme of *Volpone*, and
ultimately all the other details of the intricately wrought play
feed into this master image. Gold, for example, which is so
prominent throughout, is finally but one of the many mas-

querades. Its worshippers make of it a god, the sun, learning, honor, virtue; but it is finally no more than dull, heavy, and spiritless metal – dross – disguised to resemble the truly good. The classical references which Jonson works into his text frequently refer to some instance of 'acting' : Jacob covered with goatskins pretending to be Esau to cheat his brother of his blessing, Jove disguised as a shower of gold in order to enjoy Danaë, Lollia Paulina covered with jewels to look like starlight.

Obviously the iteration of this theme reveals that a world and men given over entirely to materialism are unreal, mere pretenses. But this is almost a moral commonplace, and Jonson's anatomizing knife cuts deeper. Volpone and Mosca, and to a lesser degree Voltore and the other fools, think of man as *homo ludens* and his genius as *ludere*, to act, to play. Where for a fool like Voltore this means no more than pretending to be the honest advocate for the cause that pays the best, for a Volpone and a Mosca playing becomes the exercise of a godlike power. Playing the roles of dying men and humble parasite are for them only rehearsals for metamorphosis, complete transcendence of reality. Volpone's belief in the powers of acting appears most clearly in his sensuous and passionate temptation of Celia, one of the best-known speeches in Renaissance drama. His imagination runs riot as he pictures for her the incredible wealth they will enjoy and the sensual pleasures they will share, if only she will submit to him. All the world will be plundered to supply them with a moment's delight, a jewel, a rare dish, a luxurious bath; and then they will pass on to the greatest of pleasures, love :

> my dwarf shall dance,
> My eunuch sing, my fool make up the antic.
> Whilst we, in changèd shapes, act Ovid's tales,
> Thou like Europa now, and I like Jove,
> Then I like Mars, and thou like Erycine,
> So of the rest, till we have quite run through,
> And wearied all the fables of the gods.

> Then will I have thee in more modern forms,
> Attirèd like some sprightly dame of France,
> Brave Tuscan lady, or proud Spanish beauty . . .
>
> (III vii 219–28)

His appetite for infinite variety and his fertile imagination
hurry him onward to describe even more shapes which she will
assume to avoid satiety: Persian, Turk, courtesan, 'quick
negro', 'cold Russian'; and he will 'meet' her,

>   in as many shapes;
> Where we may, so, transfuse our wand'ring souls
> Out at our lips, and score up sums of pleasures,
>   That the curious shall not know
>   How to tell them as they flow . . .

The action discernible in these lines is the action of human
genius as Volpone understands it: to 'flow' by means of acting, to change shapes from mere man to the immortal gods –
Jove, Mars, Erycine – and thus enjoy endless pleasures and
endless change.

Mosca is not so flamboyant as Volpone, but the achieve-
ments of his acting put Volpone to shame:

> Success hath made me wanton. I could skip
> Out of my skin, now, like a subtle snake,
> I am so limber. (III i 5–7)

But as he warms to the praise of his own acting, the ability to
skip out of his skin becomes a minor accomplishment, for he
feels that he (23–9):

>   can rise
> And stoop, almost together, like an arrow;
> Shoot through the air as nimbly as a star;
> Turn short as doth a swallow; and be here,
> And there, and here, and yonder, all at once;
> Present to any humour, all occasion;
> And change a visor swifter than a thought . . .

Here is man altogether freed by his ability to act from the

limitations reality imposes on ordinary men! Not only can he be anything he wishes, he can be several persons in several places at once!

Acting is for Volpone and Mosca a magical power, a short cut to fulfillment of boundless desire which avoids such unpleasant realities as old age, decay, satiation, poverty. Acting opens up for them a brave new world of the imagination where man can contend with the gods themselves, as Volpone boasts to Celia: 'In varying figures I would have contended/ With the blue Proteus . . .' (III vii 152–3). If their adoration of gold suggests Volpone's and Mosca's materialism, their faith in acting marks them as believers in the theory that man can make of himself whatever he wills to be, even a god. . . .

Volpone and Mosca believe their genius is most fully expressed in their ability to act, to play a part, to make of themselves what they will. Each 'act' raises them higher in the scale of being, they believe, until in Volpone's case he becomes nothing less than a god, Mars, Jove; while Mosca considers that he is able to transcend altogether the limitations of the flesh through a skill which enables him, like angels or other pure essences, 'to be here, and there, and here, and yonder, all at once'. But their progression is in fact a degeneration. In social terms this is immediately evident. Volpone begins as a *magnifico*, a noble of Venice occupying a place of dignity and responsibility in the state. In Act II he appears in the role of an itinerant mountebank, a mere quack living by his wits and without an accepted place in society. From this disguise he passes on to playing a clownish sergeant of the court, a minor hireling of the state subject to whipping. In the end he is reduced to the status of eternal prisoner confined in irons – but this is no role, it is the form which manifests finally and irrevocably the dangerous beast which Volpone has made of himself. Mosca's case proceeds somewhat differently, for as Volpone appears to degenerate socially, Mosca appears to rise. His proper place in society is that of servant. By his cunning acting he rises to the position of parasite, trusted confidant of a great man and the agent of other great men of the city. Ultimately he occupies Volpone's vacated place and becomes a *magnifico* about to marry into one of the city's great families. But this meteoric rise is all pretense and it finally melts away to the reality of the galley slave, the sentence imposed upon him by the court.

'The way up is the way down', a reverse statement of the religious belief that humility raises a man spiritually, applies to Volpone on the physical and psychic levels as well as the social. His chief disguise throughout the play is that of a sick and dying man, and it requires no particular knowledge of Elizabethan lore or the Great Chain of Being to see that the physical pretense here is the spiritual reality. In his soul Volpone is as sick as he pretends to be in body, and so, ironically, each detail of sickness which Volpone and Mosca work out and act so artfully, instead of covering reality reveals the truth about the man who has substituted gold for his God and his soul.[3] But over and above this general irony of disguise built into the play, Volpone is traced down the scale in considerable detail. . . . His understanding disappears in the opening lines, where he conceives of good as residing in gold, the material world, rather than in the soul and those institutions, religion, and society, which express man's spiritual nature. His will is immediately corrupted, for he chooses gold as his soul and his god with all the fervor of a saint choosing salvation. His higher faculties gone, it is inevitable that he will further degenerate. Common sense disappears at once as he becomes susceptible to the most outrageous flattery and forgets that he is only a mortal man with severe limitations. The remainder of the descent is accomplished by means of the disguise of sickness. Memory soon goes :

> He knows no man,
> No face of friend, nor name of any servant,
> Who 't was that fed him last, or gave him drink;
> Not those he hath begotten, or brought up;
> Can he remember. (I v 39–43)

His five senses disappear one by one – and while they may reappear if the situation requires it, the general movement is downward. Sight, the highest of the senses, goes first (I iii 17) and by Act I, scene v, he is described as retaining only touch, the lowest of the senses : Mosca advises Corvino to place the pearl he has brought into Volpone's hands because (18–20) :

> 'tis only there
> He apprehends, he has his feeling yet.
> See how he grasps it !

In Acts II and III, when Volpone resumes the disguise of sickness, his symptoms reveal even further degeneration. Act I has brought him to the level of the lowest of the animals – the parasite is the usual example given of the animal who has only the sense of touch – but now he falls below the vegetable level as his reproductive and nutritive faculties disappear. Corvino is gulled into believing that there is no danger in lending his beautiful wife to a Volpone so far gone that his sexual powers have disappeared. 'A long forgetfulness hath seized that part,' Mosca says, and 'nought can warm his blood . . . but a fever' (II vi 64–6). In Act III Corvino assures his wife, Celia, that getting into bed with Volpone involves no danger to her honor because the man is so weak that he can no longer even feed himself :

> An old, decrepit wretch,
> That has no sense, no sinew; takes his meat
> With others' fingers; only knows to gape
> When you do scald his gums; a voice, a shadow . . .
>
> (III vii 42–5)

Below the level of vegetable it would seem impossible for a man to go, but Volpone predicts his own end when he compares himself to a 'stone' and to a 'dead leaf' (III vii 84–5). By Act IV, when he is brought into the court 'as impotent', he has become simply an object to be carried about. The end is inevitable, and Volpone seeks it out with his usual pride in his genius for inventing roles. To instrument a final joke on the fortune hunters he pretends to be dead. His descent from man to mere corrupt matter is hastily completed when Mosca asks what he is to say if anyone should ask what has become of the body:

Volpone. Say it was corrupted.
Mosca. I'll say it stunk, sir; and was fain t' have it
Coffined up instantly and sent away. (v ii 77–9)

While Volpone's symptoms are pretenses, they do mirror genuine moral failings. The loss of sight and hearing suggests his moral blindness and deafness. The retention of only the sense of touch is a perfect image of his grossness and materialism: only if you can touch a thing is it real! The failure of reproductive powers reminds us that Volpone has cut himself off from society and from family. His children are those monstrous distortions of nature, the dwarf, the hermaphrodite, the eunuch, and other bastards begotten on 'beggars, Gypsies, and Jews, and blackmoors when he was drunk' (i v 44–5). His inability to feed and nourish himself reflects the very real spiritual starvation which he is undergoing, which ends in the death of the soul and the corruption of the body. Greed, lust, selfish individualism, and vulgar materialism are identified with the process of physical decay to mark the 'progress' down the ladder of being from man to corruption. And the man chose freely to trace this path, thinking all the while that he was achieving godhead.

The greatness of Jonson's play comes from his ability to bring, by means of irony, two great views of human nature into perfect juxtaposition. On one hand we have a vivid depiction in Volpone and Mosca of an exuberantly sensual delight in the physical world, here symbolized by gold, and a bursting vitality which enables man to believe that by himself he can remake world and man to conform to his own desires – here symbolized by acting. These are views which we take to be characteristic of the Renaissance, and Jonson gives them shape and language which for sheer vitality and evocative power have never been surpassed. The brilliance of phrase and the urgency of rhythms in such speeches as Volpone's praise of his gold and his temptation of Celia guarantee that Jonson himself responded powerfully to this optimism; but he was at the same time the greatest classicist of his age, profoundly committed to the principles of order and tradition in religion, society, and literature. And so he counterweights the joyful worldliness of his characters with a rigid moral system and a vision of reality built up and refined upon by pagan and Christian thinkers over two thousand years. Volpone and the views he represents were, in Jonson's time, only the latest of a long series of challenges to society and established order. They were as contemporary and shining new as a fresh-minted coin, and yet they were as old as Satan himself. And the end was the same in both cases. With the predictable regularity of a machine, each step upward in defiance of nature becomes a step downward. Mosca perfectly, though unintentionally, describes this specious progress of 'your fine elegant rascal', who, he says, 'can rise and stoop almost together'. And by the end of *Volpone*, despite all attempts to cover truth and all skill at playing, reality asserts itself once more as the impostors' physical shapes are brought into conformity with their true natures. Their own greed unmasks them, and the court locks these Proteans into the shapes they have wrought for themselves: Mosca becomes a perpetual galley slave; Volpone is condemned to prison, where, as a moral incurable, his body will be cramped by irons to fit it to his spiritual diseases; Voltore is exiled from his profession and the state, condemned to wander outside society like the outlaw he truly is; Corbaccio is confined to a monastery and treated as a moral idiot who has forgotten that he has a soul which will be held to account; and Corvino is turned into a civic joke, made to wear a cap with the ears of an ass and sit in the pillory.[4]

Source: Introduction to *Volpone* (1962) pp. 1–4, 6–13, 20–6

NOTES

1. 'Riches, the dumb god . . . That canst do nought, and yet mak'st men do all things' (1 i 22–3). The resemblance of this to Aristotle's Prime Mover is noted by Edward Partridge, *The Broken Compass* (New York, 1958) p. 74.

2. Volpone's 'cocker up my genius' is very close to Iago's declaration of his fundamental purpose, 'to plume up my will' (*Othello*, 1 iii 392).

3. The same technique is used to reveal the lawyer Voltore. In v xii, where he pretends to be possessed by a devil 'in shape of a blue toad with a bat's wings', the pretense discloses the truth about a lawyer who pleads so eloquently for falsehood and for gold.

4. The subplot has the same kind of conclusion. Sir Politic after pretending to be a clever statesman is forced to confess his pretenses and, driven by his fears, to disguising (revealing) himself as a tortoise.

Ian Donaldson

JONSON'S TORTOISE (1968)

In Act v, scene iv of *Volpone* Sir Politic Would-be is warned by Peregrine that his plot to sell the State of Venice to the Turk has been revealed, that warrants are signed for his arrest and for the search of his study. Sir Politic announces that he has 'an ingine' that will save him; he produces a large tortoise-shell, dons a black cap and gloves, climbs inside the shell, and remains there while Peregrine's three English merchants enter, to prod, moralize over, and finally expose him. The scene is usually taken to be one of Jonson's feebler attempts at farce. Soames' comment

> When in the *Fox* I see the tortoise hissed
> I lose the author of the *Alchemist*

suggests that the scene had a rough passage even in the seventeenth century. Upton in the next century criticized the whole scene as an irrelevant interruption to the plot; Scott considered it too farcical for the rest of the piece; and Rea, who summarized these criticisms in his edition of *Volpone* in 1919, could only argue somewhat desperately that at least the scene filled up the time agreeably while Mosca made the commendadore drunk and acquired his uniform for Volpone.[1] The scene continues to distress critics: a recent editor of the play, Arthur Sale, finds 'the farce is as cumbrous as the tortoise' and considers that the scene shares 'with its main plot only some such feeble common moral as "Disguises that move fall off" '.[2]

Yet in recent years it has also been generally acknowledged that at one level *Volpone* may be seen as a beast-fable, and that most of the characters have what Volpone himself calls 'morall emblemes' to their names (v viii 12). The skill with

which Jonson uses this fable to unite the play's two plots has
been sensitively and persuasively demonstrated by Professor
Jonas Barish. In the scene with the tortoise-shell, Mr Barish
argues, the notions of animal mimicry and metamorphosis
which are persistently suggested throughout the play move to
a farcical climax; Sir Politic's 'playing possum' is a reminder
of Volpone's similar stratagems earlier in the play, and Sir
Politic's unshelling anticipates the final uncasing of the Fox.[3]
Convincing though this argument is, one is left with the suspicion that Jonson may have intended the tortoise to bear an
even more precise emblematic significance, like (say) the cat
that accompanies the figure of Liberty in *Part of the King's
Entertainment*; and that when Sir Politic speaks of the
tortoise-shell as 'Mine owne deuice' (v iv 60) the word
'device' may bear the double sense of 'stratagem' and 'emblem'.
If this is so, what might Sir Politic's 'device' signify?

It seems likely that Jonson was here in fact combining three
different, though related, emblematic significances. The first
and most obviously important is that of the tortoise as an
emblem of policy : safe so long as it remains within its shell,
vulnerable as soon as it ventures any part of its body outside.
The best-known classical use of this figure is in the speech of
Titus Quinctius Flaminius, reported by Livy, in which
Flaminius attempts to dissuade the Achaeans from invading
the island of Zakynthos, counselling them to remain safe
within the Peloponnesus, as the tortoise remains safe within
its shell :

> ceterum sicut testudinem, ubi collecta in suum tegumen est,
> tutam ad omnes ictus video esse, ubi exserit partes aliquas,
> quodcumque, nudavit, obnoxium atque infirmum habere, haud
> dissimiliter vos, Achaei, clausos undique mari, quae intra Pelo-
> ponnesi sunt terminos, ea et iungere vobis et iuncta tueri facile,
> simul aviditate plura amplectendi hinc excedatis, nuda vobis
> omnia, quae extra sint, et exposita ad omnes ictus esse.[4]

This passage seems to be alluded to on the one or two other

occasions on which the tortoise is used as a dramatic emblem in Elizabethan times. In the *Gesta Grayorum* of 1594–5 Jervis Tevery is represented by the device of *A Tortois, with his Head out of the Shell*; the inscription, *Obnoxia*, recalls Flaminius's own words.[5] In Robert Wilson's *The Three Lords and Three Ladies of London* (1594)[6] there is a more explicit and altogether more interesting use of the emblem. In the opening scene of this play the shields of the three lords – Policy, Pomp, and Pleasure – are displayed; each bears an appropriate emblem, that of Policy (who is also called 'Pol') being a tortoise. Conveniently, the lord's page, Wit, explains its significance :

A Tortoyse my boy, whose shell is so hard, that a loaden cart may goe ouer and not breake it, and so she is safe within, and wheresoeuer she goes, she beares it on her backe, needing neither other succour or shilter but her shell; the woord underneath her is *Prouidens securus*, the prouident is safe, like to the Tortoys, armed with his owne defence, and defended with his owne armour; in shape somewhat rounde, signifying compasse, wherein alwaies the prouident forsee to keepe themselues within their owne compasse, my boy. (Sig. B2v)

It seems likely that Jonson knew Wilson's play and certain details (e.g. that about the cart – cf. Peregrine's 'Hee'll beare a cart', v iv 67) suggest he was remembering it when he wrote the scene under discussion.[7] *The Three Lords and Three Ladies* is an unashamedly nationalistic play, written and performed in the aftermath of the Armada; a central event of the play is the defeat of the three lords of Spain, Pride, Ambition, and Tyranny. Wilson's Policy is a hero. Wilson tries to rid the word 'policy' of the hostile connotations which it was rapidly gathering at this time; it is English policy (the prologue informs us), combined with God's providence, that has saved England from the threat of Spain. Policy *may* be a bad thing, announces Wit blandly, but

Bad *pollici's* seldom found in so Christian a common
                                                    wealth
As *London* is I trust, where my maister is a Lord.
                                               (Sig. B3)

To clinch the point, Policy marries a lady named Love, 'to
shew, that all our pollicie is for loue of *Londons* common
wealth : and so our *love* cannot be separate from our *pollicy*'
(Sig. Iv). In the sub-plot of *Volpone* Jonson reverses all the
jingoistic implications of Wilson's play. English policy is
neither 'bad' nor 'provident', it is simply laughably amateurish
and incompetent. Jonson's use of the emblem of the tortoise is
derisively ironic.

The tortoise was also commonly taken to be an emblem of
silence. The tortoise was sometimes said to be tongueless;[8] a
familiar paradox was that the animal was silent while alive
and vocal after its death (the shell being used as a frame for
various stringed instruments).[9] The one metamorphosis story
connected with the tortoise, that told by Servius in his note to
Aeneid I 505, gave further strength to this significance. This
is the story of the garrulous Chelone ('virgo . . . linguae
impatientis fuit') who refused to attend the wedding of Juno
and Jupiter, and for her presumption in deriding the marriage was turned by Mercury into a tortoise. It is appropriate
that Sir Pol, the talkative parrot ('Sir, I but talk'd so/For
discourse sake, merely', v iv 46–7) should undergo a similar
metamorphosis, being finally reduced to silence inside a
tortoise-shell. The final silencing of a highly talkative character is of course a characteristic feature in several of Jonson's
plays, the most obvious parallel perhaps being the gagging of
Carlo Buffone in *Every Man Out of His Humour*.

The third, and in Jonson's day, the best known, emblematic
significance of the tortoise is closely connected to this. The
figure of the heavenly Venus frequently appears in the emblem
books standing with her foot upon a tortoise. The tortoise is
said to symbolize the two golden qualities of the chaste

woman : she is silent, and keeps always to her house.[10] It is possible (though the scene can only suggest this indirectly) that Jonson thought the tortoise a suitably ironic emblem not only for Sir Politic but also for his loquacious and wandering wife. The theme of *keeping to one's home* is played over in many ways throughout *Volpone*. Both Sir Politic and Volpone expose themselves disastrously by not keeping to their homes :

> here, 'twas good, in priuate,
> But, in your publike, *Caue*, whil'st I breathe. (v i 3–4)

But the theme is applicable too to the women of the play. As early as the first act the contrast is pointed between the talkative and wanton Lady Would-be, who roams freely from home and husband, and the silent and chaste Celia, who is rigorously confined to house by her husband : 'Shee's kept as warily, as is your gold' (i v 1·18). Celia leaves her home only under duress, and contemplates with loathing the proposed encounter with Volpone; Lady Would-be voluntarily seeks out and offers herself to Mosca, whose final retort to her is 'Goe home' (v iii 44). Jonson's use of the tortoise in the following scene subtly gathers together the play's free-floating though related ideas about the conservation of 'political' strength and wifely integrity.

If the scene in question is feeble, then, it is not because it relies upon a pointless or juvenile piece of farce. The scene fails for more interesting reasons, because its humour is esoteric and top-heavy; Jonson has not been wholly successful in directing his erudition to comic ends. Like the sub-plot as a whole, the incident may well seem tiresome today, not because it is irrelevant but because it relies on contemporary allusions which have now lost their clarity and force. It is the kind of minor obscurity in Jonson that renders mildly ironical his frequent lofty appeals over the heads of the audiences of his own day to the verdict of posterity.

SOURCE : *Review of English Studies*, xix (1968) 162–6

J.V.—G

NOTES

1. *Volpone*, ed. J. D. Rea, Yale Studies in English, LIX (New Haven, 1919) pp. 223–4.

2. *Volpone*, ed. Arthur Sale (London, 1959) p. 176.

3. 'The Double Plot in *Volpone*', *Modern Philology*, LI (1953) 83–92. While the present article was going through the press, a further article by Lloyd L. Mills, 'Barish's "The Double Plot" Supplemented : The Tortoise Symbolism', appeared in *The Serif*, IV (Sep 1967) 25–31.

4. Livy, bk XXXVI xxxii 5–9; cf. Plutarch, *Flaminius* xvii.

5. Malone Society Reprints (Oxford, 1914) p. 67.

6. Tudor Facsimile Texts (London, 1912).

7. Herford and Simpson noted the similarity between the two phrases about the cart, though nothing more (Jonson's *Works*, ed. C. H. Herford, P. and E. M. Simpson (Oxford, 1925–52) IX 729–30). This phrase seems, however, to be used in other contemporary descriptions of tortoises, and is attributed to Palladius by Edward Topsell, *The Historie of Serpents* (1608) p. 282. C. R. Baskervill discussed Wilson's play in connexion with *Cynthia's Revels*, and thought it 'altogether probable' that Jonson knew the play (*English Elements in Jonson's Early Comedy* (Austin, Texas, 1911) pp. 249, 253–6). More recently Robert E. Knoll has independently suggested a parallel between *Volpone* and *The Three Lords and Ladies of London* (*Ben Jonson's Plays, An Introduction* (Lincoln, Nebraska, 1964) p. 100).

8. Pliny, *Nat. Hist.* XI lxviii 180.

9. Cicero, *De Divinatione* II lxiv 133, quoting Amphion's riddle from Pacuvius's *Antiope*.

10. Vincenzo Cartari, *Le Imagini dei Dei degli Antichi* (Padua, n.d. [1603]) p. 490; Andreae Alciati, *Emblemata* (Paris, 1602) pp. 874–9 (a slightly fuller account is given in the edition of 1621, pp. 832–7). The emblem is an ancient one : see Jean Seznec, *The Survival of the Pagan Gods*, trans. Barbara F. Sessions (New York, 1961) p. 101 and n. 81*a*; for its currency in Elizabethan literature see W. M. Carroll, *Animal Conventions in English Renaissance Non-Religious Prose, 1550–1600* (New York, 1954) p. 118.

Philip Brockbank

FROM INTRODUCTION TO *VOLPONE* (1968)

Volpone, or *The Fox*, was the work of a single commanding
act of the imagination, written in five weeks, making one sustained experience from a great diversity of materials and
insights. It carries an air of spontaneity and gay improvisation,
and yet it continually wins effects that stand up to exacting
reflective analysis. It is an act (to borrow Jonson's rhetoric)
'worthy of celebration', and not a 'declamatory and windy
invective'.

The dedicatory Epistle is to the 'Most Equal' (that is,
equally just and judicious) Universities of Oxford and Cambridge; the scene is set in Venice; and the first performances
were by Shakespeare's company (the King's Men) at the
London Globe. These circumstances begin to mark the lineaments of the play; it is a comedy of city-life by a scholar-
playwright, and it displays the enterprise and extravagance of
Renaissance Venice for the entertainment of a popular English audience. This way of putting it awakens certain expecta-
tions and quietens others; the play is about a way of life within
a whole society, its implicit judgements and modes of analysis
will satisfy the academic mind, and its verve and vitality will
engage and delight the public at large.

In the daunting phrases of the Epistle, Jonson may be
accounted a 'learned and liberal soul' whose office as comic
poet requires him to 'imitate justice', 'instruct to life' and to
'purity of language', and to 'stir up gentle affections'. He will
perform for London the services that Horace once performed
for Rome; but his responsibilities are equally towards his art –
he will 'raise the despised head of poetry again' and 'render
her worthy to be embraced, and kissed, of all the great and

master spirits of our world'. We may, therefore, survey the
play from the platform that Jonson himself has afforded.

THE IMITATION OF JUSTICE

Jonson speaks in his Epistle of the 'strict rigour of *comic* law'
and says that his own catastrophe (*dénouement*) may be
thought not to accord with it; but the happy ending that
would satisfy one kind of pedantry about the nature of comedy,
would leave unsatisfied those who clamour for the punishment
of vice. Jonson is content to remind his university public that
even ancient comedies do not always end happily, but the
passage may recall us to the distinct but elusive analogy
between comic justice and moral justice – they are not the
same but they are often alike. In the final scene Volpone is
exposed to the 'strict rigour' not of the comic but of the
criminal law; but Jonson insinuates that the judicious will
recognise that this is exactly what the comedy itself demands.
The comedy requires that comic justice should be executed by
the knaves before it is executed upon them.

Jonson is well aware of the contiguity between his own role
as plotter of the play's large design, and the roles of the knaves
who plot its particular mischiefs. So it happens that the excite-
ments of the play and the nature of its insights owe much to
the wit and understanding displayed by Mosca and Volpone
as it were on Jonson's behalf. The resourcefulness of the comic
playwright, the confidence trickster and the criminal alike, is
dramatic and histrionic – they are good at contriving ways out
of difficult situations, at putting on an act, and at taking
people in. Many of the gloating exchanges between Mosca
and Volpone therefore read like Jonson's compliments to his
own art – 'Good wits are greatest in extremities', 'to make/
So rare a music out of discords', 'Scoto himself could hardly
have distinguished!' But the playwright's art is decisively
more comprehensive than the knave's, in ways both obvious
and subtle.

The gull-and-knave pattern of comic episode has a long history from Aristophanes and Plautus, the Roman *fabulæ togatae* (in which the country visitor was often taken in by the city sophisticate) and the *commedia dell'arte*, through Tudor interludes and entertainments and university drama, into the popular comedy of the fifteen-nineties. But it is Jonson (with some prompting from Marlowe's *Jew of Malta*) who most fully realises its potentials. The knave of the new plays is not only like the parasite of the old classical plays – exploiting human weakness in order to prosper; he is also like the devil in the medieval moralities – exposing man's weaknesses and feeding their vices to damn them.[1]

Mosca's Justice

Mosca, self-confessedly a parasite and by Volpone called a devil, works to the ends appropriate to both. As a parasite he enjoys the limber wit of the game, its transcendental skill ('dropped from above'); but as a devil he exhibits a perverse mastery of the moral law. When he approaches Bonario under cover of friendship (III ii) he is like Hypocrisy or Dissimulation in an old play,[2] pretending to be good fellowship in order to serve the devil's ends. His mastery of the appearance and language of virtue moves him to tears and overcomes all the resistance of his allegorically named victim. There is a kind of validity, however, in his claim to 'an interest in the general state/Of goodness, and true virtue' (whether or not Mosca is punning on his different kind of interest in Bonario's estate). All four legacy hunters who attend upon Volpone through Mosca's agency are fittingly abused and tormented for vices that are almost systematically delineated; the seven deadly sins are partners to the gulls' dance but they do not come undisguised – pride, for example, is assimilated into Voltore's forensic vanity, anger finds occasion in Corvino's jealousy and lechery in his lingering upon Aretine (III vii 58–64). Envy, gluttony and sloth are subsumed into the pervasive parasitic avarice, the pre-eminent vice of the acquisitive society. Mosca professes this degree of wisdom and upon each gull in turn he passes his derisive sentence :

> Go home, and use the poor Sir Pol, your knight, well;
> For fear I tell some riddles : go, be melancholic.
>
> (v iii 44–5)

Lady Would-be does indeed (in Jonson's play as well as Mosca's) come 'most melancholic, home'; the same verdict lights upon Corvino, but touched with perverse magnanimity :

> Why, think that these good works
> May help to hide your bad : I'll not betray you . . .
>
> (v iii 56–7)

The judgement upon Corbaccio awakens exactly the sensations of physical disgust that Jonson has put to his making :

> Are not you he, that filthy covetous wretch,
> With the three legs, that here, in hope of prey,
> Have, any time this three year, snuffed about,
> With your most grov'ling nose; and would have hired
> Me to the poisoning of my patron? sir?
>
> . . . Go home, and die, and stink. (v iii 67–71, 74)

The displacement of obsequiousness by a purging arrogance (indicated by 'sir?' above) that can be roared out to the deaf ear of Corbaccio in one terrible injunction, is succeeded by the equally effacing, casual and caressing insolence bestowed upon Voltore :

> You, that have so much law, I know ha' the conscience,
> Not to be covetous of what is mine. (v iii 97–8)

The gull-and-knave structure as Jonson contrives it allows the knave, therefore, to prevail over the gull not alone because of his superior know-how, but also because of his superior moral insight. He is the scourge of inadequacies and follies, and even of crimes, that the society would have tolerated or overlooked, through inertia or defective government. About *Volpone*, the point can be made the more readily because society itself is directly gulled – both as a public in the Piazza, acclaiming the fake mountebank (himself a charlatan), and as a formal body in the Scrutineo, where the Avocatori are tricked by a knavish display of mock obsequiousness and indulgent moral indignation. The law, as Dogberry cries in *Much Ado About Nothing*, is an ass.

Jonson's Justice

From Bonario's point of view and Celia's, the happy outcome of the action is attributable to divine intervention – 'Heaven could not, long, let such gross crimes be hid'. But Jonson knows that divine intervention in a play is the playwright's responsibility ('let no god intervene', says Horace, 'unless a knot come worthy of such a deliverer') and that he must observe, in some sense, the rigour of comic law. It appears that justice is finally imitated (that is, made manifest in the theatre) not by the vigilance of the criminal law, but by the process through which the knaves finally betray each other. It can be known by its commonplace tags and proverbs ('set a thief to catch a thief', 'pride before a fall', 'thieves fall out') but Jonson explores its intellectual and imaginative dynamics, without confining attention to the punishment of vice. Volpone and Mosca are not arbitrarily struck down by their creator's whim or by his servile regard for conventional morality. Jonson's art makes it imperative that they consume themselves with the very energies and fantasies that animate them. To appreciate Jonson's justice we must look more widely at his moral judgements, his poetry and his theatre.

'INSTRUCTION TO LIFE'

Jonson's phrase may be generously interpreted to suggest all the discoveries that the comic-poet makes about the impulses and principles by which men live, both in themselves and in the society about them. Recognising that the play is about virtuosity and is itself a feat of virtuosity, what has virtuosity to do with virtue, and what openings for either did the city cultures of Venice and London provide?

The question in respect to virtuosity has been partly answered – the characteristic vices of the city money-grabbers invited the exercise of the skills of the confidence-trickster. In respect to virtue, it is best considered through the language and postures of the dominant figure, Volpone, fox and magnifico.

Volpone the Magnifico

Usually the conventions of the theatre do not allow us to attribute poetic gifts to the characters of a play (the sentiments are theirs, the arts that convey them are the poet's) but from the profane matins of the opening scene to the closing pun of the last, Volpone is a self-consciously accomplished performer. Jonson's wit plays sardonically upon itself as he touches the parallels between his own talents and his hero's – both inventive, clever mimics, plotters, public entertainers, poets, singers and critics. The mountebank scene seems to be charged with specific allusions to Jonson's own situation, but delight in the rarity of an imposture never wholly disarms judgement.

A good poet, says the Epistle, must be a good man, for it is among the offices of a poet to 'inflame grown men to all great virtues'. But 'virtue' is not an indivisible word describing a definitive group of qualities, and in Jonson's time it was the more complicated because it retained something of its radical Latin sense 'that which becomes a man', together with its current sense 'moral excellence'. There is no necessary tension between manliness and goodness, but their relationship is not a stable one, and the art of the Renaissance often explores and dramatises it; Lady Macbeth's taunt, for instance, and Macbeth's response :

> Art thou afeard
> To be the same in thine own act and valour

As thou art in desire?

I dare do all that may become a man;
Who dares do more is none.

When you durst do it, then you were a man.
                    (*Macbeth* i vii 39–41, 46–7, 49)

In a different province of moral experience, Volpone's en-
counter with Celia in the seduction scene is of the same kind.
Celia's despair finds expression in a graphic indictment of
Venetian morality :

Is that, which ever was a cause of life,
Now placed beneath the basest circumstance?
And modesty an exile made, for money? (iii vii 136–8)

Volpone, springing from his bed, offers to despise and to
transcend the bond that weds her to the impotence of Corvino; he proclaims a higher cause of life than her betrayed and
forfeit fidelity :

Ay, in Corvino, and such earth-fed minds,
That never tasted the true heaven of love.
Assure thee, Celia, he that would sell thee,
Only for hope of gain, and that uncertain,
He would have sold his part of paradise
For ready money, had he met a cope-man. (iii vii 139–44)

Because the contempt for the acquisitive merchant is authen-
tic and just, we are the more ready to entertain the elated
assurances of the 'true heaven of love', and to allow the buoy-
ant cadences of the verse to carry speech into song, unresisting.
But so to say is manifestly to yield to the seducer. The seducer's
persuasive arts have their history in Marlowe, in Catullus, and
in the garden of Eden.

   Marlowe's early plays tuned English verse to sound those

astonishing hubristic hyperboles that make it man's virtue to
be a god :

> Christian Merchants that with Russian stems
> Plough up huge furrows in the Caspian sea,
> Shall vail to us, as Lords of all the Lake.

> *Jove* sometimes masked in a Shepherd's weed,
> And by those steps that he hath scal'd the heavens,
> May we become immortal like the Gods.
> (*Tamburlaine*, 1 387–9, 394–6)

Volpone has a different disdain for merchants :

> I use no trade, no venture
> ....expose no ships
> To threat'nings of the furrow-faced sea. (1 i 33, 37–8)

and a different aspiration to Olympus :

> Whilst we, in changèd shapes, act Ovid's tales,
> Thou, like Europa now, and I like Jove,
> Then I like Mars, and thou like Erycine,
> So, of the rest, till we have quite run through
> And wearied all the fables of the gods. (iii vii 221–5)

But in the movement and range of the imagination there is a
significant continuity. Volpone can be represented as indulging the fantasies of a Marlovian hero (for much might be said
too of Faustus and Barabas) in a society of corrupt money
makers, where the merchants 'expose' their ships to danger
but themselves stay home to secure and invest their property –
including their wives. Marlowe's Elizabethan eagerness for
sovereignty over the plenitude of the earth is still finding
expression in Volpone's words to Celia :

> See, behold,
> What thou art queen of; not in expectation,
> As I feed others; but possessed, and crowned.
> (iii vii 188–90)

And Volpone has a contempt comparable with Marlowe's for 'earth-bred minds' and for the 'beggar's virtue' (conscience) that he opposes to his own 'wisdom', but where Marlowe's loves of conquest, sensual satisfaction, and knowledge are heroic :

> And every warrior that is rapt with love,
> Of fame, of valour, and of victory
> Must needs have beauty beat on his conceits.
>   (*Tamburlaine,* I 1961–3)

Volpone's conquests are amorous, his senses look for less aetherial satisfaction, and his knowledge serves for the 'cunning purchase' of his wealth.

While Volpone's vainglory looks back to Marlowe, his lyrical importunity is from Catullus, as Jonson re-creates the celebrated fifth poem (*Vivamus, mea Lesbia, atque amemus*) to convey yet more poignantly the transience of the lovers' opportunities. The prospect of an illicit affair in difficult domestic circumstances is transfigured by the song's rhythm and by its easy disdain of ordinary human values :

> Why should we defer our joys?
> Fame, and rumour are but toys.
> Cannot we delude the eyes
> Of a few poor household spies? (III vii 174–7)

Celia's resistance to Volpone's enticements feels in context like a resistance to the poet's art as well as the seducer's :

> Good sir, these things might move a mind affected
> With such delights; but I, whose innocence
> Is all I can think wealthy, or worth th'enjoying,
> And which once lost, I have nought to lose beyond it,
> Cannot be taken with these sensual baits.
>   (III vii 206–10)

And Jonson is certainly well aware of the strength of the

tradition that Volpone represents, with its sense of virtue closely consonant with virility, and sanctioned in pagan mythology by one of Volpone's patron deities, Jove. But the play encompasses both Volpone's virtue and Celia's, and before the scene ends we are made to see the Circean charm give place to gross violence, with 'lust' (the vice in Celia's view most remote from 'manliness') brutally opposed to frigidity and impotence, Volpone's versions of the rival values.

The more conventional kind of goodness embodied in Celia and Bonario is allowed its modicum of strength and resolution, but it is scarcely efficient in the play. It is enough that the master-knaves destroy themselves through over-weening wit and fantasy; like Marlowe's heroes they are over-reachers, whether in self-exhausting, self-consuming phantasmagoria :

> Our drink shall be preparèd gold, and amber;
> Which we will take, until my roof whirl round
> With the vertigo. . . .

> And I will meet thee, in as many shapes :
> Where we may, so, transfuse our wand'ring souls,
> Out at our lips, and score up sums of pleasures.
>   (III vii 217–19, 233–5)

or in self-entangling, self-betraying conspiracy :

> To make a snare, for mine own neck ! and run
> My head into it, wilfully ! with laughter ! (v xi 1–2)

Volpone's spell, however, continues to testify to a kind of virtue long after it has been seen for what it is. The bounty that he offers Celia is like that which Mammon in *The Alchemist* would bestow upon the whole of mankind, and it is a travesty of Aristotle's 'magnificence' – the virtue that can only be displayed by a man with great resources (material and spiritual).[3] Nietzsche's Zarathustra supplies the vindicating aphorisms :[4]

Your soul striveth insatiably for treasures and jewels because your virtue is ever insatiable in the will to give.

Ye compel all things to come unto you and into you, that they may flow back from your fount as gifts of your love.

But he can also supply the necessary qualification :

But we hold in horror the degenerate mind that saith :
'All for myself !'

Volpone does not, after all, honour and fulfil his role of Magnifico in the Venetian state. The tardy Venetian law does at last discover his weakness and Mosca's :

These possess wealth, as sick men possess fevers,
Which, trulier, may be said to possess them.

(v xii 101–2)

Sir Politic in Venice

The play is so contrived that the episodes of the main plot and the sub-plot seem to belong to the circumambient civilisation. Venice was famed for its mercantile prosperity, its proud resources of gold and treasure, the splendour of its architecture and exuberance of its art, the intensity and ceremony of its public life. Its fame lends resonance to many of the play's local allusions – the Portico to the Procuratia, the Arsenale, and even the Piscaria – and its reputation makes it a probable setting for luxurious living and extravagant fancy; but, as Shakespeare recognises in *The Merchant of Venice*, it is a city of commercial know-how where money can be made by ruthless exploitation.

Thomas Coryat's *Crudities* ('Hastily gobled up in five Moneths travells') is not a source for *Volpone* (it was published in 1611) but, as Herford and Simpson show, it witnesses appropriately to an Englishman's impressions of Venice at the time, and supplies circumstantial glosses on the Venetian scene – from its courtesans to its strappado (see appendix of Analogues and Documents). Coryat, while not always prefer-

ring accuracy to human interest, was a good reporter and
sufficiently experienced in the ways of the world. It may be
that Jonson nevertheless had his eye on Coryat's kind, even (it
has been suggested) upon a specific example, another English
traveller to Venice, Sir Antony Shirley.[5] However this may be,
the presence in the play of Sir Politic and Lady Would-be, and
of Peregrine (whose name means both 'hawk' and 'traveller')
reminds us of a range of self-deluding fantasies that a foolish
Englishman abroad may entertain about foreigners. The Sir
Pol episodes are intricately related to the wit of the play without for an instant losing their disarming simplicity. Primarily
they contribute to the pattern of incidents and judgements
that make the play an exercise in sophistication. A version of
the gull–knave relationship is used to expose the absurd vanity
of an aspirant to the seasoned traveller's brand of knowing-
ness. In Volpone's and Mosca's plot, however, all the gulls
fancy themselves a jump ahead of the others and believe themselves knaves. Sir Pol is from his talk taken for a naïve impostor,
by circumstance supposed a clumsy knave, and finally by
design made a gull. Peregrine is not a knave, but sophistication courts knavery when its first principle is that a man
should not readily be taken in, and that he should be good at
taking in others :

> Well, wise Sir Pol : since you have practised, thus,
> Upon my freshmanship, I'll try your salt-head,
> What proof it is against a counter-plot. (IV iii 22–4)

In Volpone's plot, the gulls are in the last phase taunted in
turn for their failures of 'wisdom' : Corbaccio (beard of
'grave length') is 'over-reached', Corvino ('traded in the
world') is caught like the crow by the fox in the fable, and the
skilled Voltore is left without a 'quirk to avoid gullage'. But
the culpable innocence of Sir Pol is less offensive than the
culpable guilt of the principal gulls; his punishment is corre-
spondingly muted as he and his wife leave the Venetian clime
and put to sea for 'physic'.

The aptness of Peregrine's plot (and Jonson's) was to be nicely demonstrated some hundred and fifty years later when Lord Chesterfield played a similar trick on Montesquieu in Venice.[6] Following an argument about the precedence of French *esprit* and English common sense, Montesquieu returned from a sight-seeing round of Venice to find a badly dressed Frenchman waiting to warn him against meddling in Venetian affairs of state :

> . . . Les Inquisiteurs d'État ont les yeux ouverts sur votre conduite, on vous épie, on suit tous vos pas, on tient note de tous vos projets, on ne doute point que vous n'ecriviez. Je scais de science certaine qu'on doit, peut-être aujourd'huy, peut-etre demain, faire chez vous une visite. Voyez, monsieur, si en effet vous avez écrit, et songez, qu'une ligne innocente, mais mal interprétée, vous coûteroit la vie.

When Chesterfield called a little while later he found that Montesquieu had burnt his papers and made arrangements to leave Venice at three o'clock in the morning.

The Chesterfield story shows that Jonson's wit might alight upon any traveller who displays innocent curiosity about a city and goes about taking notes, but also that the aspirant to political wisdom is particularly vulnerable. It suggests too a generality of application that discounts attempts to turn Sir Pol into a specific caricature. The most canvassed figure has been Sir Henry Wotton, British ambassador to Venice for most of the period 1604 to 1624, but the circumstance would mainly ensure that Wotton (who was a friend of Jonson's) would have been among the play's most amused spectators – he had more reason than most to know the extent and boundaries of Venetian political intrigue. It is not improbable, however, that Jonson did enjoy the occasional satirical glance at an acquaintance or public figure including perhaps Sir Antony Shirley, and even Wotton.[7] But there is a great difference between opportunities casually taken and systematic caricature. . . .

'PURITY OF LANGUAGE'

Something has already been said, and much implied, about Jonson's poetic language. It might be seen as bringing Marlowe's energies under Horatian rule – a technical feat that corresponds to Jonson's readiness to subdue his sympathy with Renaissance aspirations to his respect for classical canons of good sense.

The phrase 'purity of language' may remind us that among the many pointless tensions expressed in the notorious war of the theatres, there is one that had a distinct significance and continues to animate the Epistle prefixed to *Volpone* : it is between those poets who are merely 'naturals' and 'contemners of all helps and arts', and those 'true artificers' whose 'divine instinct' is tempered by study and by labour. In its cruder forms the distinction looks like a simple one between the vulgar poet and the learned; but it is capable in Jonson's hands of much refinement, under the general maxim (from a Greek fragment) that 'without art, nature can never be perfect; and without nature art can claim no being'.[8]

The Epistle expresses disgust for those who write 'with such impropriety of phrase, such dearth of sense, so bold prolepses, so racked metaphors'. Jonson was probably thinking of Marston (much of the Epistle repeats material from the Apologetical Dialogue appended to the *Poetaster*) but he could also be anticipating Dr Johnson's Augustan judgement upon Shakespeare's style – 'ungrammatical, perplexed and obscure'.

Jonson's dramatic poetry is often graphic where Shakespeare's is evocative, clear where Shakespeare is elusive, explicit where Shakespeare is mysterious. Volpone, for example, characterises the ruthlessness of society with clarity, gaiety and rigour :

> I use no trade, no venture;
> I wound no earth with ploughshares; fat no beasts
> To feed the shambles; have no mills for iron,
> Oil, corn, or men, to grind 'em into powder. (I i 33–6)

There are metaphors here – the wounded earth, the feeding of
the slaughterhouse and the grinding of men to powder, but
they are so immediately related to the phenomena they touch
that they strike with almost literal force; it would not be surprising if Jonson meant the 'men' to be raw material for bone-
meal or mummia. When Shakespeare's Pericles expresses his
sense of human tyranny in Antioch, the boundaries of the
metaphor are much less clear :

> .The blind mole casts
> Copp'd hills towards heaven, to tell the earth is
> throng'd
> By man's oppression; and the poor worm doth die for't.
> (*Pericles,* 1 i 99–101)

Jonson could not have invented a metaphor whose implications are so hard to contain; the mole seems to have been
driven from the earth's surface and therefore blinded 'by man's
oppression', its hills are a signal of protest towards heaven –
and yet it too is an oppressor, a killer of worms. Shakespeare's
metaphor obscurely suggests that oppression, protest and
suffering are laws of the natural and human worlds. Jonson
might well have found it 'racked'.

Other comparisons might be made with Shakespeare to
similar purpose, between Isabella's resistance to Angelo in
Measure for Measure and Celia's to Volpone, or between the
Duke's contempt of life in that play (III i 5–40) and Volpone's
(1 iv 144–59), and almost every page of Shakespeare offers
metaphors that Jonson would have thought indecorous. But
decorum in Jonson's art is not merely a principle by which
words are judged acceptable to polite taste; it is an energising
force requiring that every word should meet in context the
demands made upon it :

For a man to write well, there are required three necessaries –
to read the best authors, observe the best speakers, and much
exercise of his own style. In style, to consider what ought to be

written, and after what manner, he must first think and excogi-
tate his matter, then choose his words, and examine the weight
of either. Then take care, in placing and ranking both matter
and words, that the composition be comely; and to do this with
diligence and often. No matter how slow the style be at first, so it
be laboured and accurate; seek the best, and be not glad of the
forward conceits, or first words, that offer themselves to us; but
judge of what we invent, and order what we approve. Repeat
often what we have formerly written; which beside that it helps
the consequence, and makes the juncture better, it quickens the
heat of imagination, that often cools in the time of setting down,
and gives it new strength, as if it grew lustier by going back.
                                    (*Timber or Discoveries,* cxv)

Jonson's labour and accuracy confer in the end an astonishing
swiftness and power of movement. Voltore's speeches to the
Scrutineo, for example, are totally composed of forensic skill
and forensic pathos; the rhetoric is absolute, there are no
expressions or cadences that do not wholly belong to it, for
the 'invention' has been scrupulously judged :

> And, as for them, I will conclude with this,
> That vicious persons when they are hot, and fleshed
> In impious acts, their constancy abounds :
> Damned deeds are done with greatest confidence.
>   (IV vi 50–3)

The staggering check of the closing thought perfects Voltore's
malicious fantasy. It is one of the delights of Jonson's art that
fantasies are splendidly articulated, whether Voltore's of
righteous indignation, or Volpone's of sensual prodigality and
golden dissolution :

> See, here, a rope of pearl; and each, more orient
> Than that the brave Egyptian queen caroused :
> Dissolve, and drink 'em. See, a carbuncle,
> May put out both the eyes of our St Mark;
> A diamant, would have bought Lollia Paulina,
> When she came in, like star-light, hid with jewels,
> That were the spoils of provinces . . . (III vii 191–7)

The allusions to Cleopatra and to Lollia Paulina exemplify the contribution that creative imitation makes to the play, for Jonson borrows both notions of heroic indulgence from Pliny (*Natural History,* IX lviii). But the sail of the verse (reminding us that Jonson honoured Marlowe for his mighty line) confers a grace and insolence upon 'the spoils of provinces' not to be found in the matter-of-fact of Pliny's prose, although the phrase itself is translated precisely (*provinciarum scilicet spoliis pratae*).

The arts of imitation and allusion are not, as Jonson uses them, parasitic – they renew the life of the imagination both in the past and in the present. As he himself puts it, the first requisites in a poet are 'natural wit' and 'exercise' while the third is :

imitation, *imitatio,* to be able to convert the substance or riches of another poet to his own use. To make choice of one excellent man above the rest, and so to follow him till he grow very he, or so like him as the copy may be mistaken for the principal. Not as a creature that swallows what it takes in, crude, raw, or undigested; but that feeds with an appetite, and hath a stomach to concoct, divide, and turn all into nourishment.
(*Timber or Discoveries,* CXXX)

With this in mind one may browse with greater satisfaction in the literature that the play calls into service, finding (for example) that the voices of Horace and Juvenal can be heard the more clearly because Jonson had attended to them.

'THE MANNERS OF THE SCENE'

Jonson studied the theatrical art of the past as exactingly as he did its poetry, but both as playwright and as poet he made contributions decisively new. We have noticed that the conventions of Classical Comedy meet those of Tudor Interlude, and, it may be added, of the *commedia dell'arte*; brought to

Jonson's forge and file (his favourite metaphors for the poet's craft) they are fashioned into a fabric at once massively and sensitively wrought. The debt to classical comedy has been sufficiently indicated – the gull-and-knave structure, the antics of the witty parasite, the satire upon professional men, the legacy-hunting motif, all have their beginnings in Greece and Rome. Medieval and Tudor plays, on the other hand, supply something of the moral design; the Devil and his acolytes (Dissimulation, Ambidexter, Hypocrisy) are still recognisable in Volpone and Mosca, while Volpone as seducer and tempter might be seen as in a different line from Satan in Eden or in the wilderness. Thus the spectacle of Mosca exposing at once the physical and the moral frailties of Corbaccio in Act I, scene iv, might have satisfied a Roman audience or a medieval English one.

The Venetian scene made it appropriate if not prerequisite that the play should pay its respects to the *commedia dell'arte*. In part indeed it offers the *commedia* documentary recognition, as when Corvino calls Volpone's Scoto 'Flaminio', Celia 'Franciscina' and himself by the name of the stock cuckold 'Pantalone di Besogniosi', or when Volpone makes Nano his Zany and styles him Zan Fritada. More significantly, however, Italian comedy styles leave their mark on the manners and mood of the play as a whole. The play is not an improvisation but it often wins the best effects associated with improvisation; it is not a masked comedy (to name another Italian type) but it often works in the same way; it has no pantomime, but acted in silence its spectacle might still be made entertaining and significant.

The qualities of the play as emblematic spectacle owe much to its assimilation of beast fable, from Aesop or from popular lore : [9]

> vulture, kite,
> Raven, and gor-crow, all my birds of prey,
> That think me turning carcass, now they come.
> I am not for 'em yet.

> .... not a fox
> Stretched on the earth, with fine delusive sleights,
> Mocking a gaping crow? (1 ii 88–91, 94–6)

Sir Pol is a chattering parrot, and so is his wife; Peregrine is a pilgrim hawk, and the hawk (by one of Jonson's epigrams) 'pursues the truth, strikes at ignorance, and makes the fool its quarry'. Ape, ass, crocodile, mule, gennet, wolf and chameleon all have a place in Jonson's vision of human predatoriness and folly, and assist in the impression that men readily lapse into beasts and lose their distinctive manliness or virtue. Volpone's attendant grotesques – dwarf, eunuch and hermaphrodite – take on the same significance, like the rout of Comus.

Dominating the play, however, is the fox's capacity to deceive the bird of prey; it is related to the skill by which a man imposes himself on another by flattery, and therefore to all modes of deception and false appearance. There is wit in deception and there is a glory in changing shapes. Again the spectacle does much to sustain the sequence of metamorphoses – from the doctoring of Volpone's face on the stage to the prodding of the vast tortoise-shell that conceals Sir Politic. Characters and situations change appearance with exhilarating and bewildering pace until all human identities are disfigured, all relationships confused, and the truth made inaccessible to reason and law. Final disintegration threatens when the fourth Avocatore moves to match Mosca with his daughter; but within moments Venetian order is resumed with the judicial cry 'Disrobe that parasite!' The conventional comic servant discarding his master's robes becomes the symbol of Venice restored to its 'honoured fathers' – at least for the time being.

'GENTLE AFFECTIONS'

It may seem among the more surprising claims that Jonson makes for the comic poet that he should 'stir up gentle affections', for *Volpone* has not infrequently been thought sombre, grim and even 'cynical'.[10] 'Cynical' has become a carelessly used word of imprecise meaning, but since Crates (a true Cynic) is mentioned in Mosca's entertainment, it is worth remarking that the play at large cannot be regarded as cynical in the strict sense, for it does not recommend that man discard his civilised pretensions and return to his animal simplicity. On the contrary, it commends the virtues – of wit, generosity and vitality – that Volpone and Mosca both embody and pervert; it persuades us that fine energies and impulses are running into strange forms or running to waste; that reverence, bounty, love and ceremony exist still and that the English language is ripe for their expression when they return to their proper shapes. 'Gentle affections' in Jonson's critical dialect does not mean merely 'tenderness of regard' but, more fully, 'noble dispositions of feeling', and these are stirred up less by our immediate sympathy with Bonario and Celia (although that is surely present) than by our freshened insight into the nature of imposture and the precariousness of civilised values. Whoever jeers at that last commonplace, stands in Mosca's shoes.

SOURCE : Introduction to *Volpone* (1968) pp. ix–xix, xxii–xxvii

NOTES

1. For some developments of the devil and the diabolical villain in medieval and Tudor drama, see Bernard Spivack, *Shakespeare and the Allegory of Evil* (1958).

2. See, for example, *Lusty Juventus, The Disobedient Child, Cambyses, The Three Lords and Three Ladies of London,* in W. C. Hazlitt (ed.), *Dodsley's Old English Plays,* 15 vols (1874).

3. See Aristotle, *Nicomachean Ethics,* IV ii.

4. *Thus Spake Zarathustra,* trans. Tille and Bozman, Everyman's Library (1933) pp. 66–7. A comprehensive history of ideas of *Virtù, Virtus* and Virtue could reasonably begin with Zoroaster; but the relevant figures for Jonson are Marlowe and (perhaps) Machiavelli.

5. The first version of Shirley's book was : *A True Report of Sir Antonie Shirlies Journey overland to Venice, from thence to Seaton, Antioch, Aleppo, and Babilon, and so to Casbine in Persia.* It was published in 1600 but suppressed as unlicensed. A version by William Parry was authorised and published in 1601.

6. The story is fully reported by Diderot in a letter to Sophie Volland, 5 September 1762. See Herford and Simpson, IX 728.

7. The claim that Wotton is specifically caricatured is fully developed by J. D. Rea in his edition of the play (1919). For the other possibilities see Herford and Simpson, IX 681–2; like Gifford, however, they would rule out Sir Thomas Sutton the founder of the Charterhouse, who was said by Aubrey to be a model for Volpone himself.

8. See *Timber or Discoveries,* section CXXX.

9. See J. A. Barish, 'The Double Plot in *Volpone*', *Modern Philology,* LI (1953) 83–92; reprinted in *Ben Jonson* (Twentieth Century Views), ed. Barish (1963). See also D. A. Scheve, 'Traditional Fox Lore and Volpone', *Review of English Studies* (1950) and H. Levin, 'Jonson's Metempsychosis', *Philological Quarterly* (1943).

10. See Edmund Wilson, 'Morose Ben Jonson', in *Ben Jonson* (Twentieth Century Views), ed. Barish. Wilson is not strictly concerned with Jonson's cynicism but his 'anal eroticism', which he related to the avarice and sadism of Jonson's heroes and to the pedantry and arrogance of Jonson himself.

PART THREE

Reviews of Productions, 1930 to the Present

ANON. : *Volpone* at the Festival Theatre, Cambridge

Volpone	Roy Malcolm
Mosca	Frederick Piper
Voltore	Peter Hannen
Corbaccio	Dennis Robertson
Corvino	Robert Donat
Bonario	Charles Carter
Sir Politick Would-Bee	Philip Thornley
Peregrine	Evan John
Lady Would-Bee	Margery Phipps-Walker
Celia	Winifred Thompson

It is the characteristic, one might almost say the function, of a
fox to be cunning. It is at any rate the function of Ben Jonson's
Fox to be cunning, although his creator allows him to be
caught in the end. Herein is perhaps the only true psychological touch in the whole play : mischief living by its wits is apt to
overreach itself in real life as in a comedy where there are no
human types but only personified vices and virtues. Volpone is
neither man nor fox : his passions are not human, for his
avarice has no power and his lust no heat – both are mere
excuses for mischief; neither are they foxy, for the fox presumably has a taste for chicken as well as for spoiling hen-roosts.
Jonson, however, is only pretending to draw a psychological
type, just as he only pretends to ask us to be edified by the
moral to his riotous tale. At any rate those responsible for the
present revival at the Festival Theatre are quite clear that
the instruments of justice are not intended to command our
respect. Indeed, they go too far in reducing the grave government of Venice to roaring, almost to knock-about, farce.

But it is not the theme – unscrupulous cunning *versus* virtuous stupidity – that we are asked to consider, but the variations upon it. And these were played with admirable briskness
and gusto. Scene followed scene without a break, and if the
Elizabethan magniloquence was poured off the tongue with

the speed and intimacy of Shavian dialogue, it all added to the exhilaration of this exuberant comedy of intrigue.

Mr Evan John's production aimed at speed and gaiety, and achieved it consistently. Verisimilitude was strained beyond what farce allows in the court scene and in the portrayal of Voltore, who was perhaps just too gentlemanly in his manners for this particular advocate. The three birds of prey were admirably differentiated by their voices, and each was a neat study. In this matter of voice praise must especially be given to Mr Frederick Piper, the suave parasite, who bears the main burden of the play. Mosca, too, is neither man nor monster, but his confidence tricks were perfectly plausible in Mr Piper's hands. Mr Roy Malcolm played the fox himself with the light touch on which Jonson relied to win the applause for which he asks at the end in order to extricate himself from the muddle of psychology and morals in which he has lightly involved himself in creating his comic situations. Miss Winifred Thompson, a newcomer to the company, looked charming and pathetic, as she was meant to, and Miss Phipps-Walker looked absurd and made herself as *gauche* as she was meant to. Her husband, however, was not as articulate as he should have been.

Volpone was revived a few years ago at Cambridge by the Marlowe Society; it has since been done in London, Paris, and Oslo. The French admired its tidiness as compared with Shakespeare, and the consistency of its plot. We are apt to see these qualities in a different light and cannot overlook its narrowness and limitations. But we can admire its gaiety, and nowhere better than at one of the universities where 300 years ago it won its earliest successes.

(from *The Times*, 28 April 1930)

ANON.: *Volpone* at the Malvern Festival

Prologue	Elspeth Duxbury
Volpone	Wilfrid Lawson
Mosca	Stephen Murray

Voltore	Arthur Ridley
Corbaccio	Charles Victor
Corvino	Cecil Trouncer
Bonario	Donald Eccles
Sir Politick Wouldbe	Clifford Marle
Peregrine	Harold Chapin
Androgyno	Tony Halfpenny
1st Officer	Derek Prentice
2nd Officer	Norris Stayton
1st Advocate	Alan Robinson
2nd Advocate	Richard Lonscale
Notario	Reginald Gatty
Lady Wouldbe	Eileen Beldon
Celia	Curigwen Lewis
1st Saffa	Lee Fox
2nd Saffa	David Bird
Waiting Woman	Mavis Walker

In his own day Ben Jonson was an author for the few, and the English public continues, in spite of the illuminating Phoenix revival of 1923, to be estranged by the formalism of *Volpone*. Good French critics tell us that Molière might have been proud to sign this particular comedy, but we have not the French love for tidiness and simplification. We are apt to shrink from a satirist determined 'to anathematize every nerve and sinew of the time's deformity', and there is a tendency in revivals which are not first rate to emphasize the farcical portions of the play, and to abate the full force of the satire by denying to Volpone that all-pervasive intelligence which adds horror to his triumphant wickedness.

At Malvern we learn among other things how to endure our own satirical masterpieces, and there was no abatement of satire in to-night's production. Briskly as the crow, the raven, and the vulture were drawn by the clever fly into Volpone's traps, Mr Wilfrid Lawson saw to it that the farce was dominated by the sulphurous horror of an intelligence immensely alert in the pursuit of evil, and there was terror as well as laughter in the play. There was nothing of the cackling dotard about this Volpone. A fox in his flaming make-up, he was in

essence a man whose cruelty and cunning and intellect had
grown with age and were ripe for mischief on the grand scale.
Mr Lawson's performance had breadth and drive, and all the
other performances were nicely adjusted to its movement.

Volpone sets the producer who would do it full justice a
delicate problem in timing. Its farce, surely no less brilliant
than that of *The Alchemist* or *The Silent Woman*, requires to
be taken with extreme rapidity, and no actor can establish
Volpone's intellect, if he is rushed through verse whose polish
is the secret of its power. Mr Herbert Prentice had successfully
arranged that there should be two tempos running through
the performance, and Mr Stephen Murray, besides making
the confidence trick of Mosca perfectly plausible, skilfully
related these two tempos, helping Mr Lawson to accept Volpone's richness of imagery and sultry splendour of thought,
and leading the preposterous legacy-hunters a swift, exuberant
dance. These three parts were played variously and well by
Mr Cecil Trouncer, Mr Charles Victor, and Mr Arthur
Ridley; and though women have but limited uses in Jonson's
theatre, Miss Eileen Beldon as the petulant, talkative Lady
Wouldbe, and Miss Curigwen Lewis as the innocent and
much injured Celia ornamented a production which may
safely be called first rate.

(from *The Times*, 31 July 1935)

DESMOND MACCARTHY : *Volpone* Revived

O, the refreshment of hearing stage-characters whose speech
is worth listening to! The language of our contemporary
stage is insipid, skimpy, trivial; there is no joy, no exhilaration
in it, seldom even colloquial hard hitting. Pick up an averagely
good modern play and its texture is largely composed of lines
like, 'Let me make you a piece of toast', while the fantastic
genius of man's love for woman is often reduced in them to a
cry of 'Darling' and the spectacle of a squeezed kiss. The

cinema can do that. As far as the eye is concerned, the Cinema
can do everything and more than the Stage can do, and moreover it can tell a story with a far wider sweep. It can do all
save move us profoundly through the ear; so intimate is that
connection between the bodily presence of an actor and the
words he speaks. Its formidable rivalry will in the end compel
the dramatist to make wit, vigour, beauty of speech once more
the substance of his art as it was before elaborate scenery was
invented.

It was the spirited revival of *Volpone* at the Westminster
Theatre that inspired these general reflections, which may
have visited others, too, after they had chewed the cud of their
delight.

The production is better than my recollection of the
Phoenix Society's performance in 1921, though it is seldom
fair to compare impressions of ancient date with those that are
both fresh and favourable. I remember that Mr Holloway as
Volpone struck me then as particularly good; but I cannot
believe he equalled the performance of Mr Donald Wolfit.
Perhaps he did, but the impassioned gestures, gloating frenzy
and sardonic laughter of the latter are far too vividly before
me to permit me to credit that, though I am quite sure that
Mr Alan Wheatley's Mosca, whose airy agility and whispering
mephisto-gaiety were truly remarkable, excelled the merely
passable (as I recall it) interpretation of Mr Ion Swinley. His
elocution will no doubt improve in subtle finish as the run goes
on, but it could hardly be better than it was on the first night
in the soliloquy, 'I fear, I shall begin to grow in love with my
dear self', which ends in that glorious definition of 'the true
parasite', or when, ceasing suddenly to be an adoring comrade
in iniquity, Mosca resolves to devour brother 'fox'. At first I
feared Mr Wheatley would prove to be an over-mannered
Mosca, and I still think he should in the first scene be less of an
attitudinising sprite; but later on his gusto captured me completely. He might, however, make up his face to disguise a little
its natural pleasantness, and thus remind us less of a young

tennis-player; a touch of paint to the corners of his mouth
might do it. Both Mr Wheatley and Mr Wolfit (and here they
were no doubt abetted by the producer) seized on the essential
aspect of their parts: Volpone and Mosca are self-delighting
artists in iniquity. That note is struck at the opening of the play
when Volpone says he glories even

> More in cunning purchase of my wealth
> Than in the glad possession.

It is repeated again and again. It is this impulse in them both
which, even after they have attained their ends, makes them
over-shoot themselves magnificently in iniquity. Risks are their
delight. In the end they are caught through putting the finish-
ing touches to that artistry. The spirit of Volpone and Mosca
pervades the whole play; it gives to Jonson's sardonic humour
its peculiar edge. The production brought that out. Mr
MacOwan made some cuts, but if there was loss there was also
gain in his omitting those absurd English innocents Sir Politik
Would-Be and his wife who strayed into this Venetian world
of bottomless iniquity. It is a sad loss but it pulls the action
closer together. I have only one general criticism. The first part
goes splendidly, but after the one interval the production is
rather ragged. The first trial scene and the street scene in which
Volpone mocks his victims, want attention. Mr Dignam, whose
Voltore is excellent, was inaudible when he first appeared as
advocate before the owl-like judges, at least while his back was
turned to us and the cries of the accused and innocent Celia
hardly had their full effect. The triumphant moments of the
performance were Volpone's scene when disguised as a
mountebank-vendor of patent medicine (Mr Wolfit had an
inspiration in delivering that marvellous patter with a slight
American accent), and when Volpone woos the horrified
Celia in that splendid tempest of imaginative lust, where
gleams from Catullus mingle with the gorgeous hyperboles of
the Renaissance. Ah, it was good!

The world of Ben Jonson's comedy reminds me more of Balzac's *Comédie Humaine* than any other. The worlds of both writers are a phantasmagoria of monomaniacs, crammed to the muzzle with will and appetite, plaguing each other, devouring 'conies' and torturing feeble 'angels' on his or her occasional appearance among them. And the demiurges of these two worlds resemble each other in prodigious robustness and in being imaginators rather than observers, despite the circumstantial detail with which their pictures are packed. They resemble each other also in their Rabelaisian effervescence, and, above all in their hearty, though with the Elizabethan somewhat scornful, sympathy with the resourcefulness and courage of the vicious. Both also endow the vicious with such exuberant energy of intellect that we cannot but delight in their misdirected zest. 'The Fox' is, at any rate, lion-throated.

Elizabethan London and nineteenth-century Paris were, to both, places not unlike Hell, but one suspects neither would have been happy elsewhere. Hell was so gloriously entertaining to them both, but Jonson had over Balzac one advantage; his thick-skinned fortitude had behind it the support of a creed which leaves the mind free, if it chooses, to see without despair mankind as desperately wicked. A robust, tough-minded Catholic can afford to envisage human nature's vileness with scornful and possibly outrageous gaiety. Jonson's contempt for private enterprise in other-world consolations such as Balzac indulged in – Swedenborgianism, spiritualism, animal magnetism and what not – will be summary and emphatic.

It was Swinburne who remarked that Ben Jonson was a Titan, a son of earth, and that there was nothing of Olympus about him. Ben boasted he was a good hater, a good fighter and a master of his craft, and he was, superbly, all the three. The classic criticism of his work is to say that his characters are personifications of 'humours' or passions rather than complete human beings. But every dramatist or novelist (Dickens for example) who has drawn human beings with hard outline may

be so described : Tartuffe is no more a complete man than
Volpone; and in Volpone, as Swinburne said, there is that
'life-blood which can only be infused by the sympathetic faith
of the creator in his creature – the breath which animates
every word, even if that word be not the very best word that
might have been found, with the vital impulse of infallible
imagination'. Mr Eliot in his admirable essay on Ben Jonson
has gone further into this. He agrees with Mr Gregory Smith
that Falstaff and a score of Shakespeare's characters have a
'third dimension' and that Jonson's have not. 'This will mean,
not that Shakespeare's spring from feelings or imagination and
Jonson's from his intellect or invention, they have equally an
emotional source; but that Shakespeare's represent a more
complex tissue of feelings and desires as well as a more supple,
a more susceptible temperament.' He concludes that Jonson's
characters are not less 'alive', but that the world in which they
live is smaller. I prefer to put it this way : Jonson's characters
when you think of them apart from the setting in which they
appear are less complex and complete. It is not his world that
is small. That world is fiery, vital and various, full of glaring
contrasts, bustle, cruelty and laughter. It dazzles, entertains,
but it scorches. All the characters in *Volpone*, with the exception of the insipidly meek wife of the ruffian Corvino (Miss
Kempson looked and moved in character at any rate) and the
colourless son of Corbaccio, are one and all what Carlyle would
have called 'unspeakably unexemplary mortals'. This was well
brought out on the stage of the Westminster Theatre, where
we were not spared the full horror of Corvino's scene with
Celia. His bull-like brutality was well suggested by Mr Raymond Lovell, and this is important because the zest of the
whole play lies in seeing him tricked like a bull in the arena by
that agile pair of matadors, Volpone and Mosca; he and the
whole crew of crazy Chrysophilites, mad after gold. The senile
feebleness of Corbaccio is a contrast to such vigorous baseness,
but I am not sure that in marking that contrast Mr Lathbury
was not permitted to put into his part a dash too much of

pitiably laughable idiocy. *Volpone* is comedy that hovers on
the border of tragedy (Jonson wrote it after *Sejanus*, a tragic
study in parasitism), and to keep it in the key of comedy the
last scene, when punishments are distributed all round, must
not be played too heavily. True, Jonson himself was particularly proud of having insisted on the triumph of justice; but
the producer was right in avoiding a too rhadamanthine note
at the close – at least for modern audiences. He has made the
Court itself grotesque. *Volpone* is a prodigious masterpiece,
and while you sit in the Westminster Theatre you will feel it.

Only the gambols of the eunuch, the hermaphrodite and
the dwarf will miss their mark; not, I think, because the best
is not made of them, but because in one respect human nature
has improved; physical deformity no longer seems in itself
extremely funny to men. It did so till even well on into the
eighteenth century, at any rate, among the rougher sort. There
are few pages in literature which suggest 'progress' more definitely to me than that in which the old dropsical, helpless
Fielding takes for granted in his *Voyage to Lisbon* that he
should have had to endure for some hours the jeers and laughter of the riverside crowd before embarking. No philosopher,
now, would define, like Hobbes, the *essence* of laughter as a
joyful feeling 'so am not I'.

(from *New Statesman*, 29 January 1938)

JAMES AGATE : from *The Amazing Theatre*

De gustibus and so on. Speaking for myself, I had as lief see a
comedy by Ben Jonson as any by Shakespeare. Perhaps liefer,
though the unfamiliarity of the one and the over-familiarity of
the other may have something to do with it. But then I would
sooner live surrounded by Hogarths than by Watteaus, since
to me the English painter, despite the ugliness of his subject, is
warm and alive, while the Frenchman, despite the elegance of
his, is cold and not so alive. And there the analogy must end,

since, if we take Hazlitt as our mentor, Shakespeare's humour 'bubbles, sparkles, and finds its way in all directions, like a natural spring', whereas Jonson's 'is, as it were, confined in a leaden cistern, where it stagnates and corrupts'.

Still holding each to his own taste, I submit that it is possible to prove Hazlitt all wrong about this play. Consider Volpone's speech, which begins : 'Why droops my Celia?' and goes on :

> See, behold
> What thou art queen of; not in expectation,
> As I feed others, but possess'd and crown'd.
> See here a rope of pearl, and each more orient
> Than that the brave Ægyptian Queen carous'd;
> Dissolve, and drink them. See, a carbuncle,
> May put out both the eyes of our St Mark;
> A diamond would have bought Lollia Paulina,
> When she came in like star-light, hid with jewels
> That were the spoils of provinces; take these,
> And wear, and lose 'em. Yet remains an ear-ring
> To purchase them again, and this whole state.

Look over the exquisite passage beginning :

> Thy baths shall be the juice of July flowers,
> Spirit of roses, and of violets,
> The milk of unicorns, and panthers' breath,
> Gather'd in bags, and mix'd with Cretan wines;
> Our drink shall be prepared gold and amber,
> Which we will take until my roof whirl round
> With the vertigo. . . .

It seems to me that Faustus himself would not have disdained

> When she came in like star-light, hid with jewels,

and that Perdita would have been at home with

> The milk of unicorns, and panthers' breath.

Yet Hazlitt's adjectives for Jonson's verse are 'dry', 'literal', and 'meagre'. The point is that the great essayist, like every other playgoer who ever lived except me, is a sentimentalist and will take no pleasure in a play unless he can find in it some nice person with whom to identify himself :

> There is almost a total want of variety, fancy, relief, and of those delightful transitions which abound, for instance, in Shakespeare's tragi-comedy. In Ben Jonson, we find ourselves generally in low company, and we see no hope of getting out of it. He is like a person who fastens upon a disagreeable subject and cannot be persuaded to leave it.

But, in heaven's name, who wants anybody to leave a disagreeable subject if he can make it more interesting than an agreeable one?

Hazlitt thinks that the trouble with Jonson's comedy is that it is mean. This is palpably absurd, since one of the concomitants of meanness is littleness. I would rather call Jonson's comedy riotous and his humanity of the cartoonist's size. Volpone bestrides his world as Valmont bestrides that of Choderlos de Laclos and Vautrin Balzac's; the lesser rogues have still something Michael-Angelesque about them. Hazlitt denies Jonson gusto because he does not like the things the gusto is about, and because, like any other sentimental playgoer, he wants to warm himself at the spectacle of good men routing bad ones, and sees no fun in villains destroying one another. It dismays him that Volpone should be undone by Mosca, and that both should be punished by a bench of zanies. He dislikes the caperings of Volpone's minions because he would not have them behaving so in his own drawing-room.

To sum up, Hazlitt desires that comedy should make him think better of mankind, whereas I demand of comedy only that it shall make me think. So long as the comic dramatist is writing well and not ill I am indifferent whether his characters behave well or ill. 'Jonson had a keen sense of what was true and false, but not of the difference between the agreeable and disagreeable.' This proves my case against any playgoer demanding more that the things shown him in the theatre shall be agreeable than that they shall be true. Judged by the

West-End standard of popularity, *Volpone* is 'cross-grained', 'prolix', 'improbable', 'repulsive', and even 'revolting'. Yet in a critic as good as Hazlitt the critical habit dies hard, and he cannot help saying that 'this best play' of Jonson 'is written *con amore*'. This sentence clinches my argument. It is all very well for its author to recover by saying that the play 'is made up of cheats and dupes, and the author is at home among them'. The gibe comes too late; the *piece is written con amore*! So saying, Hazlitt puts himself in the position of a batsman who should at one and the same time hit the ball twice, obstruct the field, and tread on his wicket. The play is written *con amore*, and not merely to supply a demand, please a manager, or create a part for Miss Promptworthy!

In the revival at the Westminster the same boundless spirit is at large. Mr Michael MacOwan has given their heads to Mr Peter Goffin and Mr Edmund Rubbra, and, thus encouraged, Mr Goffin responds with a gold-encrusted Jacobean tableau which Mr Sickert ought to paint, and Mr Rubbra, meeting his producer more than half-way, conjures from the throats of clarinet, oboe, and bassoon a concourse of sounds even more obnoxious, in a Hazlittean sense, than the scenes they accompany. This spirit extends to the players. Mr Donald Wolfit makes a splendid mouthful of the Fox; he is right in presence, and he speaks the verse as the actor of Jonson's day must have spoken it. There must be many ways of playing Mosca, and Mr Alan Wheatley has chosen to be a silk thread among the hempen villainy. Mr Mark Dignam is the vulture-lawyer of all time, and Mr Stanley Lathbury is a most pointed, witless crow. As I wish this revival immensely well, and as at this point the praise of the acting must get thinner, I stop.

(from *The Amazing Theatre*, 1938, pp. 68–71)

T. C. WORSLEY : *The Fox*

It is a pleasure to be discussing Stratford again in terms predominantly of praise: to be arguing with them, so to speak, over interpretations, but to feel that they are arguing back, no longer from weakness but from strength. For the *Volpone* which Mr George Devine has produced, with Sir Ralph Richardson as the Fox and Mr Anthony Quayle as Mosca, is, granted the general conception, a solid success. It is well mounted, excellently staged and strongly acted almost throughout. On the other hand, the play does seem to me to have been softened and prettified. That savage streak which ought to curdle the laughter in our throats is missing. The note is antic rather than acid. But this at least fits in with – it may well have been dictated by – Sir Ralph's over-gentle handling of the main part.

Power and fire seem for the moment to have deserted this actor, but his comedy touch is still sure. So he does not even attempt that relish in sheer wickedness which Mr Donald Wolfit brings out in the part. He is not a monster practising evil on the evil; he is a rather crazy eccentric devising practical jokes, which are played with a good-humoured self-satisfaction, on some gulls who deserve nothing better. At first it seems, as a reading, to work; for Sir Ralph extracts all the possible quiet comedy from it (producing, for instance, an astonishing range of interjectory noises by the way). But as the underlying violence of the play comes through, this mildness ceases to satisfy; it doesn't match with the rapacity all about it, nor with those three terrible pets of his, and the rape scene seems wildly out of keeping. (What a curious piece of production there was in the middle of this scene, by the way, where Sir Ralph lay moaning on the ground, while Celia knelt over his prostrate body begging him to let her go.)

One obvious result of toning down the Fox is that it opens the door dangerously wide for the play-stealing part of Mosca. Lucky, then, that Mr Quayle is there in this role. Too loyal an actor to over-play but quite big enough a one to plug the gaps. His Mosca is a delightful creation, oily, sly and smooth, a Zeal-of-the-Lord Puritan with a touch of Uriah Heep, with

drooping back, rubbing hands, meek knees and a most insinu-
ating voice – and consistently played from the inside.

Mr Devine has worked with a promising new designer, Mr
Malcolm Pride, to give us a most lively production. In his
recent highly technical but very fascinating book, *Changeable
Scenery* (Faber, 1952), Mr Richard Southern reminds us that
at its first introduction in the Jacobean Court Masques the
moving of scenes was intended to take place before our eyes;
the mechanical marvels were an important part of the show.
Mr Devine and his designer restore this usage in full measure;
and a present-day audience enjoys as much as its predecessors
watching Volpone's bedroom sinking slowly down, while a
piazza, complete with foreground beggars and background
canal, slides in to take its place.

It was Jonson, Mr Southern also recalls, who led the opposition to this scenic theatre when the marvels tended to oust
the words. But he could not raise any objection on this score to
Mr Devine's production, where the action is crystal clear and
the text sacred. Too sacred, in my own view. There is a good
deal that is tedious in this comedy and which might well be cut.
I could cheerfully sacrifice much of the sub-plot centred round
Sir Politic Would-be, even at the cost to Mr Michael Hor-
dern's clever performance. Mr Devine's style runs to the kind
of detail which I personally find very trying, an excess of
miming from the mute characters, the largest crop of false
noses since Mr John Burrell produced at the Old Vic, and
rows of whinnying Ancients. But they do remain decorative
additions and don't spoil the faithful but inventive staging of
the main mass.

I have space to mention only three of the supporting per-
formances, Mr Michael Bate's amusing dotard, Mr Raymond
Westwell's advocate with nice professional frills, and Miss
Siobhan McKenna's quiet (at last!) beauty as Celia.

(from *New Statesman*, 26 July 1952)

HENRY POPKIN: *Volpone* in Sir Tyrone's Best Style

In its second season, the Tyrone Guthrie Theatre continues to entrench itself at Minneapolis. This year's four plays are *Henry V*, Shaw's *Saint Joan*, Ben Jonson's *Volpone,* and Tennessee Williams's *The Glass Menagerie.* As in most such festivals, it was not difficult to isolate the one best production, Sir Tyrone Guthrie's of *Volpone.*

This *Volpone* is so boldly stylized in its visual aspects, in the actors' make-up, their gait, and their costumes (inventively designed by Tanya Moiseiwitsch), that it could make most of its points in silence – to which I must add that full justice is done to Jonson's' words and that Douglas Campbell, in particular, gets off Volpone's set pieces with considerable gusto. He plays the title role for hearty self-indulgence, the better to contrast this quality with the symptoms of Volpone's feigned illness. All the images are sharply defined here, and not only Mr Campbell's. George Grizzard's Mosca, his crooked smile aglow, awakens his master with a fly's buzzing sounds, and from then on he maintains a feline, predatory manner that suggests the mosquito as well as the cat and the fly. We are impressively reminded how very good he is as a character actor and how necessary it is for him to keep working at this high calling and not to descend any more to the function of a straight leading man. Last year he failed as Hamlet, but his portrait of the envious Solyony in *The Three Sisters* was accurate and economical.

Others, too, support their characterizations with strong visual images. Ken Ruta's Voltore wears a sharp, prominent vulture's nose, and Robert Pastene's Corbaccio, quite deaf and nearly blind, has a non-human, grey complexion. Claude Woolman creates a nervous Corvino, alternately a coward and a bully. These three dupes are obvious figures of fun, and the actors take more than full advantage of their opportunities; accordingly, in a moment of crisis, Voltore enters antically chewing on a cloth and making wordless sounds, and Corvino, slandering his wife at the trial, speaks from notes. But Sir Tyrone always has such tricks as these up his sleeve. What is harder to do is to make something, on the stage, of the strange adventures of Lord and Lady Politic Wouldbe. Their roles are nearly uncut – a remarkable case of textual fidelity in view of the same producer's free hand with *Coriolanus* in Nottingham – and Lee Richardson and Ruth Nelson bring us a long way toward comprehension of these two simple-minded tourists who strive to be as subtle as the Venetians.

One of the production's incidental points is that innocence is a ridiculous and deplorable condition, equally ridiculous in the English tourists and in the simple-minded young folk, Celia and Bonario. We know Thomas Slater's Bonario to be a dolt even before he opens his mouth, so steadfastly does he stride on to the stage, while Kristina Callahan's Celia is sufficiently idiotic to deserve Mr Campbell's derisive rendering of Ben Jonson's celebrated song. In the programme Sir Tyrone observes that in *Volpone* 'there are no virtuous characters'. I assume that he takes Celia and Bonario to be too stupid to count at all in the moral scale.

Volpone is in Sir Tyrone's best style. It has sound bits of dramatic logic, like having Volpone take a drink too much before making the fatal error of announcing his own death. It has its comic use of offstage music when an ironically solemn chorus accompanies the pharisaical meting-out of punishments by judges who are morally no better than the prisoners. And it has one of Guthrie's best crowd scenes. The apron stage is suddenly filled with a mob in a Venetian street; Volpone disguised as Scoto addresses them, he climbs to Celia's balcony, and, when her jealous husband interrupts, he falls backwards off the balcony into the waiting arms of several accomplices who have rushed over from the other side of the stage to catch him. The stage is cleared in an instant.

(from *The Times*, 11 November 1964)

HENRY POPKIN : Black Comedy Still Has Too Much

Volpone (Fox)	Colin Blakely
Mosca (Fly)	Frank Wylie
Voltore (Vulture)	Edward Petherbridge
Corbaccio (Raven)	Paul Curran
Corvino (Crow)	Robert Lang
Sir Politick Would-be (Parrot)	Graham Crowden
Celia	Gillian Barge
Lady Would-be	Gabrielle Laye

The National Theatre has preserved *Volpone*, complete with its hills and valleys. Ben Jonson's black comedy – it passed in the days of this island's innocence for a black comedy – has so much in it, so much action, so much satire, so much vision of human folly, that no one gets it all.

No director and no cast have, to my knowledge, had the energy or imagination to get quite everything and make every moment exciting to a modern audience. Some have solved the problem by making drastic cuts. At the National Theatre, Mr Guthrie has made a brave effort to give us all of the text or nearly all of it. The intention is admirable and frequently successful.

Mr Guthrie's special approach is by way of the play's animal and bird images. He recognizes and magnifies Jonson's gallery of moral monsters, creatures so monstrous that they are no longer men but beasts or birds. Volpone the fox, clad in an appropriate shade of red, wears a savagely cunning expression and emits odd foxy yelps. Mosca the fly is waspish and dressed in black. The three birds of prey who gather to pounce on Volpone's estate begin but do not quite finish a symmetrical pattern illustrating grotesque immorality. We pass from the grim, broadwinged Voltore the vulture, ready to betray the law and the state, to Corbaccio the raven, a hideous mass of rags and feathers, ready to betray his son, and finally to Corvino the crow, who will gladly offer his wife to Volpone, and there anticlimax sets in; the last moral monstrosity is greatest, but it has no sufficient image to embody it.

The English visitors to Venice turn out beautifully, perhaps because Mr Guthrie is haunted by no memory of previous directors who have done much with them. Sir Politick Would-be is, for once, presented as he should be, as a parrot. He has the parrot's trait of inexact imitativeness, trying vainly to be like the sinister Venetians, inventing exotic plots and repeating strange news, while he remains quite oblivious of the real hard-shelled plotting in which Volpone and his dupes are enmired. Wearing a parrot's costume, he punctuates his vacuities with clucks and whistles. His wife, also dressed in parrot's colours, talks nonstop and, to overwhelm the Venetians, gives a wildly exaggerated imitation of a proper English lady's deportment. Played with great resourcefulness by Graham Crowden (with a touch of Don Quixote, and not only because of his beard) and Gabrielle Laye, these two supporting roles are the particular gems of this production.

What is best conveyed in the main plot, besides the single-minded voracity of the dupes, is the nearly innocent jollity of the Volpone gang. The fox wallows in his gold, which sticks not only to his fingers but even to his face. Mosca bounds into Volpone's lap, and the same hearty animal spirits move Volpone to bound after Celia. That level of energy and interest cannot be maintained, however; even jollity begins to pall. The Scoto of Mantua episode achieves very little, and even the last jolly scene in Volpone's household, just before Volpone makes the mistake of feigning death, is more than a little anticlimactic.

Interest in this play goes to those who are bold, or are permitted to be bold – that is, to Colin Blakely's savage Volpone, as wolfish as he is foxy, and to Edward Petherbridge's and Paul Curran's grossly caricatured Voltore and Corbaccio.

(from *The Times*, 17 January 1968)

RONALD BRYDEN : View-halloo *Volpone*

Almost inevitably, I am about to overpraise the National
Theatre's *Volpone*. Every critic has one or two plays before
which, in barely competent performance, he rolls over and
purrs with helpless, infatuate pleasure. I admit at least four :
The Seagull, Major Barbara, Giraudoux's *Ondine* and Jonson's comedy. Call the first three weaknesses if you like –
I confess a certain protectiveness about their vulnerable young
heroines and reliance on charm. But *Volpone* bowls me over,
like a playful lion, with sheer, gorgeous strength. Intoxicated,
I come away sharing momentarily the seventeenth-century
judgment that Shakespeare had a nice touch with landscape
and human emotions, but Jonson is what one really means by
art.

Tyrone Guthrie's production, I recognise, has faults. The
itch to invent and decorate which he subdued for his *Tartuffe*
last November has returned in all its mischief. Bounding out
of bed, his Volpone spends the play's opening moments wash-
ing his face in ducats, then pressing a gold piece into Mosca's
palms in malicious parody of the mass. Later, his seduction
of Celia is chopped up with comic skirmishings round the room
and lascivious wrestling-holds among the pillows, forfeiting the
cumulative incantatory force of the most superb poetic tirade
outside Marlowe.

Perhaps most serious, Guthrie caricatures right up to the
final curtain the four Venetian judges, destroying the crucial
effect of a return to impersonal order. Here, ringingly, Jonson
gathers up all the play's hinting references to Pythagoras in an
affirmation of the true gold Volpone's excess mocks and fears :
the golden mean of measure, temperance and justice. It is
done in a moment, but for that reason needs the more impressive underlining. Guying it, Guthrie blurs the play's point.

But in general, his production has the virtue most vital to the
comedy – energy. Usually, directors get carried away by the
Venetian setting and play for spectacle and grandiloquence.

Guthrie, helped perhaps by his Irish farming, detects the brisk, coarse Englishness beneath. It is a fox-hunt : a yelping, hallooing run to earth, invigorating as an icy morning in the shires, callous and rank with predatory animal odours.

His Volpone was artfully chosen. I've never understood how Olivier has resisted so long the one great role left him in the English repertoire, but Colin Blakely brings to the part a fierce, grinning gusto complemented rather than handicapped by its superimposition on his rather stocky, squirearchic physique. As he springs bright-eyed and bare-foot from his reddish fur covers, he is both Reynard and his heavy, red-cheeked pursuer.

Boldly, Guthrie has taken Jonson's animal caricatures literally. In costume and gesture, he has turned his cast into a human bestiary – I'm told they spent hours at the Zoo studying their various models. I can imagine the horror this will rouse in Method circles, but the result is brilliant theatre. In the younger actors particularly, the disguise has released inhibitions to produce some of the most memorable supporting performances we're likely to see this year.

The funniest are Graham Crowden's and Gabrielle Laye's Sir Politick and Lady Would-be. Sir Pol (get it?) becomes a parrot, all clicks and kettle-whistles as he waddles pigeon-toed in pursuit of the true Italianate manner. His mate, a tall, beaky county gawk in flamboyant tweeds, swoops across the stage like a giant, flapping macaw. Paul Curran's Corbaccio is a moulting, verminous old raven from some elm-darkened churchyard, while Robert Lang's Corvino has the spruce vulgarity of a crow strutting on a dungheap.

But the finest of all, I'd say, is Edmund Petherbridge's Voltore, a hunched, sunken-eyed vulture whose hands claw at those near him with the sudden, frightening deliberation of Captain Hook's gestures of friendship. At his first entry, he hops, spread-eagled and voracious, to balance on the side of Volpone's bed. When finally discomfited by Mosca, he sweeps out into the dark like a great, rustling bomber taking off. It's impossible to tell where the human character ends and the bird begins, and the proud, hooded eyes tell that both natures are tragic. . . .

He has the advantage, too, of speaking Jonson's verse so as to verify T. S. Eliot's derivation of it from Marlowe's mighty line. Colin Blakely has yet to master it, and Frank Wylie as Mosca is kept too busy dancing and darting round the action to keep his breath. But on the whole, the strength of Jonson's great play is captured. It bowled me over as usual. If you can suspend the belief that great drama depends on knowing the number of Lady Macbeth's children, it should you.

(from *The Observer*, 21 January 1968)

SUGGESTIONS FOR FURTHER READING

Una Ellis-Fermor, 'Dramatic Notes', *English*, II (1938) 41–3.

Arthur Sale (ed.), *Volpone* (University Tutorial Press, London, 1951) Introduction, pp. v–xix.

Louis Kronenberger (ed.), *Volpone* (Oxford, 1952) Introduction, pp. v–xii.

H. R. Hays, 'Satire and Identification : An Introduction to Ben Jonson', *Kenyon Review*, XIX (1957) 267–83.

Alan C. Dessen, '*Volpone* and the Late Morality Tradition', *Modern Language Quarterly*, XXV (1964) 383–99.

William Empson, '*Volpone*', *Hudson Review*, XXI (1968–9) 651–66.

Jay Halio (ed.), *Volpone* (Oliver & Boyd, Edinburgh, 1968) Introduction, pp. 3–6.

Alexander Leggatt, 'The Suicide of Volpone', *University of Toronto Quarterly*, XXXIX (1969) 19–32.

NOTES ON CONTRIBUTORS

JAMES AGATE (1877-1947). Wrote drama criticism for the *Sunday Times* from 1923 until his death, and served as drama reviewer for the B.B.C.

JONAS A. BARISH. Professor of English at the University of California at Berkeley. He has written on Jonson and the Elizabethan drama, and edited plays by Shakespeare and Jonson.

PHILIP BROCKBANK. Professor of English at the University of York. He has edited Marlowe's *Doctor Faustus* and the poems of Pope.

RONALD BRYDEN. Formerly Theatre critic of *The Observer;* has published a collection of reviews and essays entitled *The Unfinished Hero*.

IAN DONALDSON. Professor of English at the Australian National University, Canberra, and a former co-editor of *Essays in Criticism*. His publications include *The World Turned Upside Down*, a study of English comic drama; and he has edited Jonson's poems for the Oxford Standard Authors Series.

T. S. ELIOT (1888–1965). Pioneered not only in poetry in this century but in literary criticism. His *Elizabethan Essays* may be said to be the fountainhead of nearly all subsequent criticism of their subject in English.

JOHN J. ENCK (1923–66). Was Professor of English at the University of Wisconsin. His critical study of Wallace Stevens appeared in 1964; at the time of his death he was at work on Dryden's tragedies.

S. L. GOLDBERG. Professor of English at the University of Melbourne, Australia; is the author of *The Classical Temper: A Study of James Joyce's 'Ulysses'*.

C. H. HERFORD (1853–1931). Co-editor of the monumental Oxford *Ben Jonson* (1925–52); earlier wrote criticism on Wordsworth and romantic poetry, and edited Shakespeare and Spenser.

ALVIN B. KERNAN. Professor of Humanities at Princeton University published two books on satire, several play collections, essays on Elizabethan and later drama, and the volume on Elizabethan Drama in the Methuen History of English Literature.

L. C. KNIGHTS. King Edward VII Professor of English Literature at the University of Cambridge, 1965-73. Besides *Drama and Society in the Age of Jonson* (1937), he has published books on Shakespeare and collections of essays on seventeenth-century literature.

HARRY LEVIN. Irving Babbitt Professor of Comparative Literature at Harvard University. He has written on a wide range of literary subjects. His publications include *The Myth of the Golden Age in the Renaissance*, and *Shakespeare and the Revolution of the Times*.

SIR DESMOND MACCARTHY (1878-1952). A prolific man of letters, historian of the theatre, and critic of the drama; reviewed plays for the *New Statesman*, and wrote books on Shaw and other theatrical subjects.

S. MUSGROVE. Professor of English at the University of Auckland, New Zealand. He has written a study of T. S. Eliot and Walt Whitman, and edited plays by Jonson and Shakespeare.

EDWARD B. PARTRIDGE. Professor of English at the University of Iowa. He has edited *Bartholomew Fair* for the Regents Renaissance Drama, and *Epicoene* for the Yale Ben Jonson.

HENRY POPKIN. Has for several years been the regular New York drama correspondent of *The Times*. He teaches at the University of Buffalo, New York, and has published many essays and reviews on modern drama.

G. GREGORY SMITH (1865–1932). Wrote scholarly studies of Scottish history and literature, and edited the still indispensable *Elizabethan Critical Essays* for Oxford in 1904.

T. C. WORSLEY. Has published two studies of English education and a collection of theatre reviews entitled *The Fugitive Art: Dramatic Commentaries 1947–1951*.

INDEX